A BRIEF HISTORY OF
BALI

PIRACY, SLAVERY, OPIUM AND GUNS:
THE STORY OF AN ISLAND PARADISE

WILLARD A.HANNA
With a new introduction & epilogue by Tim Hannigan

TUTTLE Publishing
Tokyo | Rutland, Vermont | Singapore

CONTENTS

Bali Sea

Menjangan I.

West Bali
National Park

Labuhan Lalang
Resort

Batu Ampar
Resort

Ketapang

Hot Spring

Natural Gas

Gilimanuk

Jaya Prana
Grave Site

Pura Pulaki
Pura Melanting

BULELENG

Seririt

Pura Bakungan

Brahma
Arama
Vihara

Busung Biu

Protestant
Community

Bali Strait

Eka Sari

Catholic
Community

JEMBRANA

Pupuan

Buffalo Races

Negara

Mendoyo
Dangin Tukad

Pura Rambut
Siwi

Medewi Surfing
Beach

INDIAN OCEAN

Bali

20 km
10 miles

Singaraja
Sukasada
Lovina
vina
ach
ng Sing
aterfall
Gitgit Waterfall
BULELENG
Bali Handara Kosaido Country Club
Lake Buyan
Lake Tamblingan
Lake Beratan
Botanical Garden (Kebun Raya)
Pura Luhur Beratan
Budugul
Bukit Mungsuindah

Kubu
Tambahan
Tejakula
Amed
Kintamani
Mount Batur 1412m
Trunyan
Batur Selatan
Lake Batur
Bali Aga Village, Gede Pancering Jagat Temple
Mountain View
BANGLI
Tulamben
Tulamben Marine Reserve

B a l i

Pura Luhur Batukaru
Candi Kuning
Petang
TABANAN
Pura Yeh Gangga
Hot Spring
Holy Spring
Tampak Siring Rice Terraces
Tirta Empul
Traditional Village
Gunung Kawi
Cempaga
Demulih Undisan
Bangli
Abuan
Apuan
Mount Agung 2867m
Pura Besakih
Pura Pasaran Agung
Besakih
KARANGASEM
Rendang
Selat
Tirta Ayu
Culik
Pura Lempuyang
Amlapura
Puri Taman Ujung (Floating Palace)
Ujung Beach

Butterfly Park
Marga
Sembung
Monkey Forest
GIANYAR

Dance Performances, Palaces
Gedong Marya Theater
Sangeh
Blahkiuh
Ubud
Peliatan
Abian Semal
Bedulu
Goa Gajah
Gianyar
Kerta Gosa
Semarapura (Klungkung)
Padangbai
Candidasa
Kuan I.
Gili Bio/Kambing I.
Marine Reserve
Goa Lawah (Bat Cave Temple)

Tabanan
Kerambitan
Mengwi
Sibang Kaja
Blahbatuh
Gamelan Maker
Tulikup
Bona
KLUNGKUNG
Kusamba

Kaba-kaba
BADUNG
Singapadu
Craft Market
Sukawati
Guwang
Beraban
Batu Bulan
Ketewel

Pura Tanah Lot
Ubung
Kerobokan
DENPASAR
Dangin Puri
Dauh Puri

Legian Beach
Legian
Sanur
Sanur Beach
Ceningan Reef Surf Break
Nusa Lembongan
Cavehouse
Toyo Pakeh
Pura Ped
Kuta
Kuta Beach
Serangan Island
Nusa Ceningan
Spring
Karangsari Cave
Ngurah Rai International Airport
Jimbaran Beach
Jimbaran
Tanjung Benoa
Tanjung Benoa Beach
Nusa Penida
Pura Batu Madan
Pura Batu Kuring
Sabuluh Waterfall
KLUNGKUNG
Bingin Beach
BADUNG
Nusa Dua
Nusadua Beach
Pecatu
Ungasan
Nusa Batujinengan
Pura Luhur Uluwatu
Bali Camel Safari

Introduction

Bali at the start of the 1970s was still a sleepy sort of place as far as most foreign visitors were concerned. The traffic was relatively light: a modest flurry of puttering motorbikes and three-wheeled bemo; a battered truck or two; the occasional rattletrap bus. At the airport—its extended runway inaugurated as an international gateway just a couple of years earlier—each arriving flight still felt like a special event. Somewhere, out of sight and out of mind, a team of French experts were putting the finishing touches to a tourism development masterplan for Bali. But for now there was only a modest crowd of moneyed holidaymakers at Sanur, staying at the stark white hulk of the Bali Beach Hotel or in the growing clutch of low-rise competitors nearby; a gaggle of long-haired young Westerners permanently installed amongst the palm trees and magic mushrooms of Kuta on the other side of Bali's southern isthmus; and the first of a new generation of artistically inclined expats, settling into an Ubud where it was easy to imagine that nothing had changed since the 1930s. All of them were inclined to think of the place as paradise.

Way out east in Karangasem, swathes of countryside were still scorched and flayed following the 1963 eruption of Mount Agung, and battered local communities were still struggling to put fields and lives back together. But few foreign visitors traveled that way. Similarly, few visitors were aware that even more recently Bali had been consumed by an episode of human violence far more devastating than any volcanic explosion. The Balinese locals—and there were just over two million of them at the time—knew all about the violence, of course, for they had been both its perpetrators and its victims. But had any of the tourists asked them, they would have been thoroughly disinclined to talk about it.

One foreign visitor who did know of the recent violence—and a good deal more about the island's past besides—could be spotted in that early 1970s scene, flitting from palace to temple to government office with a notebook in his shirt pocket. He was a lean, fair-headed American with a beaky nose and thick-rimmed glasses. He was in his early sixties, approaching the end of a 22-year career with the American Universities Field Staff in Southeast Asia. His name was Willard Anderson Hanna.

Willard Hanna was born in 1911 in the little township of Cross Creek in Washington County, Pennsylvania. In this eminently tranquil and temperate rural setting, he developed an unlikely fascination for all things Asian, and as soon as he had graduated college he winged his way to China to work as an English teacher. Four years later he came home, and in very short order completed a master's degree in English literature, a PhD and a novel set in contemporary China. When the USA entered World War II, he joined the Navy, received training in the Japanese language and found himself posted to Okinawa in the wake of the Allied victory over Japan.

After the war Hanna served with the US State Department, and for seven years he was an information officer in Asia. His postings included Tokyo and Manila, but the bulk of his time was spent in Indonesia. He was on hand in Jakarta to watch the post-war turmoil as the resurgent Dutch colonialists and the rising Indonesian nationalists tussled for control of the country. He was there to observe the new nation's faltering first steps in the early 1950s. And, naturally, he made visits to Bali.

In 1954, newly married, Hanna resigned from the State Department and joined the American Universities Field Staff. This improbable project, funded by a consortium of august American colleges and a body of private subscribers, sounds today like a heavenly employment prospect for any writer with globe-trotting tendencies and a lively interest in events past and present. Its aim was "To develop, finance, and direct a corps of men to study mainly at first hand the contemporaneous affairs of significant areas of the world and, through reports and their personal services, to make their knowledge available." This corps of men—and they were all men—were dispatched to the far corners, from where they would send back their missives to the colleges and subscribers, covering the politics, culture, economics and history of wherever it was that they found themselves. During his time with the AUFS, Willard Hanna and his wife Marybelle lived in Kuala Lumpur, Hong Kong, Singapore and, above all, Indonesia.

If the idea of "field reports" sounds ominously dry, Hanna's background as a literature scholar and sometime novelist ensured that his AUFS offerings were anything but. When penning accounts of the past, in particular, be it Jakarta's colonial heritage, the blood-spattered backstory of Maluku, or the dramatic saga of nineteenth-century Bali, he went at it like the finest of popular history writers. He had a sharp eye for the color and the character that can turn a succession of historical facts into a ripping yarn.

During his final years with the AUFS, Willard Hanna gave much of his attention to Bali. In 1976, his very last year with the service, his tales of the island's history were collated in a single narrative and published as *Bali Profile: People, Events, Circumstances 1001–1976*, later reissued as *Bali Chronicles*, and now republished here in fully updated form as *A Brief History of Bali*, complete with new chapters, modernized spellings and a few long-standing errors of fact and nomenclature ironed out.

Hanna's account of Bali drew from a formidable range of colonial-era sources in Dutch and other European languages, with added information from the first-hand accounts of local royals and politicians, tourist industry pioneers and veteran expats in the 1960s and 1970s. It was delivered with a snappy prose style, a leavening dash of authorial subjectivity and a parade of vivid character sketches—of everyone from Danish adventurers to feuding kingly cousins. It was, in short, narrative history writing par excellence and it remains one of the most entertaining and accessible accounts of Bali's past available today.

Hanna's book was originally billed as an account of "the entire history of Bali since the beginning of recorded time." But his real focus was the last 500 years, and his central theme was that of Bali's often traumatic interactions with the outside world, from its testy relationships with the old courts of Java, through the piratical first encounters with European colonialism, to the grim experience of Japanese occupation during World War II. In preparing this new, updated edition, picking up the baton where Willard Hanna set it down in the early 1970s with new chapters carrying Bali's story to the end of the twentieth century and beyond, an attempt has been made to continue his central theme, though Bali's outsider antagonists are now foreign tourists, Jakarta politicians and the faceless forces of globalization rather than Dutch traders, soldiers and missionaries. But the new section at the end of this book does diverge from Hanna's text when it comes to the subject of the supposed fragility of Balinese culture.

As a regular visitor at the dawn of Bali's modern tourism boom, Willard Hanna was troubled by a notion that has been preoccupying admiring outsiders since at least the 1930s, and which continues to concern the latest crop of aficionados today: the idea that tourism is likely to "ruin" Bali. He was particularly horrified by the hippies at Kuta—"wan apostles of latter day savagery" he memorably called them—and fearful of the unimaginable prospect of 500,000 annual tourist arrivals (Bali currently gets something like four million foreign tourists a year and possibly twice that number of domestic arrivals). It was probably these concerns that prompted Hanna to sign up for a view first voiced by early nineteenth-century orientalists and then formally codified by Dutch officials and promulgated by expat artists and anthropologists in the 1930s: the idea that the island's distinctive Hindu-Balinese culture was a fossil, a static, fragile thing, unchanged since the sixteenth century and likely to be "broken" by the arrival of a few hundred thousand Australians with sunshades and surfboards.

It was a curious line for him to have taken, given that he had spent so long exploring the ever shifting, never static patterns of Bali's past, and had surely recognized the way that the litany of external impacts had already altered the island without "destroying" it. What was "traditional" in the early 1970s was not exactly the same as what had been "traditional" in the 1930s or the 1830s; nor is it entirely identical to what is judged "traditional" today. The idea that Bali could be "ruined" by anything ignores the flexibility of all cultures, especially those of Indonesia. The people of Bali have been connected to and influenced by the outside world since the moment the very first band of hunter-gathers set up camp in a limestone cave on the Bukit Peninsula. No man is an island, they say, and when it comes to the ebb and flow of history no island is an island either, least of all Bali. That's what this book is all about.

Bali Beginnings

In the beginning, the wandering bands of Melanesian hunter-gathers heading eastwards—and the tigers traveling in the same direction—would have been able to pass across the shallow valley between the great Ijen volcano complex of East Java and the green ridges that stretch westwards from Bali's Mount Batukaru without getting their feet wet. Further east there was a deep channel, stirred by fierce currents. But the body of land that would one day become Bali itself was part of a great shelf of territory that stretched all the way to modern Thailand and which is known by modern geologists as Sundaland.

But then the polar icecaps started to melt and the sea levels rose. It took many, many centuries for the shorelines of modern Bali to be formed, of course. At first that connecting valley would simply have narrowed, hemmed in north and south by swamps and mangroves. Then the valley would have become marshy, the tall stands of old-growth forest giving way to weedy thickets, rooted in mud. Then, during the highest tides and the fiercest storms, a murky, brackish current would have washed right across from one side to the other. After that, the inundations would have become so frequent that nothing more would grow on what was now a tidal isthmus rather than a valley. And then, finally, perhaps around 12,000 years ago, even the sandbar would have ceased to raise its crown above the level of the lowest tide and any new hunter-gatherers who wished to visit Bali would have had to do so by boat. A small population of tigers was left marooned on the eastern shores of the strait.

The island carved out from this furthest promontory of Ice Age Asia had a bank of formidable volcanic peaks for a backbone, rising beyond 7,000 feet at their highest summits. To the north, these mountains angled steeply downwards to the sheltered shores of the Bali Sea. To the south, meanwhile, they sloped more gently towards the island's tapering southern terminus. Busy streams coursed down the inclines, cutting deep ravines into the fertile soil. In the far south, a narrow neck of land stitched the rest of the island to a raised limestone plateau that was originally a fragment of the Indo-Australian tectonic plate, torn off during a monumental collision some 70 million years ago and known today as the Bukit Peninsula.

It was in the craggy caves of the Bukit that some of the earliest humans to reach Bali had set up camp, perhaps 50,000 years ago, back when the island was still connected to Java and the rest of Asia. They left pebbles and flakes of andesite and volcanic tuff, roughly worked to create cutting edges, along with shell scrapers and crude tools made of antler and bone. But it was the people who came after the deluge, when Bali was already an island, who created the first proper settlements. They were part of a great Austronesian ethnic and linguistic expansion, which began in southern China some 7,000 years ago, passing by way of Taiwan, and which eventually stretched beyond Indonesia to the furthest reaches of the Polynesian world. The Austronesians brought with them, amongst other things, the knowledge of how to farm pigs and how to grow rice.

The earliest Austronesians may have reached the northern coast of Bali over 3,000 years ago. They ate fish and kept chickens and dogs, and by the dawn of the Current Era they had created a large settlement at Gilimanuk, the spot that had once lain on the eastern side of that shallow connecting valley and which was still within a mile and a half of Java. It was Bali's closest point of contact with the outside world, and the people who lived there were by no means isolated.

Amongst their possessions were amber-colored carnelian beads and pots marked with rouletted patterns which had been made in towns in southeast India, which were themselves linked by trade all the way to the Greco-Roman civilizations of the Mediterranean.

These early Balinese communities also found themselves tied into trade networks stretching to mainland Southeast Asia, and from around 2,200 years ago intricately worked bronze goods—heart-shaped spearheads, flamboyantly splayed axes and huge ceremonial kettledrums—from the Dong Son civilization of northern Vietnam began to reach Bali. In the wake of these imports came the technology and raw materials required to replicate them, and by the early centuries of the Current Era Balinese people were making their own bronze tools and ornaments. Rice growing technology was becoming more sophisticated, too, and as it did so new centers of Balinese life developed away from the littoral, particularly in the furiously fecund middle catchments of the Petanu and Pakrisan rivers which run south from the slopes of the central Batur caldera.

The local cultural practices of the time fitted a pattern which spanned the wider archipelago, in which ancestors and volcanoes were the objects of veneration. The dead were often placed in hulking stone sarcophagi along with precious grave goods, a process accompanied, in all probability, by extravagant funerary rites. Up on the mountainsides, meanwhile, terraced platforms were carved out for the worship of the ancestral spirits dwelling on the summits above, platforms later to support the foundations of more elaborate mountain temples. These patterns and practices would not vanish altogether in the centuries to come; they would leave traces and outlines in an elaborately syncretic culture forged, in Willard Hanna's fine phrase, as Bali underwent "the contagion of civilization." By the middle centuries of the first millennium CE, it was not just beads and pots and bronzes of Indian origin that were washing up in Bali, but also ideas, political and social concepts and religious beliefs. The scene was set for the eventful story of Bali's encounters with the outside world.

—*Tim Hannigan*

CHAPTER 1

THE DEWA AGUNG
AND THE RAJAS
(PRE-1800)

I sland Setting and Cultural Background
The island of Bali is celebrated for the peculiar splendor of its
Balinese-Hindu culture, a highly developed and artistically embellished
system of life and worship which was arrested in the sixteenth century
at the very moment of its finest flowering and preserved into modern
times with little perceptible loss of vitality. This life of medieval
pageantry is still the living tradition of an island population made
up of extraordinarily handsome and gifted people. The island itself
is an enclave of such pristine natural beauty as to be suggestive, as
Jawaharlal Nehru poetically put it, of "the morning of the world." No
one can very satisfactorily explain just how this miracle happened,
how it was that one idyllic little island created and sustained a rich
civilization that was in certain significant respects as anomalous in
former times as it is anachronistic today, but one which has never until
recently been tainted with artificiality.

The most plausible conjecture with regard to Bali's good fortune
is that the island and the islanders profited enormously from a quite
fortuitous combination of involvement and detachment. Bali was exposed to the great early civilizing influences of Southeast Asia, but up

until very late in the colonial era it was insulated against the intrusion of European explorers and traders. The island, furthermore, is as fertile as it is scenic, and the islanders are industrious as well as artistic. It must be conceded that ancient evils such as superstition, slavery and suttee long persisted, but there have also been compensations. One of these has been the animistic conviction that the divinities of nature are more disposed to be protective than vindictive.

Bali lies just a mile and a half off the eastern tip of Java on the direct trade route between the spice islands of the Maluku and the Asian entrepôts which long distributed their cloves, nutmegs and mace to a spice-hungry world. From early times the island was visited by Indian, Arab, Chinese, Japanese, Bugis and other Eastern traders who brought with them not only their goods but their manners and customs. But once the island was really inhabited, Bali and the Balinese did more to repel than to attract any considerable number of later settlers. Along most of its sea coast Bali enjoyed the natural protection of high cliffs and continuous coral reefs. The nearby seas were notorious for sudden storms. They were also known to be shark- and barracuda-infested. The Balinese people themselves were physically vigorous and likely to be ferocious in battle. They regarded the seas as the abode of demons and monsters and were little inclined either to explore them or to extend aid and comfort to alien voyagers. One of the beliefs of the island was that whatever and whoever the waves tossed up on the shore were destined to become the property of the kings, shipwrecks being meant for plunder and castaways for enslavement. Bali, therefore, remained little known to the outside world and not especially inviting to better acquaintance. The early Asian and the later European seafarers preferred generally to sail on past Bali to other islands that offered surer, safer profits.

Notwithstanding their suspicion of what the seas bore them, the Balinese were quick to accept certain outside influences, which they ingeniously adapted to their own requirements, meanwhile devoting themselves to the development of their lovely and fruitful island. They began the planting of rice at least two millennia ago and achieved a scientific and artistic standard of cultivation unmatched in the region. At least a millennium and a half ago they began to transmute their native animism by adopting Hindu rites. By the sixteenth century they had achieved a distinctive civilization matched in miniature, if it did not indeed surpass anything in India itself or Indianized Southeast Asia. The microcosmic Balinese-Hindu world survived intact up until the nineteenth century and did not then really shatter when it felt the full impact of Dutch colonialism. Even in the modern era the illusion, if not the actuality, of the traditional Bali persisted.

The early history of Bali is a matter of theoretical reconstruction of the precise origins of the population and the evolution of the society. The Balinese are clearly a blend of the various Austronesian peoples who moved into insular Southeast Asia long before historic times. Their well-integrated society is the creation of an animistic, agricultural people inspired by vigorous priests and princes. The first great outside influence upon the early Balinese was exercised by Indian or Indianized traders and travelers who brought with them the Hindu learning. Bali shared very generously in the great wave of Indianizing influences that spread throughout most of Southeast Asia in the latter half of the first millennium. In politics and religion the Indians introduced the key concept of the God-King, whose capital reflects the splendors and perfections of Heaven and whose people prosper only so long as the ruler conducts himself in conformity with natural and divine law. Every Balinese ruler, therefore, had his monumental *kraton* or *puri* (palace) from which he exercised spiritual and temporal power through a hierarchy of courtiers and priests who not infrequently deposed an evil ruler and replaced him with a better one.

Indianization and Javanese Influences

The conversion of primitive Bali into an Indianized society was the result not of conquest and colonization but rather of the contagion of civilization. The rulers found in Indian culture the religious and administrative practices which exactly served their purposes, and the people responded with such enthusiasm as to prove the appropriateness of the choice. India provided the literary, the artistic, the social as well as the theological and political model for an evolving Balinese society. The Balinese exercised their own creative adaptations while still retaining much of the Indian original.

The Indianization of Bali was a process of many centuries. The most pervasive influence was exercised not by India itself but by nearby Java, which had been subject even earlier than Bali to an even more extensive Indianizing process. The documented history of Bali during this period is mainly a catalog of names of obscure royal personages and imprecise references to forgotten events. Modern archaeologists have reconstructed the approximate historical sequence from fragmentary inscriptions in Sanskrit or classical Balinese on various objects of stone and metal, most of them temple treasures. By an amazing exercise of erudition they have matched up names, dates and events to create a chronological outline which meshes with a rather more detailed table similarly constructed for the island of Java and other regions.

One thus learns that certain Indianized rulers invoked certain Indian deities in commemorating their own succession to the throne, in building or endowing a temple, in winning a battle or in celebrating other events. It is clear that by the year 1001, or perhaps 991, when the first reasonably well authenticated historic event occurred, Bali was already very extensively Indianized. In that year, presumably, was born Airlangga, the son of a Balinese king, Udayana Warmadewa (also known as Udayana and sometimes identified with King Udayadityavarman of Cambodia who was exiled in about the year 1000, perhaps to Bali), and his Javanese queen, Gunapriyadharmapatni (also known as Mahendradatta). In his early youth Airlangga was sent for education and marriage to the court of Medang in East Java. When the ruler of Medang was overthrown in the course of civil wars, Airlangga was invited to succeed him. He devoted himself to rebuilding the empire and in so doing he added his home island of Bali to the Javanese domain, ruling it through a regent who was probably an uncle, brother or cousin. Airlangga thus inaugurated a period of close Javanese–Balinese political and cultural contacts which continued, to Bali's very great advantage, for well over three centuries. The relationship was not without its conflicts. The Balinese several times asserted their autonomy and the Javanese Singhasari emperors, or their successors in Majapahit, as often reasserted their own hegemony. Balinese rulers, in whose veins flowed varying proportions of Balinese and Javanese blood, were always implicated in dynastic rivalries which Majapahit was not infrequently called upon to settle. The Javanese ruler Kertanagara, for instance, found it necessary to pacify and reunify Bali in the year 1262 (or 1284), as did the great general, Gajah Mada, in 1343. Majapahit imposed more and more of its own institutions upon its far from un-receptive dependency. Eventually, when the Majapahit Empire itself collapsed in 1527, migrations from Java to Bali resulted in still more massive cultural transfusion.

Majapahit Conquest and Early Rulers

With the Majapahit period Balinese history begins to assume clearer content and pattern although much remains legendary. Gajah Mada constituted Bali a province of the empire with a Majapahit governor. Kapakisan, the first incumbent, and, according to Balinese legend, the offspring of a stone Brahma and a heavenly nymph, became the founder of a line of princes who ruled the island more as supporters than as subordinates of the Javanese state. Kapakisan and his successors sometimes used the Javanese title of Susuhunan (Emperor), but more commonly the Balinese title of Dewa Agung (Great Deity), thus more than merely implying that they ruled independently and by divine right. Kapakisan built his *kraton* (Javanese term) or *puri* (Balinese) in Samprangan and ruled firmly but justly over the whole of the island. He was succeeded by his son, Sri Aji Kresna Kapakisan, about whom nothing is known except his name. Kresna Kapakisan was in turn succeeded by his own son, Dalem Samprangan, about whom nothing is known which does him credit. Dalem Samprangan, the third Dewa Agung, was so given to vanity, frivolity and venality that his counselors encouraged his young son, Dalem Ketut, to build a separate *kraton* in nearby Gelgel and gradually to usurp the powers which his father was too dissipated to exercise. Dalem Ketut succeeded in restoring royal authority and prestige. He is especially celebrated for having journeyed to Java to participate in a solemn imperial council called together by Emperor Hayam Wuruk (r. 1350–80) to consider the gathering troubles which were already shaking his empire and were to overwhelm and destroy it a century later.

The fall of Majapahit signaled the rise of Mataram, a new Javanese empire built out of small kingdoms newly reinspired and reinvigorated by the advent of powerful Islamic influences. A number of Majapahit Hindu priests, nobles, soldiers, artists and artisans fled from Java to Bali to escape their Muslim conquerors. In Bali they gave fresh impetus to an already strongly Indianized culture which was thus able to enrich and maintain itself. Hindu Bali and Muslim Java became implacable enemies. The East Javanese state of Blambangan, separated from Bali by a mile-wide strait which was both difficult and dangerous to cross, became a buffer region. The Balinese claimed and occasionally half conquered Blambangan. Mataram often threatened but usually failed to mount a counter invasion, and for centuries Balinese–Javanese relations remained readily inflammable.

Dewa Agung as Emperor and Symbol

At the end of the fifteenth century, then, the Dewa Agung and his remote court at Gelgel, who suddenly fell heir to the still glittering legacy of the vanquished and vanished Majapahit Empire, achieved previously undreamed of splendor and authority. The sixteenth century was destined to be Bali's golden age. Under Dalem Baturenggong, who became the Dewa Agung in about the year 1550, the various Balinese principalities were welded together into a strongly centralized kingdom. Baturenggong followed up his successes at home by launching military expeditions abroad. He conquered Blambangan, where he installed a vassal ruler and supported him against Mataram's counter attack. Then he turned his attention eastward to the islands of Sumbawa and Lombok, which he both conquered and colonized. Political and military triumphs of Baturenggong's reign were more than matched by a cultural renaissance. The Balinese transformed the Majapahit influences to conform to their own special needs and abilities. They created what is, in fact, the contemporary Balinese culture, endowing it with that special element of Balinese genius, the secret of eternal renewal of youth. The Balinese still share with the Javanese many common traditions of language, music, dance, sculpture and literature, but the gap between Hindu Bali and Muslim Java is almost as wide as that between youth and old age. The older, the Balinese-Majapahit culture, paradoxically preserved its freshness and animation while the younger, the Javanese-Mataram society, grew both sober and somber. It is the riddle and miracle of Bali that the fires should have been ignited—and still burn bright in the neighbouring islet—from the embers of Majapahit Java.

Emergence and Divergence of Eight Rajadoms

Gelgel's golden age flickered during the reign of Baturenggong's son, Dalem Bekung, and died out under his grandson, Dalem Di Made. Dalem Bekung engaged in an ill-advised adventure in Blambangan which all but provoked a full-scale invasion by Mataram of Bali itself. He lost the respect of the other Balinese princes, who became openly defiant, and he played host to the first Dutch visitors, whose arrival eventually proved to have been an omen of evil. But it was Di Made who suffered the undeniable, the irreparable reverses. He lost Blambangan, Sumbawa and Lombok, and he lost also the allegiance of the other princes. Di Made's successor, Gusti Sideman, abandoned the *kraton* of Gelgel, which was clearly under a curse, built a new one in nearby Klungkung and sought to rule as grandly as had his predecessors. But it was already too late. The Dewa Agung was to be less prominent thereafter than various of his presumed vassals. Klungkung therefore never matched Gelgel in glory, but Bali's silver age, which set in when Klungkung was founded, saw the island-wide dissemination of the Gelgel culture.

The Dewa Agung and his court in Klungkung continued to symbolize Hindu imperial grandeur but never again imperial power. The other princes became the Dewa Agung's rivals and even his enemies. Their own *punggawa* (chiefs) at times presumed to virtual autonomy while the *pendanda* (priests) sometimes assumed almost independent temporal power over villages and groups of villages which fell theoretically within the domain of the rajas. The ruling families, princely and priestly, were polygamously intermarried and easily provoked to blood feuds. Divination, prophecy and mere superstition were factors of comparable significance to jealousy, intrigue and military conflict in conditioning personal and state affairs. As the domain and the authority of the Dewa Agung diminished, there emerged a dozen more or less clearly defined little independent rajadoms. Eight of these still survive as geographic and political entities (now administrative districts). They are Gianyar, Badung, Bangli and Tabanan in addition to Klungkung in the south-central region and Buleleng, Karangasem and Jembrana in the north, the northeast and the northwest respectively.

The history of these eight Balinese rajadoms of modern times—and those of adjacent Lombok—is closely linked to that of Dutch colonial penetration. It is a story which remains as yet to be very accurately reconstructed from fragmentary and conflicting records, many of which are still lost in Dutch and Indonesian archives. Some inspired student may one day search out the sources in order to write what could be a classic of East–West relations as revealed in the vivid Balinese microcosm. For present purposes and with present resources, it must suffice merely to identify the protagonists and to establish the progression by reference to rajas and rajadoms.

The Dewa Agung and his rajadom of Klungkung survived but did not flourish, for the Dewa Agung himself was powerless and his kingdom was minute. Little Gianyar rivaled Klungkung as a center of traditional Balinese culture and even presumed at times to military might. But until the latter part of the nineteenth century, Gianyar was never at the focus of Balinese events, and neither were the neighboring states of Bangli, Tabanan or, except for brief intervals, Badung. These states shared with Gianyar and Klungkung the fertile rice lands of the southern slopes of the central mountains and shared also the rich culture which rich rice lands nourished. Mengwi, a state of the center, enjoyed occasional prominence but overreached itself and was partitioned among its neighbors (1891), surviving today only in the loyalty of the people to the family of the traditional ruler and to the state shrines. The Dewa Agung's military and political powers passed first to Buleleng, the large northern state which was the first focus of foreign commerce and international competition; next to Karangasem, the large eastern state which came to dominate also the island of Lombok; and eventually to the Dutch. Buleleng and Karangasem, sometimes friends, sometimes enemies, generally under the rule of members of the same royal family, were to become the two power factors of modern Bali.

Gusti Panji Sakti, who came to the throne at the end of the seventeenth century, was primarily responsible for Buleleng's assertion of island hegemony. By skillful political and military maneuvers he extended his own authority throughout most of Karangasem and Jembrana, exacted deferential treatment from the southern states, and concentrated next upon Blambangan. He listened sympathetically to an appeal from Mas Purba, the heir-apparent to the throne of Blambangan, who sought military aid in ousting a rival and resisting Mataram pressures. Gusti Panji Sakti sent an expedition to Java (1697), which placed Mas Purba more or less securely on the throne, but succeeded more convincingly in establishing his own claim to succession to the Dewa Agung's former power. But Gusti Panji Sakti's son-in-law, Gusti Agung Sakti, the ruler of Mengwi, presently usurped his father-in-law's own kingdom of Buleleng (1711). He went on to consolidate his position by another adventure in Java, where Mas Purba had wavered in loyalty and flirted both with Mataram and the Dutch. The joint rajadom of Buleleng–Mengwi flourished for the better part of the eighteenth century but then separated again and forfeited power to Karangasem.

Karangasem began its rise to prominence by seizing the opportunity to champion Balinese interests in Lombok at a time when Buleleng was preoccupied by exploits in Java. Upon slipping from Balinese control in the time of Dalem Di Made, Lombok had fallen under the domination of Sumbawa and Gowa (Makassar), sometimes one, sometimes the other, sometimes both. It had been subjected by and through these states to strong Islamizing influences. The paramount raja was converted to Islam along with various of his court. Aided if not, in fact, compelled by soldiers from Sumbawa and Gowa, the raja then attempted to expel the large Balinese-Hindu population already living in the island. The new Muslim clique in Lombok had to contend meanwhile with very troublesome little rebellions among the warlike Sasak tribes people, who made up the greater part of the population. Karangasem found this situation conducive to its own endeavors to bring Lombok once again under Balinese control, an objective which, after half a century of intermittent effort, it quite clearly accomplished. By the mid-seventeenth century Lombok was parceled out among four weak little rajadoms, each ruled by a Balinese prince who owed his allegiance to Karangasem.

It may be of help in fixing in mind the main currents of Balinese history to do as many of the Balinese themselves do, which is to accept a much abridged version of events from Majapahit times onward and to dwell upon a simplified pattern of conflict mainly between the north and the south. According to popular Balinese accounts, the Majapahit conquest of Bali and collapse in Java occurred in quick succession and the leading characters in the former, Gajah Mada and Arya Damar, accompanied Brawijaya, the fallen Majapahit emperor, to Gelgel to re-establish his court. In appreciation for his distinguished services, Brawijaya named Arya Damar as Prime Minister and assigned him extensive lands to be divided among himself and his followers. Arya Damar received, in fact, virtually the whole of the lush rice growing area of the south which then constituted the states of Tabanan and Mengwi, from which later split off Badung and Bangli. To Gajah Mada went the large but not so desirable central mountain region and the coastal areas beyond, out of which, presently, were created the rajadoms of Buleleng, Karangasem and Jembrana. Gajah Mada's services in the Bali campaign had not been deemed especially meritorious for he had idled away his time in various pleasures leaving it to Arya Damar to fight the major battles and to lead the main invasion forces southward from Buleleng. Thus there originated the jealousies and rivalries of two different sets of rulers, those of the south, who stemmed from Arya Damar, and those of the north, who stemmed from Gajah Mada. The latter all but openly repudiated their allegiance to the Dewa Agung in the mid-eighteenth century. The former continued to pay homage and tribute, however meager, up until the late nineteenth or very early twentieth century.

Decline of Dewa Agung's Authority

The conspicuous decline of the Dewa Agung's own power and prestige, according to this reading, dates from approximately the year 1750 when there occurred a series of incidents which shocked all of Bali. The Raja of Karangasem, an ascetic sage of repulsive physical habits and appearance, generally so engrossed in meditation that he let his excrement drop where it might, paid a visit of homage to Klungkung in the course of which he greatly shocked and outraged the Dewa Agung. When the Raja set out again for home, the Dewa Agung gave orders that he should be ambushed and assassinated, and the Raja was accordingly murdered. His three filial sons immediately sought to take vengeance. They raised an army and marched into Klungkung to besiege the *puri*. Some residue of respect for tradition deterred them from either killing or deposing the Dewa Agung or even depriving him of much of his realm. But they made virtual declaration of independence and returned home to rule Karangasem without much further regard for the Dewa Agung's authority. The eldest son succeeded as raja. Presently, he conquered Buleleng, where he made his younger brother raja, and then Lombok, which he assigned to the other. From that time on, Karangasem, Buleleng and Lombok were more often hostile than amenable to Klungkung. But at the time of the Balinese–Dutch wars of 1846–9, both Karangasem and Buleleng, but not Lombok, solicited and reciprocated the Dewa Agung's support.

The long and the short versions of centuries of Balinese history, much of which, technically, is pre-history, converge upon one famous personage, Gusti Gede Ngurah Karangasem, Raja of Karangasem at the turn of the nineteenth century, the gadfly of the Dewa Agung and the kingpin of a new coalition. Once having made himself master of Buleleng as well as of Lombok and having made his brothers the rajas, he next added Jembrana to his domain. He did so over the vigorous protest of Badung, which had recently treated that state as an appendage of its own but had tolerated the rule of a Bugis prince from Makassar named Kapitan Patimi. Karangasem put pressures upon other states as well and stirred up widespread resentment and resistance.

By this time the patterns of Balinese power and politics were becoming almost incomprehensible even to the Balinese, as is still further indicated by the sudden emergence in the late eighteenth century of the state of Gianyar as a rival to Klungkung and a military threat to Buleleng, Karangasem, Mengwi and Bangli. Buleleng itself soon rebelled successfully against Karangasem (1823) and the Raja of Karangasem, Gusti Gede Ngurah Lanang, was forced to flee to Lombok. There he built a new *puri* and attempted to impose central authority over the mutually jealous little Lombok rajadoms, which welcomed his defeat in Bali as an invitation to defiance. At the same time he sought to force his one-time vassals in Bali itself yet once again to recognize him as ruler. Gusti Gede Ngurah Lanang thus did much to create the insular and inter-insular turbulence which the Dutch found conducive to the imposition of Western rule.

CHAPTER 2

WESTERN INTRUDERS (PRE-1800)

E **arly Portuguese and Other European Visitors**
Up until the time that the Dutch seriously interested themselves in Bali, which was at a very late date in their colonial history, Western contacts with the island were infrequent and transitory. The early Portuguese explorers, adventurers, merchants, missionaries and conquerors who reached Malacca in 1509 and Maluku in 1511 all but bypassed Bali in their eager rush to acquire riches, souls and territory. So did the Spaniards. The Magellan expedition (1519–22) sighted an island, probably Bali, which it identified as "Java Minor," but apparently no one went ashore. Fernando Mendez Pinto, the great Portuguese navigator and Munchausen-like narrator, may have visited Bali briefly in about the year 1546 but the evidence is not clear. Various others of the pioneer Portuguese and Spanish no doubt sighted Bali even if they did not actually explore it, and they made due notation of the island under various names (Boly, Bale, Bally) on the early charts. Sir Francis Drake called briefly in 1580 and Thomas Cavendish perhaps visited Bali itself as well as its East Java dependency of Blambangan in 1585, but they left no written record.

The Portuguese were the first to entertain any designs upon Balinese trade and territory. The Malacca government fitted out a ship to dispatch to Bali in 1585 with soldiers and merchants, building materials and trade goods, the intent being to build a fort and to open a trading post. The ship foundered on the reef off the Bukit Peninsula and most of the ship's company were drowned. Five survivors found their way to shore, where they were pressed into the service of the Dewa Agung, who treated them quite kindly, providing them with homes and wives, but refused to permit them to return to Malacca.

Houtman Expedition of 1597; Shore Party in Kuta and Gelgel

In 1597, twelve years after the ill-fated Portuguese enterprise, Cornelis de Houtman, the earliest of the Dutch explorers and traders in the East Indies, paid a visit. The record of his expedition—an official report and a detailed personal letter by one of the ship captains—constitutes the first substantial body of information about the island available to the Western world. Although its two-year voyage had been punctuated by mutiny, murder, piracy, brigandage and such ill-natured haggling over prices of local produce that it failed ever to find cargo, the expedition's conduct in Bali was almost blameless. Cornelis de Houtman, the braggart and scoundrel to whom the leadership had fallen after the mysterious demise en route of several predecessors, was so moved by the beauty and wealth of the island that he indulged in an unaccustomed but characteristically inappropriate flight of poetic fantasy and christened it Jonck Hollandt (Young Holland). It was a description so evocative of misapprehension as to lead later Dutchmen to fancy that in introducing Dutch civilization and commerce they were guiding the islanders toward their manifest destiny.

The three surviving ships of the expedition, the *Hollandia*, the *Mauritius* and the diminutive pinnace, the *Duifje* (Little Dove), with company of 89 men (out of the original 249), arrived by relays in Balinese waters: the *Mauritius* on December 25, the *Hollandia* on January 27 and the *Duifje* shortly thereafter. The *Mauritius* anchored first off the coast of Jembrana and the *Hollandia* first at Kuta. The *Duifje* for a time shuttled in between. All three presently assembled in the safer waters of Padang Bai.

Four members of the Houtman company spent most of the period February 9–14 on shore, mainly in Kuta, but they made one trip to Gelgel and went on one expedition into the countryside, along with Balinese escorts, to hunt wild birds. They had been sent ashore to negotiate with the Balinese rulers for opening of trade, an enterprise which came to nothing since the Balinese could offer only a very limited quantity of spices and the Dutch, as usual, were too parsimonious in their bids for other goods. The four men on shore actually gave little thought to trade but occupied themselves in quite agreeable and informative intercourse with the hospitable Balinese. The rulers treated them as honored guests—also as prized hostages, Houtman himself having already seized three Balinese whom he was holding on shipboard—and made many occasions to elicit information about European life and customs. They were especially skillful about exacting gifts, most notably a chart of the world which the Dutch repeatedly promised and only belatedly delivered, declining, however, to sell the Dewa Agung the big ships' guns which he was eager to buy.

Arnoudt Lintgens, Captain of the *Hollandia*, was the ranking member of the shore party. Emanuel Roodenburg, a sailor from Amsterdam, was the messenger between sea and shore and the carrier of

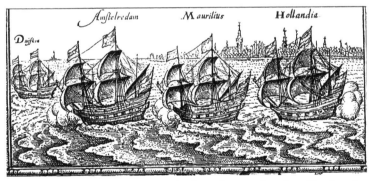

Detail from an engraving showing the four ships in the "First Fleet" under Cornelis de Houtman, from G. P Rouffaer and J. W. IJzerman (eds), *De Eerste Schipvaart der Nederlanders naar Oost-Indië onder Cornelis de Houtman, 1595–1597*, The Hague, 1915–29.

Houtman's gifts. Jan the Portuguese, a Mestizo "slave" who had come on board at Banten as interpreter, participated in all the more significant encounters, and Jacob Claaszoon, an ordinary seaman from Delft, gained historical fame along with Roodenburg by jumping ship just as the expedition was about to set sail back to Holland.

Lintgens, Roodenburg and Jan the Portuguese were guests of the Kijloer, the chief official of the Conick, that is, the Dewa Agung. Both the Dewa Agung and the Kijloer were then in residence in Kuta, where they were readying an expeditionary force of 20,000 men to send to the relief of their Javanese dependency, Blambangan, which was under siege by the Susuhunan of Mataram.

The Dewa Agung, whom Lintgens described as a tall, dark, stout, vigorous man of about forty, astounded the Dutch with his wealth, power and magnificence. He lived ordinarily in a huge palace in the walled town of Gelgel, surrounded by his harem of 200 wives, his troupe of 50 misshapen dwarfs (their bodies deliberately deformed to resemble the grotesque figures of *kris* hilts) and his many noblemen, who ruled in his name over the 300,000 people who then populated the island. His state *kris*, said Lintgens, was especially notable for the splendor of its jewels and the weight (two pounds) of its intricately wrought golden hilt. The handle of his state parasol was equally showy, and in his palace were to be found many other *kris*, lances, parasols, vessels of gold and silver and miscellaneous treasures such as would be the envy of any king in Europe. When the Dewa Agung ventured outside his palace, he was accompanied by a procession of scores of lance and banner bearers and rode either in a palanquin or in a cart drawn by two white oxen which he himself drove. He held the love and respect of his people and his courtiers and was famous for the clemency of his rule, having only recently, it was said, spared certain conspirators who had plotted against his life, commuting their sentence from execution to exile on a nearby islet.

Audience with Dewa Agung and Lesson in Geography

Once it was determined that the visitors would bear gifts and exactly what those gifts would be, the Kijloer escorted the three—Lintgens, Roodenburg and Jan the Portuguese—to an audience with the Dewa Agung in his Kuta palace, where all of the high nobility had assembled as witnesses. The Dewa Agung was delighted with the gifts: a large gilt-framed mirror, a print of a ship resembling the *Mauritius* (which he had viewed from the shore), several lengths of plain colored velvet (not as fine as the flowered velvet which had already been presented to the Kijloer, of which the Dewa Agung was jealous), six pieces-of-eight (the "coins of the Dutch"), a rifle and the much coveted chart. The rifle had to be demonstrated at once, much to the satisfaction of all of the court, but it was the chart which was the real sensation. The Dewa Agung, reported Lintgens, regarded it as evidence of the "subtilty of our nation". When he found a globe pictured in one corner he was even more astonished and insisted that the Dutch must bring

The king of Bali in his carriage pulled by two white buffaloes, as seen by the Dutch in their first expedition to the East Indies, from Cornelis de Houtman, *Verhael vande Reyse ... Naer Oost Indien*, Middleburgh, 1597.

him one on their next visit. He himself proposed to write a letter of appreciation to the Dutch king and to send him a *kris* and a dwarf, none of which are mentioned again in the records.

The Dewa Agung called at once for a lesson in world geography, and Lintgens was happy to oblige. The lesson started with the islands of Southeast Asia, the Dewa Agung expressing great disappointment to find that Bali "showed so small." Next came the Empire of the "Great Turk," which mightily impressed him. Finally came the European continent, Lintgens being required very clearly to explain about the Netherlands and the port of Amsterdam and then the route by which the expedition had traveled to the East. Upon being queried by the Dewa Agung which was the larger, China or Holland, Lintgens replied by tracing boundaries of the Netherlands so imaginative as to include Scandinavia, Austria and a generous portion of Imperial Russia.

The audience developed into a prolonged interview in which the Dewa Agung demanded detailed information about the King of Holland (Prince Maurits), his age (30), his marital status (single, much to the Dewa's amazement), his armies (50,000 foot soldiers, 30,000 cavalry and 150 pieces of heavy artillery), his commerce (700 large ships a day visiting Amsterdam), the Dutch climate (with elucidation of the strange phenomenon of ice), and much, much else, including personal information about his immediate callers and other members of the expedition, the nature of the vessels and their guns. Since, said the Kijloer, the Dewa Agung made a point of surrounding himself with foreigners and requiring all newcomers to visit him and perhaps also to remain in Gelgel, he was especially pleased to learn that the expedition had brought with it two young boys from "St Louwerens Island", whom, said Lintgens, he might see if he wished.

Entertainment by Kijloer; Interview with Portuguese Merchant

Before and after the audience with the Dewa Agung and a subsequent visit to Gelgel, Lintgens, Roodenburg and Jan the Portuguese were entertained in the splendid Kuta and Gelgel palaces of the Kijloer, who served lavish feasts (one being brought in by twelve of the Dewa

A Balinese slave of Batavia, ca. 1700, from Cornelis de Bruin, *Voyages de Corneille le Brun...*, Amsterdam, 1718. The proliferation of new Balinese kingdoms and the power of kings was clearly related to the number of peasantry obtained as slaves by a local lord.

Agung's wives) and was fully as curious as was the Dewa Agung him-self with regard to European customs, including the system of justice and the punishments meted out to thieves and murderers. The Kijlo-er informed his guests about previous European visitors: the English (presumably Sir Francis Drake) and the Portuguese. One morning he suddenly produced for their inspection Pedro de Noronha, a mer-chant from Malacca who had been in the service of the Dewa Agung ever since the shipwreck of 1585. Pedro told them something of his life story, inquired about conditions in Portugal, and allowed that al-though he had been eager at first to return to Malacca he was now quite content to remain in Bali together with his Balinese wife and their two children. He had been forbidden, nevertheless, to establish any contact with the Houtman expedition until the Kijloer himself introduced him.

For reasons which the record does not make clear, Cornelis Hout-man himself seems to have gone ashore only once, a few days be-fore setting sail again for Holland. There he met with the brother of the Dewa Agung, engaging in desultory conversation and the con-sumption of fruits and sweets while his Balinese hostages were being brought ashore so that Lintgens and his companions would be permit-ted to go back on shipboard.

Desertion of Roodenburg, Claaszoon and Jan the Portuguese

The Houtman expedition departed from Bali on February 20 without Roodenburg and Claaszoon, who had vanished. They had remained ashore to enter the service of the Dewa Agung, perhaps of their own volition, perhaps not, most probably quite willing to be induced to forgo the rigors of the voyage back to wet, cold, gloomy little Holland in preference for the pleasures of equatorial Bali. In any event, they both settled in Gelgel, took Balinese wives, learned the Balinese lan-guage and attended upon the Dewa Agung. When the next Dutch expedition appeared, that of Jacob van Heemskerck in 1601, Rooden-burg joined it as interpreter and translator, also as general informant and advisor. According to vague contemporary accounts, Heemskerck appears to have shown his appreciation for Roodenburg's services (and unspecified services of Claaszoon) by "buying them free." Roodenburg, but not Claaszoon, subsequently reappeared in Holland as a humble clerk in an Amsterdam office, an unlikely sequel to his Bali idyll.

Heemskerck Expedition of 1601; Roodenburg as Interpreter; Dewa Agung's Letter to Prince Maurits

The Heemskerck expedition left no such detailed records as those of its predecessor, but Heemskerck himself was a more perceptive and sympathetic visitor than Houtman and served as his own ambassador. He carried a letter from Prince Maurits which he presented in person to the Dewa Agung together with the usual presents, thus eliciting a gracious letter of acknowledgment from "*den conick van* Bali" to "*den conick van Hollandt.*" The Dewa Agung advised the King of Holland that he was pleased to comply with his request for permission to open trade and stated, further, apparently in reply to a suggestion of political relationship, that he concurred that Holland and Bali should "be one." Heemskerck (or Eemskerck) promptly dispatched the original letter in Balinese together with the Dutch translation by Roodenburg (or Rodenburch) back to Holland as evidence of the success of his mission. The somewhat obscure text of the translation reads as follows:

7 July 1601

God Be Praised
The King of Bali sends the King of Holland his greetings. Your Admiral Cornelis van Eemskerck has come to me, bringing me a letter from Your Highness and requesting that I should permit Hollanders to trade here as freely as the Balinese themselves, wherefore I grant permission for all whom You send to trade as freely as my own people may when they visit Holland and for Bali and Holland to be one.

This is a copy of the King's letter, which was given to me in the Balinese language and which Emanuel Rodenburch has translated into Dutch. There was no signature. It will also be sent from me to you.

Cornells van Eemskerck

The Raja also presented van Heemskerck with a typical token of royal favor—a beautiful Balinese female slave. Van Heemskerck seemed unaccountably indisposed to accept, at least until Roodenburg explained that to decline would be impolitic. Neither van Heemskerck nor his successors proved reluctant to accept the Raja's far from naïve consent to reciprocal trading conditions as a charter for one-way trade or his offhand endorsement of Dutch hopes for unity as acknowledgment of an alliance. Although nothing much came of the contact for almost two and a half centuries, it was on the basis of this document that the Dutch assured themselves that they had special rights in the island.

VOC Factory and Free Burghers from Batavia

The Netherlands (or United) East India Company, known in the East as the VOC (Vereenigde Oost-Indische Compagnie), manifested little interest in Bali even though it took vigorous and often violent measures to establish itself firmly in Maluku, Java and Sumatra. It does seem to have opened some sort of trading post in about the year 1620, but there is very little indication of subsequent activities or of any continuing European presence. The first merchant, Hans van Meldert, was instructed to purchase "rice, beasts, provisions and women," but he aroused such suspicion and hostility on the part of the rajas that he was very soon recalled, having acquired, it seems, as the total result of his enterprise only one consignment of fourteen female slaves. For the next two centuries, Balinese commerce was mainly in the hands of Chinese, Arab, Bugis and occasional Dutch private traders. These latter were the Batavian "free burghers" who came to be tolerated on the fringes of the Company's base at Batavia (modern day Jakarta) and

were permitted to deal in goods which the VOC itself found either profitless or objectionable, although it did at times quietly and indirectly
participate. In the case of Bali, this meant mainly slaves and opium.

Trade in Slaves and Opium; Missions of Oosterwijk and Bacharach

The very skimpy records of Dutch contacts with Bali during the seventeenth and eighteenth centuries relate mainly to the appearance in
Batavia and in Bali of various slavers and opium runners, the acts of
mutiny, piracy and treachery which their activities provoked, and the
inconsecutive and ineffectual efforts of the VOC officials either to ban
or control and restrict the trade. Other records refer to the rapidly
growing Balinese community in Batavia itself—by the end of the eighteenth century a total of about 1,000 Balinese members of the Dutch
colonial army, some 1,500 free Balinese residents and very many Balinese slaves. This entire community traced its origins either to slaves
sold as soldiers, who earned their freedom after five to ten years of
faithful service, or household slaves, who were commonly freed by
their masters or declared free upon the death of their masters, open
sale generally being prohibited. The free Balinese population of Batavia
was fourth in size of all the racial sectors, the first being the *Mardijkers*
(creolized Portuguese), second the Dutch and third the Chinese. The total
population of the city was then about 30,000, half slave and half free.

Balinese Community in Batavia; Senopati; Balinese–Javanese Wars

The most famous member of the Balinese community in Batavia was
Senopati, a Balinese in fact only by association, a folk hero of the late
seventeenth century whose history is half legendary. Senopati seems
by birth to have been a Javanese prince, but he fled to Bali in early
youth to escape from the cruelty of his uncle, the Susuhunan. Settling
in Jembrana, he became the foster son of the Chinese Syahbandar
(harbormaster). Later, in a spirit of pure adventure, he permitted himself to be sold as a slave and shipped to Java. In the course of the voy-

age he earned the admiration and gratitude of the slaver by fighting off pirates, but upon reaching Batavia he consented nevertheless to be sold into the family of a wealthy Dutch merchant. He served his Dutch master faithfully up until the time that he fell into a complicated set of difficulties by reason of rejecting the amorous advances of the daughter of a Dutch general. Entering the Dutch army he fought bravely in the colonial wars until he became so outraged by the arrogance of the Dutch that he raised an insurrection against them. Eventually, he founded his own kingdom in East Java in rivalry to the Susuhunan.

The story of the Balinese trade in slaves and opium was punctuated with romantic episodes such as those associated with Senopati and others which are merely squalid. It is one with regard to which the records are far from numerous or detailed, but it warrants effort at explanation. The Balinese rajas enjoyed and exercised the traditional right to enslave and to sell as slaves all such people as would constitute an encumbrance or an embarrassment to the state. This general category included criminals, castaways, outcasts, orphans, drifters, debtors and even the widows and children of men who died without leaving enough property for their support. It was regarded as both the right and the duty of the rajas to make sure that such people did not impose a burden upon society but rather contributed to it, and when Western reformers later interfered with the system the Balinese neither understood nor approved. Balinese slaves, furthermore, were highly prized both in Bali and overseas. A Balinese healthy young slave was about 100–150 rijksdaalder at home and five to ten times that amount in overseas markets. The Dutch themselves wanted Balinese slaves both as recruits for their colonial army and as household servants in Batavia. But the biggest market of all was in French Mauritius, to which as many as 500 slaves would be sent by a single ship. The slavers often found it most convenient and profitable to make payment with opium, a commodity which found ready market among Balinese royalty and even more especially among Javanese, Bugis and Chinese smugglers, who distributed it throughout the archipelago in defiance of Dutch attempts to enforce a monopoly. The island of Bali, of course, had more to sell than slaves and wanted to buy other goods as well as opium, especially arms, but the slave–opium link-up was extremely important to the development of its commerce. The first commercial center was the northern port of Buleleng. Here the rajas recognized the advantages of foreign contact and a small resident community of Chinese, Arab and Bugis merchants facilitated it.

The intermittent presence in Bali of certain Batavian merchants and the reports they brought back with regard to the wealth and power of the rajas several times stirred the VOC to make overtures of alliance. In the year 1633 the Governor-General, Hendrick Brouwer, heard from the Batavian free burgher Jeuriaen Courten that the Dewa Agung was preparing a great military expedition against the Mataram Empire in Java, with which the Dutch themselves were at war. Brouwer determined to provide the Balinese with assistance in the expectation of so weakening Mataram's power that the Dutch forces could win an easy victory. He therefore dispatched a special ambassador, Van Oosterwijk, to offer the Dewa Agung provisions for his troops and ships to transport them to East Java. The mission was accompanied by Justus Heurnius, a missionary on his way to Ambon, who later reported briefly, favorably and quite inaccurately about the readiness of the Balinese to accept Christianity, a report that was filed away in church and state archives and forgotten, which was just as well. Van Oosterwijk, who remained in Bali only briefly, and Captain Jochem Roloffszoon van Deutecom, who was sent as his replacement, both failed to achieve their purpose. Certain of the Dutch in Batavia intimated that the Governor-General had been impulsive and gullible and his emissaries clumsy. In fact, the visitors arrived at a most inauspicious time, just when the Dewa Agung and his court were altogether preoccupied with preparations for the cremation of a favorite wife and two royal princes. The emissaries had brought a fine Persian horse as a gift for the ruler and they hinted that a gift of an elephant might be delivered later, but nothing availed to gain them an audience. They had to content themselves with a bit of trading by which they acquired, among other things, 2,000 skeins of cotton, 460 pieces of woven textiles and 1,200 measures of rice.

In 1639, when Mataram suddenly invaded Bali, the Dewa Agung appealed to Batavia for assistance. For reasons now unknown, the Dutch withheld their aid, but the Balinese themselves succeeded in repelling the enemy forces. In 1651, when the Dutch were momentarily at peace with Mataram, they sent another ambassador, Jacob Bacharach, with instructions to negotiate an alliance with the Dewa Agung just in case of future need. Again nothing came of the mission.

In the course of the next century there were frequent outbreaks of hostilities between the Dewa Agung and the Susuhunan, and both Bali and Mataram applied repeatedly for Dutch assistance. The Dutch never obliged—at least not openly. But in the years 1717–18, when Balinese troops were roaming East Java and Madura, causing great destruction and dismay throughout the region, the Dutch themselves launched little clean-up operations which helped to chase the intruders back home. If the Dutch refrained from intervening in the Balinese–Javanese wars, the English did not, or at least the Dutch believed that the English did not and that they were providing the rajas with arms. They were also selling opium and buying slaves. The northern Balinese port of Buleleng, according to vigilant informants of the Dutch, was becoming a hotbed of British–Balinese anti-Dutch intrigue.

The persistent intrusions of the English into Balinese waters caused the Dutch the most excruciating seizures of political and financial agony. The English, they were convinced, were seeking to colonize and would seize any opportunity which they themselves might overlook to establish some British monopoly of their own in competition with those of the VOC. The Dutch were forced therefore to live with the awful suspicion that the predatory English were about to pounce upon some new island, large or small, among the thousand islands known or unknown, which they themselves regarded as the indisputable patrimony of the Netherlands. They entertained the recurrent premonition that the choice would probably fall upon Bali, a rich and strategic little island which they had never yet really explored even though it lay only one nautical mile off the tip of their stronghold of Java. Dutch and English rivalry over Bali was indeed to play a part, even though a very minor part, in the great new English–Dutch conflict which preceded the actual opening of the island to massive Western impact. But that was an eventuality which somehow managed to postpone itself from the early seventeenth to the early nineteenth century. During that interval, except for a few episodes such as those mentioned above, Bali enjoyed the priceless benefits of European neglect.

CHAPTER 3

RECRUITMENT, TRADE AND TRAVEL (1800-1830)

Distant Effects of Napoleonic Wars

At the beginning of the nineteenth century Bali remained relatively unaffected by the Western influences which were already transforming much of the Indonesian archipelago. Bali's sixteenth-century Hindu civilization was still inviolate to any serious religious, commercial or political infiltration either by Muslims or by Christians. In the early decades of the century, however, there came intimations of what by mid-century amounted to the breaching of all the island's defences. What happened in Bali was a remote, tragic and elsewhere almost unnoticed side effect of the Napoleonic Wars.

The early triumphs of Napoleon occasioned the fall of the Netherlands, the extension of French influence not only into Holland itself but also into the Dutch possessions overseas, and a challenge to English power everywhere in the world. The English determined to protect themselves in India by seizing Java, thinking to foil Napoleon's design of converting the Dutch colony into a base of Asian military operations of his own. This Java enterprise, in which the English succeeded brilliantly, several times focused incidental English and Dutch attention upon Bali. It served ever so slightly but significantly to illuminate and therefore to diminish the obscurity by which the island had previously been sheltered. Coming events were foreshadowed when the French–Dutch defenders of Java and the English challengers began to compete for Balinese allies in the forthcoming battle. The subsequent loss of Java to the English (1811) was a critical setback to French interests in Asia and a far from unimportant episode in the defeat of Napoleon's ambition to dominate the world. The eventual restoration of Java to the Dutch (1816) revived their own determination to dominate the whole of the Indies, inclusive of Bali, where their failure as yet to establish themselves very securely exposed them to the possibility of being forestalled by their presumed English ally. It is doubtful whether Napoleon himself had ever heard of Bali and the Balinese never identified him as their antipodal demon, but it may still be said, without doing grave damage to historicity, that Bali's relatively serene isolation from the much troubled international scene was one of the casualties of Napoleon's campaigns.

Daendels' Design for Recruitment; van der Wahl's Visit

Napoleon quite clearly signaled his own intentions with regard to Java by sending out French civilian and military personnel who quickly infiltrated the colonial administration. Napoleon himself picked a new Dutch Governor-General, Marshal Willem Daendels, appropriately known as the "Iron Marshal" and almost equally hated by the Dutch and the Indonesians. On behalf of the French, Daendels undertook enormously costly defence works which resulted in the swift completion of a military highway stretching the length of Java, the strengthening of many military garrisons and the deaths of thousands of Javanese conscripted for *corvée*. Napoleon sent French troops under French commanders to reinforce the long neglected and badly demoralized Dutch garrisons which were stationed in all the important settlements. Daendels himself devised a scheme to import Balinese manpower to support the European troops. He commissioned a certain Captain van der Wahl of the Dragoons as his special agent to negotiate with the Balinese rajas.

Captain van der Wahl arrived in Bali in 1808 with instructions, it seems, merely to arrange with the rajas for recruitment (presumably by purchase) of Balinese soldiers and workers (i.e. slaves) for service with the joint Dutch–French forces. The doughty captain brilliantly over-fulfilled his mission. He succeeded in negotiating a very curious treaty of friendship and alliance with the Raja of Badung, who, as will be noted later, was always the most susceptible of all the rajas of the time to European blandishments. In return for the promise of military aid against his enemies, both domestic and foreign, and in return also for recognition as Susuhunan (Emperor) of Bali—a dignity which attached traditionally to the Dewa Agung, the Raja of Klungkung—the Raja of Badung placed himself and his realm under the personal protection of Marshal Daendels and the personal direction of Captain van der Wahl. At the same time the Raja designated van der Wahl as his private representative for dealing with foreigners, handling commerce and working administrative reforms. The terms of the treaty reward word-by-word reading as an exercise of self-projection into the psychology of early Western negotiations with Balinese royalty:

Treaty of Friendship between Sri Paduka Gusti Ngurah Made Pemecutan, Raja of Bali Badung, and Captain of the Dragoons van der Wahl, Commissioner of Willem Daendels, Marshal of Holland, Privy Counselor of the Foreign Service, Holder of the Great Cross of the Order of the Dutch Kingdom, High Officer of the Legion of Honor of the French Kingdom, Governor- General of the Indies and Commander-in-Chief of the King's Army and Navy therein.

(1) Sri Paduka Gusti Ngurah Made Pemecutan, Raja of Bali Badung, in consideration of the trust and fatherly concern which the Dutch Government has constantly manifested in him as a friend and associate, and also in consideration of the high qualities and honorable sentiments of His Excellency Herman Willem Daendels, Marshal of Holland and

concurrently Governor-General of the Indies, joins himself and his entire kingdom with the Dutch Government, seeking not only that he himself be taken under His Excellency's personal protection but also his children, in life and death to be regarded as friends and kinsmen of His Excellency the Marshal and Governor-General, who accepts him and his into his most estimable fatherly protection.

(2) Captain of the Dragoons van der Wahl undertakes that in half a month after the signing of this treaty Sri Paduka GMM Pemecutan, Raja Bali Badung, shall be proclaimed as Susuhunan of all Bali, the act to be signed by His Excellency the Marshal and Governor-General over the Great Seal.

(3) Sri Paduka GMMP, Raja of Bali Badung, authorizes Captain of the Dragoons van der Wahl to build houses, forts and batteries, to land cannons and troops of such kind and number as His Excellency the Marshal and Governor-General may see fit.

(4) Sri Paduka GMMP, Raja of Bali Badung, as of now places under Captain of the Dragoons van der Wahl all Chinese and other foreign residents with the power of administering them for their own well-being.

(5) Sri Paduka GMMP shall receive from the Captain of the Dragoons van der Wahl all that he has need of from Batavia and Semarang, paying for it the price set by the aforesaid Captain.

(6) Sri Paduka GMMP requests the aforesaid Captain to assume responsibility for the increase of the kingdom's revenues and the improvement of its internal policy.

(7) Captain of the Dragoons van der Wahl undertakes in the name of His Excellency the Marshal and Governor-General to protect Sri Paduka GMMP, Raja of Bali Badung, against his foreign and domestic enemies.

One of the rajas or rulers of Bali, from Thomas Stamford Raffles, *The History of Java*, London, 1817.

(Translated from the Dutch text as published in Annex C of Dr E. Utrecht's *Sedjarah Hukum Internasional di Bali dan Lombok*, Bandung, 1962, pp. 306–7.)

Had this quite outrageous agreement ever been implemented, the island of Bali would have been converted into a fiefdom of the Iron Marshal with the dubious Captain of the Dragoons as regent. But Daendels was recalled and replaced shortly thereafter, the Captain vanished, the English conquered and ruled the Indies, and it served everyone's purposes to forget this improbable arrangement. Nor did the Dutch choose to revive it when Napoleon was overthrown and the English handed back their empire in order to bolster the post-Napoleonic Dutch–English alliance in which the Dutch, without the Indies, would have been a crippled and crippling partner.

A Balinese girl wearing earrings made from rolled lontar leaves, from Thomas Stamford Raffles, *The History of Java*, London, 1817.

English Occupation; Raffles and Crawfurd

Whether or not he was aware of Daendels' overtures to the Balinese, and in all probability he was, Sir Stamford Raffles, the mastermind of the English invasion and the Lieutenant Governor-General of the occupation (1811–16), entered into preliminary personal correspondence with certain of the Balinese rajas to entice them to favor the English side in the coming conflict. The rajas were at first disposed to be receptive to English advances. They sent a certain Nyoman Bagus of Buleleng to meet with Raffles in Malacca, where he was induced to accept the rank of major in the invasion forces. After dispatching and perhaps forgetting Nyoman Bagus, who never reappears in the records, the rajas remained aloof from the campaign and from the occupation. Bali itself fell just outside the sphere of English administration and the far-reaching changes which Raffles introduced affected it only indirectly. But one of Raffles' reforms, the abolition of inter-island slave trading, threatened to deprive the rajas of an important source of revenue. The Rajas of Buleleng and Karangasem, motivated apparently by indignation at the loss of a slave market, in February 1814 mounted one of their periodic little military expeditions against Blambangan, where they clashed with British sepoys. Small bands of armed Balinese, in fact, roved into other parts of East Java, occasioning no little consternation. In May, therefore, Raffles sent Major General Nightingall to Bali with a small contingent of troops to make a show of force and to receive prompt assurances, which nobody took very seriously, of Balinese "submission." The English stationed no garrison in Bali, however, and made no further attempt to impose their control.

In early 1815 Raffles himself paid a visit of a few days' duration and exhibited his usual energy in collecting data for his historical and cultural studies. His administrative subordinate and literary rival, John Crawfurd, had visited the island somewhat earlier and had engaged in similar activities. In their published works, which included sections on Bali, neither Crawfurd nor Raffles, unfortunately, attained their usual standard of accuracy and perceptiveness. Both restricted themselves mainly to comment on Hinduism on the basis of observations made, apparently, not in Bali but in India.

Dutch Demarches of 1817, 1824, 1826; Kuta Post

In 1816, over Raffles' vigorous protest and obstruction, the Dutch regained control of the Indies. One of their first moves was to dispatch a mission to Bali to establish formal relations with the rajas. Their most immediate and compelling consideration was the well-founded suspicion that Raffles was casting about for some new island to colonize. Raffles eventually chose Singapore, but by then the Dutch had already made what they regarded as a successful preemptive move to reserve Bali for themselves. They had drawn up certain "contract concepts" which they interpreted to signify sweeping concessions on the part of the rajas, who had merely discussed but had not accepted the Dutch proposals.

The contract concepts of 1817 were the work primarily of H. A. van der Broek, a revenue officer who was named special commissioner. Van der Broek arrived in Bali in mid-1817 accompanied by Heer Roos as his aide and by Lt Lotze heading a party of twenty well-armed soldiers. He had been provided with impressive credentials authorizing him to negotiate formal agreements with the rajas.

The van der Broek visitation was not altogether unsolicited. Gusti Gede Karangasem, Raja of Buleleng, had himself sent a mission to Batavia seeking aid for relief of famine and intimating interest also in arms. The shortage of food and weapons in Buleleng was occasioned, it seems, by British interference with the slave trade, from which much of the Raja's income was derived, and the Raja had been experiencing certain economic and political difficulties in consequence. The Dutch, happy for once to repair an English oversight, shipped off a modest quantity of rice, receiving in return the gift of three slave girls whom they generously freed. They then decided that the time was appropriate for an official mission.

The van der Broek visit was not a success. He arrived in Bali just as war broke out between Buleleng and Karangasem, a war in which Klungkung and Mengwi supported the latter and the other southern states the former. He found the rajas unresponsive to his suggestion of political alliance and most of them unwilling even to receive him in audience. He attributed their hostility not to any recent experience with Daendels' Captain of the Dragoons or his own evasiveness about military aid but rather to defamatory reports which, he believed, the English had spread and were, in fact, still inspiring. Eventually, van der Broek prevailed upon the Raja of Badung to intercede with his peers in Mengwi and Gianyar to join him in hearing what the Dutch wished to propose. In 1818 the southern rajas themselves sent a mission to Batavia, under escort of Heer Roos, to confer with the Governor-General. Van der Broek remained in Bali, where his stay was made most uncomfortable by reason of various petty annoyances, one of them the interception of supply shipments meant for himself and Lt Lotze's soldiers. The atmosphere, in fact, was distinctly unfriendly. Nevertheless, as a result of various obscure maneuvers both in Batavia and in Bali, the Dutch drew up two somewhat different but very formalistic sets of contract concepts. They assumed that selected paragraphs would be incorporated, with, or preferably without alteration, into the series of treaties which they envisioned with the individual states.

The treaties did not materialize, for the rajas reverted to their non-cooperative stance. Nevertheless, the rejected contract concepts achieved a sort of quasi-validity in the minds of their Dutch authors. Nothing much resulted from this diplomatic exercise other than the demonstration that Western and Eastern concepts of appropriate treaty provisions were all but irreconcilable and that Western concepts would probably prevail. The rajas were interested in occasional military aid against Lombok, Mataram and one another, whereas the Dutch wanted to assert sovereignty and to assure themselves that Balinese political and commercial contacts with the outside world would remain in all perpetuity under their own exclusive control. Neither side quite understood what the other was driving at save that it was altogether unacceptable.

A few years later, in 1824, the Governor-General tried again. This time he chose as his agent not a Dutch official but an Arab merchant from Surabaya, a far-roving trader named Pangeran Said Hassan al Habeshi, who knew from long experience how to deal with Asian royalty from Bengal to Maluku. Habeshi visited the Balinese rajas and reported back to his principals that, save only in Badung, not even the promise of great profit would elicit any interest in a treaty. If Pangeran Hassan failed to achieve his major purpose, he returned good value for the Dutch outlay upon his rather expensive travel arrangements by bringing back important intelligence relating to a second subject in which they were very much interested: the size and strength and hideouts of the pirate bands which then infested the waters of East

Java, Bali and Lombok. Hassan reported that he had counted ninety pirate *perahu* manned by conglomerate crews of ruffians from Sulawesi, Borneo and the Sulu Archipelago, who found aid and comfort in Balinese port towns to which they retreated when Dutch marine pursuit became too hot. He suggested that the Dutch could deal definitively with these vicious sea rovers only by asserting effective control over the whole of Bali and Lombok. For the time being the Dutch contented themselves with sending warships to harass the pirate fleet, and also to reconnoiter and map the Bali coast—first the frigate *Komet* in 1825, then the schooner *Iris* in 1827. They succeeded so well that in 1828 some 300 pirates abandoned Bali to reestablish themselves in the little archipelago of Pulau Laut about halfway between Singapore and Borneo, where they became the concern primarily of the British.

In 1826 Batavia sent yet another Dutch agent, a Captain J. S. Wetters, who managed that year to negotiate a simple agreement whereby the Raja of Badung permitted the recruitment of soldiers, at a royalty of five guilders per head, and the opening of trade. Wetters himself settled briefly at Badung's leading port town of Kuta, not far from the palace of the Raja. Thus began the modern Dutch presence in the island and the emergence of Kuta to compete in trade with the northern port of Buleleng.

The Kuta post did not prosper. Its main purpose was the recruitment of a proposed total of 1,000 Balinese on five-year contracts to serve in the colonial army. Most, if not all of the recruits, it is to be presumed, would be purchased as slaves and would earn their freedom after five years of military service. At just this time, however, the Dutch wound up their long but intermittent war against the Mataram Empire and decided that they no longer required so many more Balinese. The Kuta post, which therefore purchased few slaves, seems also to have sold little merchandise. For these and other reasons, relations between the Dutch and the Balinese were strained by mutual suspicion and at times overt animosity. Wetters' successor, Pierre Dubois, who managed the post from 1827 to 1831 with one Dutch sergeant and a few soldiers as his companions and guards, reported despondently that

Kuta attracted few European traders (a total of exactly three during the entire period) and kept petitioning the government to close it down. To support his case he reported incident after incident of actual or threatened robbery, arson, murder and plunder, and almost daily scenes of amok. Dubois regarded the local ruler, Gusti Ngurah Ketut, the nephew of the Raja of Badung, with a combination of apprehension and contempt. He charged him with all manner of villainy, of which, by report other than that of Dubois, he seems in fact to have been guilty. The local population, according to Dubois, consisted mainly of criminals and ruffians. It seemed to be a matter mainly of chance, however, whether the incautious visitor would be done in by violence or by pestilence, for the location was as insalubrious as its inhabitants were unsavory. Before he conclusively established his point that European survival was unlikely, Pierre Dubois himself was transferred. In 1831 Batavia notified the Raja that it was closing its Kuta station, requesting that its properties be reserved for discretionary Dutch use thereafter, a request which seems to have been ignored.

Visit of Dr Medhurst and His Report

Despite early Dutch failures it was now apparent that Bali could not much longer expect to remain isolated from Western impact. Dutchmen and other Westerners were visiting the island in ever increasing numbers and reports were beginning to circulate in the outside world. One report in particular attracted much attention and realerted the nervous Dutch to the danger that if they themselves did not soon take Bali the British could be expected to do so. It was a study prepared by Dr Medhurst, a much-traveled English medical missionary from Malacca, who spent three months (late 1829 to early 1830) in Bali in company with a Reverend Tomlin studying the northern regions, especially the rajadom of Buleleng, which, as noted above, was the traditional center of foreign contact and trade.

Dr Medhurst's report was published originally in certain English missionary journals and then reprinted (anonymously) in Singapore, first in the *Singapore Chronicle* (June 1830), later in J. H. Moor's famous compilation, *Notices of the Indian Archipelago* (1837). It was also translated into Dutch and republished in the Netherlands. Dr Medhurst attempted, within the brief scope of his essay and the limits of available information, to do for Bali what Raffles had recently done for Java and other English writers were occasionally doing for other little-known lands. He adopted the classical approach of the generalist, dealing with matters of geographical, historical, ethnographical and commercial interest and introducing such particulars as he had been able to assemble from local sources. His historical sketch focused mainly upon the family of the ruling Raja of Buleleng, in whom all Western visitors, naturally, were very much interested. Dr Medhurst portrays this young gentleman, the 20-year-old Gusti Ngurah Made Karangasem, as a princeling so sunken in torpor and licentiousness as to seem little better than an imbecile. Unattractive as he was, he seems to have been preferable as a ruler to various of his uncles and cousins who were his immediate predecessors. One cousin, Gusti Gede Ngurah Pahang, had occupied himself principally in quarreling and battling with another uncle, Gusti Gede Ngurah Lanang, the Raja of Karangasem.

Royal Family of Buleleng; Its Blood Feuds

Dr Medhurst's report is perhaps a bit over-ornamented with picturesque detail obligingly furnished by fanciful Balinese informants. But if it does not reveal exactly what it was that had happened quite recently in northern Bali, it does show what perceptive foreign visitors were quite prepared to believe had happened. The blood feud between Gusti Gede Ngurah Pahang and Gusti Gede Ngurah Lanang, according to Dr Medhurst, lasted for years and resulted in widespread disorders which had seriously affected the entire northern region. Ngurah Pahang, a high-spirited youth of vulgar tastes, became so enraged that he took a great oath to drain and drink his uncle's blood, reserving a small part of it for his beautiful young sister to employ, more delicately, for washing her lovely hair. Ngurah Lanang, not to be upstaged, vowed to cut off his nephew's head, slice his body into small pieces, send these morsels as admonitory gifts to neighboring royalty, then to build a temple of thanksgiving to be ornamented with the bones and skins of his nephew's retainers.

The fortunes of war first favored Ngurah Pahang until, in dalliance between battles, he committed incest with his sister, and the balance then shifted toward Ngurah Lanang. In the course of a particularly audacious campaign, Ngurah Lanang captured his unfilial nephew and proceeded, while professing grief at having to fulfill so impetuous a vow, to detach the head and to mince up the body to provide mementos for friends and relations. He then set out to accumulate the bones and skins necessary for his memorial monument. But Ngurah Lanang's soldiers began to fear for their own hides and bones and many of them deserted. With his still loyal companions, Ngurah Lanang retired into a nearby forest, where he made a sacrificial offering to the gods of fifteen plump infants upon whose roasted remains he and his party banqueted. This gruesome ceremony was so repugnant to others of his countrymen that the Raja found it advisable to flee to Lombok. He did not actively object when his nephew, Gusti Made Oka Sori, was elevated to the throne of Buleleng or when the new raja was deposed by his unhappy subjects and replaced by his nearly catatonic brother, the above-mentioned Gusti Ngurah Made Karangasem.

Such was the gist of Dr Medhurst's gory account, which the present writer has made no effort to reconcile with less excruciating chronicles.

Dr Medhurst did not acquire, or he did not choose to report, any such intimate details with regard to the other royal courts. But he did mention, for instance, that the little rajadom of Gianyar (population about 10,000) was at war with Klungkung (population about 50,000) and that travel into and through the south, which he would have liked to visit, was therefore cut off. He was able, nevertheless, to accumulate a remarkable amount of information concerning geography, agriculture and trade, and he gave genuine insight into manners and customs. He reported, for instance, on the large mountain lakes, the ingenious system of irrigation, the network of roads and trails, the bountiful produce of the land, the imports and exports and the system

Two *brahmana* wearing products of Bali: hand-loomed *songket sarongs*; *kris* tucked into the back of the sarongs; and hand-woven mat pouches.

of administration and taxation. The revenues of the Raja of Buleleng, he said, included the following items: annual customs duties equivalent in value to 4,000 Indian rupees; a tax of two rupees per acre on rice lands; a fine of one rupee to 200 rupees levied upon bridegrooms for engaging in the traditional practice of kidnapping their brides (usually with the bride's consent and collusion); the proceeds of the sale of personal property, including female members of the family, of subjects who died without male heirs; and the proceeds from sale as slaves of all indigent people.

Bali's important products, according to Dr Medhurst, were rice, cotton, corn, tobacco, salt, cattle, pigs, fowl, fruits and vegetables, all of which were abundantly available for export. The island conducted a flourishing trade with Java, Sumatra, Ambon and other islands. Most of the traders were transient or resident Buginese, Arabs and Chinese, but Europeans also participated occasionally. The major items of export were cattle, beef, salt, cotton, cotton thread and goods imported from the east for re-export. The imports were textiles, porcelain, iron and opium, of which Buleleng took twenty chests annually from Singapore. Bali's most noteworthy manufactures were hand loomed textiles, *kris* blades of superior style and quality and gun barrels skillfully bored by hand. In the local market one could purchase rice at the equivalent of one rupee per pikul (132 pounds), fine fat cattle for four rupees each, sturdy little ponies for 15–20 rupees and coconuts at the rate of one rupee per hundred. The actual currency of the market was not rupees but Chinese "cash," the rate of exchange being one to six hundred. A man could live very, very comfortably in Bali, Dr Medhurst said, on an income of fifteen rupees per month.

In his account of the Balinese people and their customs, Dr Medhurst made special mention of the males' predilection for cockfighting, drinking and gambling, while allowing women to perform the manual labor. He described the improvidence and extravagance of the islanders as contrasted with the prudent accumulation of wealth by the Chinese and Arabs, who generally found it wise to resettle elsewhere when their properties attracted very great interest on the part of the rulers. He deplored the arrogance and ofttimes, he said, the rudeness of the Balinese, at least of the northerners, in dealing with foreigners, and the swiftness of their being moved to passion or violence. He gave some description of the Balinese costume—generally scanty and coarse, he said—and of the homes, palaces and temples, all of which he deemed dilapidated and in none of which did he appear to observe any evidence of sophisticated art or architecture. He reported on the elaborate cremation ceremonies which the islanders were given to staging for the rajas, and the spectacular more or less voluntary practice of suttee on the part of the rajas' widows. But his account of the Balinese religion was so inadequate as to indicate that he was virtually unaware of the major role of religious ceremonies in daily life. Or perhaps he was merely indisposed to discourage his missionary associates by reporting the degree of commitment of the Balinese to their Hindu practices. His report led, in fact, to the assignment of an English missionary, a Rev. Ennis, who arrived in Buleleng in 1838 but remained only a very short time and apparently exerted no influence.

The major shortcoming of Dr Medhurst's admirable pioneering study is his failure to describe or apparently to appreciate the peculiar beauty and vitality of the Balinese culture and the special charm of the Balinese way of life. He depicts Bali as an island of great plenty, suffering occasionally from earthquake or volcanic eruption but not from famine or pestilence, experiencing misrule but not repression, offering opportunity to Western enterprise, including, by implication but not by explicit reference, that of Christian missionaries. But he misses the magic. In pointing out this omission it must be reiterated that Dr Medhurst was unable to visit the southern part of the island, where the splendors of the Balinese civilization are almost everywhere manifest, as is the marvelous accommodation of man to nature and to art. But the one place in the south where this phenomenon was least visible, the port town of Kuta, was the one spot which Dr Medhurst particularly wished to visit. He would have liked to observe the activities of the Dutch agent whom he presumed to be no better than a slaver. It was Kuta that other Western visitors were already beginning to visit

From earliest times, cockfighting has been a favorite pastime of Balinese men, including royalty. These photos were taken in the 1920s.

and describe. The very fact that early reports on Bali related mainly to the less attractive spots—Buleleng and Kuta—which the presence of foreigners did not necessarily enhance, may help to explain how Bali as a whole continued in the first few decades of the nineteenth century to enjoy its relatively serene detachment.

CHAPTER 4

MONOPOLY AND SOVEREIGNTY, PLUNDER AND SALVAGE (1830-1843)

Dutch Alarm Regarding Western Interlopers

Dr Medhurst's illuminating report on conditions in Bali in the year 1830 commanded a remarkably widespread audience for an article published originally in obscure ecclesiastical journals which one might expect to be read only by village clergymen. Bali was already becoming known, however, to the international world of traders and travelers, among them the ships' companies of English and American whalers which were beginning to frequent waters adjacent to Bali and sometimes sent parties ashore to purchase provisions in the port towns or to hunt deer and *banteng* (wild cattle) in the mountains. The recently established English colony of Singapore, which most of these voyagers eventually visited and from which no few of them came, was especially curious about its not so distant neighbor, hence the quick Singapore reprints of the Medhurst report.

Enterprising individuals from Singapore were making tentative efforts to establish themselves elsewhere in the Indonesian archipelago than just Batavia and Surabaya, where certain English merchants had managed to stay in business even after Raffles handed Java back to the Dutch. The Singapore concern of Dalmeida and Company, of which the proprietors were Portuguese by origin, was especially active. It sent its ships frequently to Bali and may have had a resident Europe-an or Eurasian agent for a time in nearby Lombok. The Batavia- and Surabaya-based firm of Morgan, King and Company, the enterprise of a pair of not very reputable English traders from Bengal, also seems to have traded extensively throughout the eastern islands. George Po-cock King, one of the partners, did regular business both in Bali and in Lombok and may have established his own trading post in Bali as early as 1831. There were others as well, but one of the most aggres-sive of all Western traders in Asian waters at the time was a Scottish sea captain, John Burd, who affiliated himself with the Danish East India Company to trade under the Danish flag in Singapore, Macau, Canton, Batavia and wherever else profit offered.

John Burd and Mads Lange in Lombok

Captain John Burd recruited an especially energetic and promising young Dane, Mads Lange (b. 1807–d. 1856) of Rudkobing as one of his ship's officers and presently made him a business partner. Lange sailed with or for Burd on several voyages to the East and persuaded his three younger brothers, Hans, Karl Emilius and Hans Henrick, to join him. In late 1833 Captain Burd set out on the heavily armed 800-ton merchant vessel *de Zuid* on a voyage to China and the Indies with Mads Lange as First Officer and the three other Lange brothers as members of the ship's company. In early 1834 *de Zuid* visited Lombok and probably also Bali. It was decided that Mads Lange would estab-lish a permanent trading post ashore in Lombok as the focus for re-gion-wide commerce which John Burd would develop. The pair would build up a shipping fleet of their own, captained by themselves, the three younger brothers and other willing adventurers.

The enterprise was an instant success. Lombok was a happy choice as a commercial center. It was strategically located on the direct sea route between Singapore and Australia which was beginning to carry very heavy traffic. It was rich in rice and other local produce for which there was great regional demand. It was also a convenient provision-ing and servicing center for the many ships' captains who preferred, if possible, to avoid the heavy charges and suspicious scrutiny of the Dutch in such ports as Batavia and Surabaya. Mads Lange established cordial relations with the Raja, accepted service as his *Syahbandar* for the port town of Ampenan, built a factory (trading post), set up a shipyard and very soon became a man of such wealth and influence that he inevitably became known as "the White Raja of Ampenan."

Pak Jembrok's Espionage Report

The Dutch, naturally, were far from pleased with this development. A Javanese spy named Pak Jembrok, who was then in the employ of Rollin Couquerque, the Resident of Besuki, East Java, in 1836 brought in a detailed and disturbing report. Between May 20 and December 27, 1835, Pak Jembrok had observed the arrival in Ampenan of fifteen European vessels—nine three-masters, three brigs and three schooners—of which three flew the French flag and the others the English or the Dutch, some of those which flew the Dutch flag being English-owned vessels from Singapore. These ships brought in large cargoes, inclusive, said Pak Jembrok, of arms, ammunition and opium. At Tanjung Karang, a point in Ampenan Bay where Lange had built his shipyard, Pak Jembrok noted two more ships, a schooner and a brig, the latter under the command of Captain George Pocock King. Pak Jembrok further reported that when he visited the island of Bali shortly thereafter he encountered the same Captain King in the market places in Badung with sixteen casks full of Singapore-minted coins (superior, he said, to the "cash" from China), with which he was buying up quantities of goods for export.

Pak Jembrok's upsetting report almost stirred the Dutch to immediate action to forestall any more foreign interlopers. But they procrastinated long enough that Mads Lange had time to acquire invaluable experience and contacts. By the time they took action, Lange was a seasoned and toughened operator, not in Lombok from which he had had to flee in the course of civil wars, but in Bali where he settled himself at almost exactly the same place and time as did the Dutch themselves, that is, at Kuta in mid-1839.

Dutch Policy of Economic–Political Penetration

The Dutch in The Hague, Amsterdam, and Batavia, having engaged in a prolonged exchange of government and company papers formulating various policy alternatives with regard to Bali, concluded this rigorous intellectual exercise by taking a somewhat clouded decision. It was, in effect, that they would first infiltrate traders and presently assert sovereignty. The exact line of demarcation between commerce and politics was left so vague that a few years later the NHM (Nederlandsche Handel-Maatschappij, the successor to the trading interests of the long since bankrupt and defunct VOC), claimed but only after prolonged and acrimonious negotiations collected the sum of fl. 172,194.39 for losses sustained in Bali in pursuit more of governmental than of company interests.

Governor-General Merkus first considered proposals such as one for designating Banyuwangi, East Java, as a free trade entrepôt to enable the Dutch rather than the English in Singapore to realize the profits of exporting opium, arms and coins to Bali and Lombok in exchange for the islands' cheap and plentiful rice. He half rejected the idea on moral and pragmatic grounds, but half accepted it for commercial and political reasons. He authorized—in fact, he prompted—the NHM to establish its own factory in Bali in the expectation that it would be permitted to trade openly in opium, arms and coins. The company was later to claim that the non-fulfilment of this expectation was one important reason for its losses. Another was the necessity for housing, entertaining, sponsoring and otherwise providing logistic support for the political missions whose activities it in part cloaked and in part promoted. It was mainly for the sake of these visitors that it had to place a special vessel at the disposal of the factory, build fine residential quarters protected by a high stone wall and dispense expensive gifts and favors to the local rulers.

For this two-pronged colonial offensive against Bali (also neighboring and closely related Lombok), the Dutch could and did allege other motives, in particular humanitarianism. They proposed, they said, to impose peace and order for the benefit most of all of the local population, pointing to the serious disturbances in Lombok and Bali's continuing involvement in them as evidence of the need. They also mentioned four highly laudable specific aims to which no one except, perhaps, the people of Bali and Lombok could take exception. They were resolutely determined, they said, to wipe out opium smuggling and arms running, Bali and Lombok being the transshipment points for opium and arms from Singapore which found their way to Java and other Dutch-held islands in which the Dutch opium and arms monopoly presumably protected the public from many abuses. They were as resolutely determined to wipe out the two associated evils of plunder and slavery, pursuits in which the opium smugglers and arms runners also vigorously engaged, in diversification of their sources of income.

The special circumstances in Bali with regard to slavery and plunder have already been referred to in an earlier context. The Balinese rajas routinely enslaved and sold indigent or unwanted people. The Dutch themselves had been among their most importunate clients, for Balinese slaves, male and female, made excellent household servants and the males made splendid recruits for the colonial army. But Raffles had caused the colonial Dutch uneasy twinges of conscience, to which they paid special attention when their worrisome wars with the Mataram Empire ended and they no longer had much need for Balinese slave-soldiers.

With regard to plunder, from the Dutch point of view the material and metaphysical considerations were equally clear. The Balinese rajas entertained a traditional concept of ship salvage which seemed to the Dutch to combine the worst features of slavery, piracy, plunder and lese majesty. In accordance with their principle of *tawan karang*, honoring Batara Baruna, the sea deity, the rajas accepted as a gift of the gods whatever ship came to grief on the treacherous reefs which ringed their island. They took the ship, the cargo, the crew and the passengers as their personal properties, sharing, naturally, with those who actually performed the act of salvage or rescue but entertaining no doubts at all regarding the sanctity of the deed. From the Dutch point of view it was bad enough if the Balinese exercised their so-called reef rights (Dutch: *kliprecht)* upon a Chinese, an Arab, a Bugis or a Javanese craft, many of which sailed under the Dutch flag and expected Dutch protection. It was quite intolerable if the ship in question was Dutch owned and operated. And it was acutely embarrassing even if it flew the English flag. The British then promptly and sternly protested. They were even so tactless as to intimate that if the Dutch presumed to sovereignty over the Indies, they were obliged to provide security and to suppress slavery and piracy, unless, that is, they preferred the English to do so for them.

At the end of the 1830s all circumstances combined to prompt the Dutch to address themselves quite earnestly to discussion with the Balinese rajas of the delicate subjects of trade and politics, slavery and plunder, and to try to blanket these various topics with treaties of friendship and commerce, in fact, recognition of Dutch sovereignty and monopoly. Batavia therefore dispatched three separate missions, first a small probing expedition headed by Captain J. S. Wetters (former recruiting agent at Kuta), then a commercial mission under G. A. Granpré Molière, the NHM Agent in Surabaya, and finally a political mission under H. J. van Huskus Koopman, a specially designated Commissioner for Bali and Lombok. Captain Wetters, who visited both Lombok and northern Bali between July 5 and September 3, 1838, reported that the time was at hand for some decisions. Molière and Koopman followed in due course.

Granpré Molière's Mission and Company Trade

Granpré Molière arrived in Bali on December 6, 1838. He traveled on the brig *Ondernemer*, chartered to the NHM for fl. 2,500 per month, but he had decided to spare the expense of the war schooner *Zwaluw*, which was originally assigned to him as escort. On shore he practised no economies, for he traveled with four to six horses and thirty to sixty porters, carrying with him everything needful for his comfort and dignity. Between December 6 and January 1 he made the rounds of the royal palaces of Badung, Karangasem and Klungkung, but he failed to get an audience in which to present the impressive credentials with which the Governor-General had provided him.

Molière was not an inexperienced trader, so he resorted to well-tested devices for opening Asian palace doors. He poured out samples of ginever, demonstrated a music box and distributed a few firearms as keepsakes. The Dewa Agung and the Raja of Badung became friendly. Both received him in audience and they even began to manifest a healthy spirit of rivalry in representing the respective merits of Kusamba, Klungkung, and Kuta, Badung, as the site of the factory which, Molière hinted, would be well stocked with other trinkets. It developed that what the Dewa Agung had in mind was no trinket. The Dewa Agung craved a rhinoceros, a creature which did not exist in Bali but was necessary nevertheless for an especially solemn state ceremony which he was hoping to conduct. Even apart from its ritualistic significance, a rhinoceros would be a sensation among all Balinese connoisseurs of curiosities, and the Dewa Agung's badly frayed prestige would be immensely enhanced if he, and only he, possessed one. Molière, disguising his dismay, promised to deliver one live rhinoceros.

The Raja of Badung, an earthier type than the Dewa Agung, yearned for one hundred pikuls of lead. He intended, he said, to cast it into balls for use with the bronze cannon which, it seemed, Wetters had promised but neglected to deliver. Wetters' oversight accounted for the coolness of his original attitude toward Molière, who seems to have convinced him, however, that the promise still held good. A daughter of Raja Pemecutan (a minor ruler of Badung) wanted quantities of linen and offered advance payment of three pikuls of tobacco, adding, as an afterthought to clinch the deal, three slaves. In view of the government's disapproval of slavery, Molière might have passed up this first trading opportunity except that the slaves insisted upon attaching themselves to him.

All in all, Molière judged his visit a success. On the basis of his own experiences he anticipated certain unpredictable difficulties, but he thought that a factory in Bali might flourish and he so reported to the NHM and the Governor-General. He kept a meticulous record of his expenses, for which the NHM was later to claim compensation. Inclusive of gin, guns and incidental items like payment of ship charter, but not allowing for the rhinoceros (later procured and delivered at a cost of fl. 839.25), the trip cost exactly fl. 9,738.58.

Schuurman, the Rhinoceros and the NHM Factory

After Molière's visit, the NHM moved fast to establish a factory at Kuta, where the Raja of Badung had promised to prepare quarters for its representative. The company designated one of its brightest young men, D. Boelen Schuurman, as its Kuta factor at a salary of fl. 500 per month, placed an order for a factory trading ship, the *Merkurius*, to be completed and delivered at an early date, and meanwhile chartered the bark *Blora* at fl. 1,800 per month to get men, goods and equipment moving Baliwards. On July 30, 1839, the *Blora* appeared off Kuta, carrying Heer Schuurman, his assistant G. W. Veenman Bouman, trade goods to the value of fl. 42,000 (inclusive of the linens for the princess), construction materials for a company warehouse and one healthy young rhinoceros for the Dewa Agung.

Heer Schuurman hustled hopefully ashore only to discover that the Raja had made no provision whatever for his reception. He made his way wearily on foot to Kuta, then by horse to the *puri*, where the Raja allowed him to wait at the gate, much to the diversion of the public, while deciding whether to receive him. The Raja, whose intelligence in matters of commerce was better than his memory of his own promises, seems already to have been informed that although the ship's manifest listed one gift rhinoceros, it showed no lead and no cannon.

Schuurman, who may have deemed a rhinoceros token enough of company esteem not just for the Dewa Agung but for all the lesser rulers as well, spent a few frustrating days trying to interest the Raja in his factory and his residence. It finally occurred to him to make a present of a fine sword and to renew assurances of the NHM intentions with regard to the lead and the cannon. The cannon was, in fact, to be delivered two years later. It cost the company fl. 1,007.95, and it had been cunningly miscast so that the Dutch need never fear looking this gift gun in the mouth. The Raja himself seems never to have tested it out. He made it the nucleus of what was to become rather an extensive palace armory, to which, in 1849, in appreciation of his good behavior during the Dutch–Balinese wars, the government added a mate. The second cannon probably was not miscast. It seems to have come out of current military stock with which the Dutch themselves had just subdued the island.

Heer Schuurman underwent many harrowing experiences highly educational to a young trader in the course of his first few months in Badung. He spent the early weeks as a not especially welcome and certainly an uncomfortable guest in rather a dingy pavilion inside the Raja's *puri*. Eventually he persuaded the Raja to assign him a scrap of property in Kuta, a run-down compound with one fairly habitable clay hut. But when he started building his factory, he had to rely upon the crew of the *Blora* and later that of the *Merkurius* for skilled labor which the Balinese themselves could not or would not provide. His precious rhinoceros had proved enormously difficult and costly to offload, and the people of Badung seemed more interested in obstructing than assisting. The eventual delivery to Klungkung, fortunately, was a great success. On his way back from Klungkung, however, Schuurman decided impulsively to drop in on the Raja of Gianyar. The Raja, no doubt apprised of the massive tribute to his near but undear neighbor, allowed the perplexed merchant to wait for an hour at the palace gate and then to go away unreceived and unenlightened. Schuurman's subsequent commerce in Kuta did not flourish and he was no happier than Pierre Dubois had been before him. The Balinese, the Chinese and the Bugis visited his factory in droves, impelled, however, by curiosity rather than by a desire to purchase. They took their trade to the Danish factory which Mads Lange was opening up just next door.

Schuurman could not complain that his life was either inactive or uneventful, and being young, vigorous and ambitious, he labored mightily during the first year or two to make his factory a success. He had to adjust to the fact that his assistants were usually less rugged than himself. The first of them, Veenman Bouman, fell seriously ill almost immediately upon arrival and had to return to Java. The second, J. A. Santbergen, was his mainstay and remained in Bali until the end of the period of NHM operations, well after Schuurman himself had been transferred. The third, Andries Beetz, died shortly after arrival and was buried at Kuta. Intermittently, there were others, and always there was an armed guard, but only Santbergen was of much comfort or assistance.

The factory itself gradually expanded although its business did not. It became rather too overawing and fortress-like to create a very favorable impression upon the Balinese or upon certain later and highly critical Dutch visitors. At enormous expense, with materials and labor imported from Java, Schuurman built a high stone wall and behind it placed a big stone warehouse, providing also residential quarters for the staff and for visitors. From the very first the factory catered more to visitors than to customers, much better serving Dutch political than commercial purposes.

The first important guests were the officers of the government steamship *Phoenix*, who arrived on October 29 on a visit of inspection and wished to pay courtesy calls upon the rajas. It was an exercise which cost Schuurman much effort and many gifts and yielded no discernible results. Next, in early April 1840, came Navy Lieutenant Van Oostervijk accompanied by the important Pangeran (Prince) Hamid of Pontianak, Borneo, who also wanted to meet the rajas. In between these visits Schuurman took delivery of his own factory ship, the *Merkurius*, and sailed off on a trading cruise of all of Bali and Lombok, hoping to stir up more business than at Kuta, but with equally meager results. Then, on April 27, 1840, there arrived in Kuta, traveling presumably on the *Merkurius*, the soon to be famous political agent Heer H. J. van Huskus Koopman. Schuurman and the NHM factory played thereafter the support role in the evolving drama of Dutch colonial penetration.

Huskus Koopman, the Contract Maker

H. J. van Huskus Koopman, famous in Dutch colonial history as the *contractsluiter* (contract maker), had received his appointment on December 10, 1839, as special commissioner for Bali and Lombok, at a salary of fl. 700 per month, plus fl. 300 for expenses, with instructions to perform what seemed at first rather a vague and innocuous mission. He was "to bring the rajas ... into such a relationship with the government [of the Netherlands Indies] that they will be removed from foreign influence." The foreign influence from which they were to be removed and isolated was mainly that of the English. The relationship into which they were to be brought and held was that of colonial subjects. These Dutch objectives, which were to become precise and categorical as time went on, were formulated into various sets of highly legalistic "contract concepts" which Huskus Koopman was charged with explaining to the rajas in order to elicit their concurrence. The preliminary contract concepts were to be converted into perpetually binding treaties just as soon as there was an agreed-upon text which both the Governor-General and the rajas had ratified.

Huskus Koopman's job was essentially that of the traveling salesman. It was the Governor-General's expectation that the Dutch-drafted texts would be endorsed with little if any necessity for modification. These Western documents, however alien they might at first appear to the Balinese mentality, would form the basis for an enduring new commercial and political relationship agreeable both to the Dutch and the Balinese without occasioning anything so distasteful to both as a military campaign. As it turned out, the rajas gave their preliminary concurrence, the Governor-General ratified, the rajas refused to ratify, the Dutch–Balinese wars followed and Dutch might prevailed. But by then Huskus Koopman, who had been awarded the Order of the Netherlands Lion for his services, was already in his grave. So too was Governor-General Merkus, as were numerous of the offending Balinese princes, and a great deal of history had happened.

Impasse of 1840; Treaties of 1841; Afterthoughts of 1842

Huskus Koopman's first visit to Bali (April 27–late December 1840) was almost a complete failure. With Schuurman to guide and introduce him, he made the rounds of the courts, starting with the Dewa Agung who not only refused to receive him but dispatched a letter to the other rajas instructing, or perhaps merely advising them to do likewise. In November he voyaged to Buleleng, where the Raja also denied him an audience but did send a message (as did the Raja of Karangasem) saying that he would permit trade. The Commissioner meanwhile had picked up the clue which enabled him to dangle before the eyes of the rajas the political equivalent of Molière's rhinoceros. It was the intimation that the rajas might induce the Dutch to provide them with military aid for an adventure which they were eagerly anticipating—the reconquest of Lombok, where the recent civil wars had gone against Balinese interest.

The Raja of Karangasem dispatched a mission of his own to Batavia to inform the Governor-General that he was already raising troops to invade Lombok and to invite the Dutch to participate. When Huskus Koopman himself returned to Batavia to report the futility of offering political without military alliance, the Governor-General ordered him back to Bali to exploit what seemed like a favorable opportunity. Neither the Governor-General nor Huskus Koopman seems ever to have made any explicit commitment about military aid. But on his return trip Koopman did not actually discourage the Balinese from awaiting favorable response to their request for Dutch ships, arms and men to help re-subdue their former dependency. Later on, in Lombok, he did not encourage the Raja to think that the Dutch would decline to underwrite exactly such an enterprise.

Since Bali–Lombok animosities dovetailed very neatly with Dutch designs, on his second visit to Bali (May 1–December 15, 1841), Huskus Koopman achieved what seemed for a time like almost total success. His fortunes were further enhanced, it seemed, by an otherwise woeful event—the wreck of the Dutch frigate *Overijssel* on the Kuta reef and the plunder of some of its cargo. Koopman promptly demanded fl. 3,000 in compensation from the Raja of Badung, who paid no money but did rather suddenly concede (July 26) that he might accept the contract concepts which Koopman had just been rather laboriously and as yet unproductively explaining to him. With Badung all but signed up, Huskus Koopman journeyed to Klungkung. The Dewa Agung too was amenable, at least up to the point of giving his approval (July 30) to the Badung negotiation. With this prestigious backing Koopman next treated successfully with the Raja of Karangasem (November 11) and the Raja of Buleleng (November 26), both of whom were impatient to get on with the scheduled invasion which they expected soon to follow.

Having accomplished his purpose in Buleleng and Karangasem, Koopman traveled yet again to Klungkung. There, on December 6, he persuaded the Dewa Agung himself to enter into the same preliminary arrangement and to state that whatever contract he might eventually sign would be binding also upon those of his vassal states which had not entered into similar agreements of their own. To the three original clauses of the contract concept, Huskus Koopman added three more which, with the approval of the Dewa Agung, automatically became part of the agreement with any of the other states. These contract concepts, to which the Dewa Agung and the rajas gave preliminary and tentative but by no means final approval, were later to be converted unilaterally and arbitrarily by the Governor-General into binding agreements which provided a pretext for subsequent demands.

The full text (inclusive of Article 7, which applied, of course, only to Klungkung) read as follows:

The following are the terms of a treaty between Hendrick Jacob Huskus Koopman, duly constituted Komisaris of the Government of Netherlands India, and Sri Paduka Ratu Dewa Agung Putra, Emperor of the Islands of Bali and Lombok ruling with full powers in the state of Klungkung:

1. We, the Emperor of the Islands of Bali and Lombok acknowledge our domain to be that also of the Netherlands India Government.

2. Therefore when any ship or boat enters any harbor of this domain the Dutch flag will be raised.

3. In accordance with this agreement, we, the Emperor, will never surrender to any other white people whomsoever or enter into any agreement with them.

4. We promise never to accept any other flag over our lands except that of Holland.

5. The Dutch merchants who are now in Kuta with our consent we shall always assiduously protect.

6. Should the Government of Netherlands India encounter difficulties in warfare the rajas of Bali are obliged to assist them to the best of their abilities.

7. Finally, we approve the provisions of the treaties which have already been made by Komisaris Huskus Koopman with the rajas of Buleleng and Karangasem and Badung.

Thus transpired in the palace of Klungkung on Monday, the 21st day of the month of Shawal in the year 1257 (i.e. 6 December 1841).

Ratu Dewa Agung Putra

Witnesses:
Cokorde Dewa Agung Putra
Ratu Dewa Agung Gede
Anak Agung Ketut Rai
Pedanda Wayahan Pidada
Ida Wayahan Sidaman

(Translated from the original Malay of the treaty text found in the National Archives in Jakarta and published as Annex G (pp. 321–3) to Dr E. Utrecht's *Sedjarah Hukum Internasional di Bali dan Lombok*, Bandung, 1962.)

Huskus Koopman returned to Batavia in early 1842 in full expectation of receiving the warmest congratulations of the government and of being honorably discharged from his arduous mission. But the Governor-General refused just then to ratify, and Koopman found himself formally accused of negligence. It was all because of the unfortunate *Overijssel* incident, which had aroused the greatest of indignation and outrage in the Netherlands and in Batavia. The Governor-General himself was therefore under strong pressure to get categorical assurance from the rajas that they renounced reef rights and would refrain from plunder. The question of reef rights having been deemed of secondary priority, the Governor-General had not dealt with it in the original contract concepts. And even though Huskus Koopman had seized upon the *Overijssel* incident as pretext for pressuring the rajas into accepting his contracts, he had not considered it advisable to insert a special clause to deal with a problem which, once Dutch sovereignty were exercised, might be expected to resolve itself. But the furor over the *Overijssel* had caused the Governor-General to draw up a very lengthy and detailed set of new contract concepts which amounted virtually to a codified law of salvage, with stipulation of rules of conduct and scales of payment, and he was determined to make these a part of the original package. He therefore ordered Huskus Koopman to return to Bali to renegotiate with the rajas, those of Lombok as well as Bali, for he put no faith at all in his Commissioner's assurances that the Dewa Agung could speak for all of his presumed vassals and he was determined to leave no loopholes.

On July 31, 1842, Huskus Koopman wearily embarked on his third voyage. Once he arrived in Bali he very quickly persuaded the rajas to approve if not actually to read and study his rules of ship salvage. In October he traveled onward to Lombok. There he got the raja's consent to renunciation of reef rights but failed to convince him to forgo sovereignty as well. That required a fourth voyage (January 1843) and the rather thinly veiled threat of force. Then, to his great dismay, it was necessary to make yet a fifth trip (September 1843) to get acceptance of a clause which had been inadvertently omitted from the Lombok copies. This time all was complete. The Governor-General wearily approved and hastily ratified, Huskus Koopman got his Netherlands Lion and soon died, and the Balinese rajas repudiated the whole *Bali-bundel*, as some of the more irreverent Dutch were already beginning to refer to the documentary coups of their highly skilled *contractslui-ter* and *traktaatsluiter,* who could so artfully transform concepts into irrevocable commitments.

Once they had a chance to reflect, the rajas decided that they had been hustled, threatened, tricked, cajoled, deceived and betrayed in making commitments which they never intended. What upset them most was the mysterious and sinister matter of sovereignty, which remained both ill-understood and ill-explained. They had acknowledged their own domain to be the domain also of the Netherlands. They had been offered Huskus Koopman's standard explanation: "You say your realm is your friend's realm, and so it is with sovereignty." But as a clarification of the concept of sovereignty, the remark seemed on careful consideration to be singularly specious. The Dutch word for domain, as used in the treaty texts, was *eigendom* (property) and the Malay word was *negeri* (country), but it made as little sense in Dutch as in Malay to say that the raja's eigendom or negeri was also the Dutch eigendom or negeri without adding further mystification such as only a constitutional lawyer could have provided. There was no attempt to render the text into Balinese, in which the mystical significance of this imprecisely shared sovereignty over domain might at least have been endowed with symbolical validity.

What the rajas began to realize and indeed also to assert was that they had never intended to raise the Dutch flag over their ports and palaces (they themselves flew not flags but banners), or to elevate the Dutch crown over the many-tiered royal umbrellas (tiers signified rank but a crown was a suspicious alien device suggestive of black magic), or to seat a Dutch official on a golden chair as ornate as that of the raja, let alone one even more ornate and placed on a higher level. And it was one thing to say that their realm was their friend's realm but quite another for the friend to move in to stay. It was to take three

Dutch military expeditions to persuade them to think or at least to act more like the loyal and tractable protégés of the Dutch Crown which they were already destined to become.

The eigendom–negeri conundrum was illuminated for them by the *tawan karang* (reef rights) episode of the *Overijssel*, which the rajas deplored as deeply as did the Dutch but for different reasons. It had demonstrated to their own subjects that they were powerless to prevent the Dutch from intervening in affairs either more or less innocent than the ancient practice of taking possession of a stranded ship. The *Overijssel* had yielded them little in plunder but had cost dearly in prestige.

Shipwreck and Plunder of the *Overijssel*; Kuta Scene

The sad tale of the *Overijssel* began on July 19, 1841, when the vessel, on the hundredth day of its maiden voyage from Plymouth to Surabaya with a valuable cargo of machinery for a sugar factory in Java, hit the Kuta reef and was promptly plundered. Subsequent Dutch outrage served in part to cloak their humiliation that a large and heavily armed frigate was wrecked by reason of an egregious navigational error, the captain having mistaken the coast of Bali for that of Java, and that the ship was looted notwithstanding the presumed vigilance of the ship's company against exactly that contingency. The captain, Govert Blom, was soon to publish a highly controversial and quite incoherent "impartial" account of his experience. He blamed poor visibility, poor charts and poor judgment. It was not his own poor judgment, as others alleged, but that of Heer Huskus Koopman, who failed to control the rajas; of the NHM factory personnel, who neglected to save the cargo and salvage the ship; of the Dutch naval Captain Willinck, who delayed in responding to call. Captain Blom had good words only for Mads Lange, who provided good advice and good company and eventually purchased the wreck to cannibalize it for repairs to other vessels.

For a period of a week the *Overijssel* incident much enlivened life in Kuta. Lange and Santbergen both showed up on the beach to welcome the castaways, to warn them against Gusti Ngurah Ketut's gang of ruffians, and to offer them the shelter and the hospitality of their respective factories. The Balinese plunderers went to work on the wreck just as soon as did the company salvagers, the one crew apparently working by day and the other by night but to equally little advantage. The main cargo of heavy iron machinery and boilers was not salvageable by any Kuta methods and much of the rest of the cargo and ship's fittings were lost on the dangerous reef.

The Raja of Badung caused much excitement by sending an order commanding the Europeans, on pain of death, to desist from their efforts to remove property which now belonged to him; he rescinded the order on receipt of strong protest from Santbergen and Huskus Koopman; he revalidated it the next day under pressure from the Kuta looters. The dispute over salvage soon became academic as both ship and cargo were beyond hope of recovery. The NHM factory bought up for fl. 197.50 what little salvage was offered for sale, and Lange, as mentioned, bought the wreckage. As Huskus Koopman pointed out in his own self-defence, the goods were very heavily insured (for fl. 170,000).

The *Overijssel* incident offered social as well as commercial, political and economic diversion to the minute European community in Kuta, which suddenly found itself entertaining a total of 57 passengers and crew, among the former the large and important family of Colonel Lucassen—husband, pregnant wife, five children and nursemaid—the Colonel being the owner of the cargo. Captain Blom and most of the ship's company remained in Bali until July 25, when they left for Surabaya on the factory schooner *Merkurius*. Captain Blom was to return briefly later on to try to repair his ship and his reputation.

The family Lucassen remained until August 9, when they departed for Surabaya on board a government vessel, the *Sylph*. Vrouw Lucassen, meanwhile, had given birth to her child—the first European child to be born in Bali—and the event had been celebrated by a champagne dinner attended by 24 Europeans. These familial and festive events, which, according to one account, occurred in the NHM factory, and according to another in Lange's establishment, no doubt greatly enlivened Kuta and comforted the castaways. But they did nothing to appease the wrath of the Governor-General, at least not until Huskus Koopman brought off the second series of what seemed at the time to be major coups of diplomacy.

More Complications; More Treaties

The Governor-General had scarcely even promulgated the still unratified contract concepts and terminated his long correspondence with The Hague over the *Overijssel* incident when the Balinese rajas quite deliberately defied him by reverting to vigorous exercise of reef rights. In 1844, therefore, the year in which the rajas were scheduled by the Dutch to send a mission of homage to Batavia, there arrived instead in Bali a newly appointed Dutch Commissioner, J. Ravia de Lignij, the Assistant Resident of Banyuwangi. His mission was to protest the most recent outrages and to demand the ratification and observance, without further delay or discussion, of the Huskus Koopman contracts. Commissioner de Lignij made his call at Buleleng, where the latest reef incidents had occurred, meeting there with the Raja and his council of state. It was at this meeting that the great modern hero of Bali identified himself. He was Gusti Ketut Jelantik, a dramatic, dynamic young prince, the younger brother of the Rajas of Buleleng and Karangasem, who defied the Dutch Commissioner in the following, perhaps apocryphal words:

> Never while I live shall the state recognize the sovereignty of the Netherlands in the sense in which you interpret it. After my death the Raja may do as he chooses. Not by a mere scrap of paper shall any man become the master of another's lands. Rather let the *kris* decide.

The upshot of this warlike declaration will be described in Chapter Six, but first let us examine events across the water in Lombok, where a protracted power struggle had been underway.

CHAPTER 5

BALINESE AND EUROPEANS IN TURBULENT LOMBOK (1824-1843)

B alinese Conquest and Rule of Lombok

The island of Lombok is the disadvantaged counterpart of the island of Bali. It is remarkably similar in natural and cultural features but it lacks Bali's great wealth of scenic and artistic endowment. In the late sixteenth century Lombok was conquered and colonized by the Balinese, and for the next hundred years it was subjected to very strong Balinese cultural influences. But in Lombok the Hindu Balinese, a 5 to 10 percent element in the population, collided with the Muslim Bugis from Makassar, seafaring traders who were aggressively exporting their own manners, customs and religion. The Sasak tribes people were converted to Islam and the island slipped almost altogether from Balinese control into that of Makassar and Sumbawa. At the turn of the nineteenth century Lombok was reconquered by Balinese armies and again subjected to massive Balinese infiltration. Gusti Gede Ngurah Karangasem, Raja of Karangasem-Bali, who made himself the paramount ruler of northern, eastern and western Bali, made himself also the paramount ruler of Lombok. As Raja of Karangasem-

Lombok he installed other Balinese princes as rulers of the numerous little states into which the island was divided and named his own daughter, known as the Cokorda (a title, not a name), as regent.

Shortly after it re-emerged as a Balinese dependency, Lombok emerged also as a regional center of trade. The island was strategically placed on the heavily trafficked Europe–Asia and Singapore–Australia shipping routes, and its chief port of Ampenan, located in the big, sheltered Ampenan Bay, began to attract regional and international visitors. In the early 1830s several Westerners settled in the island as resident merchants. The most important of these were the Englishman George Pocock King, who fled to Lombok in 1834 to escape his debts in Surabaya, and the Dane Mads Lange, each of whom also introduced more or less permanent associates. Lange and King became bitter commercial rivals and attached themselves to the leading but rival local rulers. Civil wars were already inevitable, and the advent of the Europeans signified that they would come sooner, last longer and prove more costly. Civil wars and Western traders' involvement in them meant, furthermore, that the colonial Dutch in nearby Java would interest themselves and therefore intervene in Lombok's affairs. Lombok, like neighboring Bali, was therefore destined sooner rather than later to become a Dutch colonial possession.

The domestic situation in Lombok in the 1830s was far from tranquil and equally far from transparent. The presence of the Western merchants enormously complicated the already involuted island politics, which is to say the intrigues of the feuding members of the Balinese royal house of Karangasem who ruled the various principalities, for, with and against whom conspired also various of the princes of Bali itself. The house of Karangasem, unhappily, was especially vulnerable to violent animosities because it was not only arrogant and aggressive but also degenerate, being given to that most heinous of moral offences, the crime of incest. Whoever would start a war had only to allege incest to condemn his enemy and thus justify himself. Conspiracy, commerce and incest, then, were the prime factors in the Lombok Wars of 1838 and 1839 which led directly to Dutch colonialism. These bizarre circumstances require an attempt at summation, even at risk of oversimplifying without actually clarifying.

Hostile Rajas and Rival Merchants

Gusti Gede Ngurah Karangasem, the founder of the modern ruling house of Karangasem, died in 1806, bequeathing to his numerous and mainly dissolute progeny an apparently endless series of quarrels over his domains both in Bali and Lombok. One of his sons, Gusti Gede Ngurah Lanang, who made himself briefly and bloodily the ruler of Karangasem-Bali, committed such hideous crimes (allegedly both incest and cannibalism) that in 1824 he had to abandon his throne in Bali and seek shelter in Lombok. There he found himself almost equally unwelcome, but he did manage to assert his authority over a small state on Ampenan Bay. He made repeated and more or less polite requests to his sister, the Cokorda, to terminate her regency and yield him the throne of Karangasem-Lombok, then later to join him in the reconquest of Karangasem-Bali. Instead, she invited their own half-brother, Ratu Ngurah Panji, to join her as royal consort, and when this particular paramour died (1835), she chose his son, Ratu Gusti Ngurah Panji, as his replacement. Ratu Gusti Ngurah Panji himself compounded the incest by taking his own sister also into his harem. The outraged Raja Lanang appealed urgently and regularly to Anak Agung Ketut Karangasem, the Raja of Mataram, the second most important state of the island, to assist him in deposing his abominable sister and her abandoned consort and in establishing his own claim. The Raja of Mataram declined to undertake the military action which would certainly have been necessary for any such dynastic rearrangement.

Raja Lanang died in 1837, bequeathing his claim and little else to his son Ida Ratu, who continued to press the reluctant Raja of Mataram to overthrow the wicked Cokorda. Mads Lange, the Danish merchant, meanwhile, had built up his commercial enterprises under the patronage of Raja Lanang and his son with the apparent consent of the Cokorda and her paramours. George Pocock King had attached his fortunes to those of the young, vigorous and apparently much more admirable Raja of Mataram. This ambitious young ruler proved far from unresponsive to King's suggestions that the time had come to overthrow the Cokorda and to establish Mataram's political—and King's commercial—hegemony over the island. It took only a minor crisis to spark a war—a routine quarrel over boundaries and water rights. In early 1838 the affair escalated into widespread conflict both by land and by sea, with King becoming the Commander-in-Chief and Admiral of the Fleet for the Raja of Mataram, and Lange, after a critical interval of hesitation, playing the same role for the Cokorda.

Wars of 1838; Cokorda's Defeat; Lange's Decline

The course of hostilities proved only slightly less mystifying than had been the preliminaries. Karangasem, with twenty times the population of Mataram, could and did raise about 10,000 troops, but the royal house of Karangasem was widely detested and its fighting men could easily be induced to defect. Mataram seemed an almost harmless challenger until King suddenly began importing soldiers from Bali, to an eventual grand total of about 10,000. Along with the troops, King imported also Gusti Bagus Karang, recently and briefly Raja of Karangasem-Bali, who, having been deprived of his throne, was willing to join Mataram in the fight against Karangasem-Lombok. King also imported Nakhoda (Captain) Ismaila, a Bugis merchant, pirate and slaver, who brought with him a gang of 200 Bugis ruffians to serve as a special task force. For payment of fl. 125 per day he chartered his private bark, *Pleyades*, as flagship of a small fleet of European and Asian vessels, some of whose captains were only with difficulty induced or impressed into service, which were used to transport troops from Bali and arms from Singapore. Lange and his partner, John Burd, meanwhile deployed their heavily armed merchant vessels, the *Falcon* and *de Zuid*, to blockade the Lombok coast. King, in riposte, set up powerful shore batteries in Ampenan Bay to keep them out. Presently Burd sailed off to Batavia to appeal to the Dutch to come to the aid of the beleaguered Cokorda.

The Dutch had already heard disquieting rumors of what was happening in Lombok, but they had contented themselves with sending a mission to investigate. They had had a report, for instance, from the Dutch captain of the *Monkey*, on an English-owned ship from Semarang. The captain had engaged, more or less voluntarily, on behalf of the Mataram-King faction, in transport of troops from Bali. But certain events had convinced him that he had best confess all, and perhaps more than all, to presumably vigilant Dutch colonial authorities. His fourth voyage had ended in a bloody shipboard uprising when the Balinese troops began to suspect, perhaps with reason, that they were being kidnapped to be sold as slaves. The captain's rather extravagantly embroidered and self-exculpatory report was not much more fanciful than what was actually happening in Lombok, but the War of 1838 was over before the Dutch investigators even arrived to check the various reports.

The decisive battle occurred in early June 1838 when the Cokorda mounted a badly timed and ill-coordinated offensive by land and sea, relying upon hundreds of soldiers and scores of *perahu*, most of which never turned up, Nakhoda Ismaila's task force having surprised them on their way to the rendezvous. Mataram thus won the war, but the Raja, who was shot in the head in the course of a minor skirmish, did not live to profit from his victory. Nor did the Cokorda survive defeat. When her capital was besieged, she set fire to the *puri*, plunged her *kris* into the heart of her consort, then turned it upon herself, inspiring some 300 members of the court to emulation in the traditional rite of the *puputan*—the self-destruction of a royal household when other disaster seems certain.

The Raja of Mataram was succeeded by his son, Gusti Ngurah Ketut Karangasem, who selflessly placed the former pretender, Ida Ratu, on the throne just vacated by the Cokorda, but rather less selflessly made it quite clear to him that the overlord–vassal relationship had been reversed: Mataram was now the paramount state and Karangasem was the subordinate. There also occurred a beginning of reversal in the respective positions of Lange and King. King, the ally of the winner, was not about to let the commercial rewards of victory fall to Lange. Western shipping had begun to seek out Ampenan Bay again in even greater numbers just as soon as King silenced the shore batteries and Lange lifted the blockade. But King was unable to persuade the young Raja to expel Lange, or at least not just yet. The Raja, who knew the Dutch fixation about English penetration, feared the Dutch reaction to any move which would seem to favor an English trader. He was already having difficulty enough with tiresome Dutch investigators.

The first Dutch mission to Lombok was headed by Army Captain J. S. Wetters, who was already familiar with the region, having negotiated the agreement of 1826 with the Raja of Badung for recruitment of Balinese soldiers. Captain Wetters arrived in Lombok on July 5, 1838 on the schooner *Kameleon*, impressively escorted by the corvette *Hippomenes*, the iron steamships *Etna* and *Hekla* and the adventuresome *Monkey*. After visiting the ruins of the Cokorda's capital and *puri*, Wetters proceeded to Ampenan. There King received him, shadowed him and monitored his very unilluminating conversations with the Raja. Wetters' trip to Lombok was productive of nothing except a side excursion to Bali, where he reconnoitered the situation in Buleleng and Karangasem in advance of Granpré Molière's visit.

The second Dutch mission to Lombok (December 1838) was headed by Navy Captain A. C. Edeling, who was sent with the corvette *Triton* and the schooner *Castor* to make stern representations in the case of the murder of a Chinese sea captain, Kouw Si An, and the looting of his vessel, the *Fatal Berakat*, which flew the Dutch flag. The incident had occurred in Ampenan on October 10, 1838. According to the report made by members of the crew when the ship reached Surabaya, the murderer was one of Nakhoda Ismaila's Bugis ruffians. He had been relieved of his loot (opium and money), given shelter and presently enabled to escape by George Pocock King. But the Dutch investigators in Ampenan were quite unable to pin down the facts. The Raja and King both professed themselves eager to see Dutch justice done but declared themselves unable to produce the alleged murderer, who had fled, they said, to Bali. The investigators were unconvinced, nor were they overly impressed with the fact that whereas Lange flew the Danish flag, King flew the Dutch. They had already been informed by reliable witnesses that during the recent war, when King had two shore batteries in Ampenan Bay, he flew both the Dutch and the English flags and trained the gunners, in the course of target practice, routinely and symbolically to shoot down the former. The Edeling mission was not a success, nor was that of Granpré Molière, who called at Lombok after his visit to Bali but was unable to travel to the capital to meet the Raja.

Wars of 1839; Fall of the House of Karangasem

The Lombok War of 1838 had not really resolved either political or commercial rivalries; it merely provoked the war of 1839. The Raja of Mataram, as paramount ruler, distrusted and detested the Raja of Karangasem, his ungrateful and therefore presumably rebellious subordinate; King distrusted and detested Lange; and everybody was suspicious of Gusti Bagus Karang, the ex-Raja of Karangasem-Bali who had helped the Raja of Mataram make the once forlorn pretender, young Ida Ratu, the now pretentious Raja of Karangasem.

Gusti Bagus Karang held that he had abandoned claims to his own throne in Bali to see justice done in Karangasem-Lombok, only to find himself later rejected and maligned. He made his resentment so unmistakable that both the Raja of Mataram and the Raja of Karangasem automatically assumed that he was conspiring to overthrow them in order to rule all of Lombok in his own right and perhaps Bali as well. The rulers of Karangasem-Bali and Buleleng-Bali, who had no reason to wish him well, decided to make his downfall a certainty. Justly or unjustly, they accused him of incest and secured the blessing of the Dewa Agung of Klungkung upon anyone who would depose him from the few scraps of Bali domain over which he ruled. The Raja of Mataram, after more or less scrupulous investigation of the incest charges, publicly pronounced him guilty. But Gusti Bagus Karang still had it within his capability to provoke certain local disorders which, in early 1839, developed into a small-scale civil war. A half dozen prominent princes of Bali and Lombok raised a much more powerful army than was really necessary and marched upon their lone adversary. It was a little ten-day war which climaxed in a *puputan,* with Gusti Bagus Karang ending his own life with greater dignity than he had lived it. The splendid *kris* with which he killed himself was sent, along with the rest of his regalia, back to Karangasem-Bali, from whence, it was hoped, no more troublesome refugees would come.

The ten-day war of February 1839 was followed by the four-day war of June. The Raja of Mataram decided that the time had come to depose the Raja of Karangasem, an enterprise in which he had the enthusiastic assistance of King, who had determined upon a definitive settlement with Lange. The Raja led one wing of his army and King led the other in an attack upon the *puri.* The Raja elected escape rather than the *puputan* and fled to the interior, where he was captured and imprisoned and six months later (December 1839) murdered. Lange, meanwhile, had been given exactly one hour in which to settle his affairs in Ampenan and depart from Lombok forever. He made it within that deadline to his schooner, *Venus,* and sailed off to Bali. Or, according to a more heroic version of the story—his own—he fought his way through his enemies, leaped onto a fast horse, swam the horse out to sea, boarded his yacht, but still sailed off. Lange's partner, John Burd, tried to revisit Lombok later that year in order to collect debts and information, also perhaps to rescue the imprisoned Raja, but his vessel, *de Zuid,* was fired upon by King's *Pleyades,* and he thought it wise to withdraw.

George Pocock King and the New Dynasty

King remained in Lombok as Syahbandar to the Raja and as proprietor of the factory and shipyard which had once been Lange's, becoming, just as he had intended, the new merchant king and "White Raja" of Ampenan. He succeeded well enough in overcoming Dutch distrust that they did not put him out of business and actually at times engaged his services. He won Dutch confidence and gratitude mainly because he brought men and arms from Lombok to reinforce the Dutch armies in Bali in 1849. But he experienced increasing difficulty with his own patron, the Raja of Mataram, who showed evidence of being determined to be the master of his own kingdom. The Raja expelled King's friend, the arrogant and violent Nakhoda Ismaila, together with his gang of Bugis, the Nakhoda having, in fact, proved troublesome to King as well as to the Raja by reason of his attempts to share in the profits of the opium trade.

King apparently left Lombok in the mid-1850s, when he vanishes from the historical records. It seems probable that he sold his commercial interests to another Englishman, named Cooper, who had been associated with him from time to time over the years. When Alfred Russel Wallace made his famous visit to Lombok (June–July 1856), he stayed with a certain Mr Cooper, who was the proprietor of a commercial establishment. Wallace encountered three other Europeans: a second merchant whom he identified only as "Mr S"; an unnamed "Dutch gentleman"; and Mr Ross, an Englishman better known later as "the King of the Cocos Islands," who had been engaged by the Dutch to settle the affairs of a bankrupt Dutch missionary. Evidently, the European population of Lombok continued even after the time of Lange and King to include people about whom one would wish to know much more. But Wallace was uncharacteristically reticent and other records are lacking. There were no European residents in the 1890s when the Dutch returned in force to add Lombok to their other colonial territories.

Dutch Investigations; Huskus Koopman's Contracts

After the visits of Wetters, Edeling and Granpré Molière, the next Dutch démarche upon Lombok was that of Huskus Koopman, the accomplished *contractsluiter*, whose assignment it was to induce the rajas of Bali and Lombok to acknowledge Dutch sovereignty and thereafter, among many other concessions, to renounce the traditional practice of reef rights and to engage instead in more conventional ships salvage. Huskus Koopman made five separate voyages (1839–43) into the region before he fully accomplished his mission, but on the first two trips he visited only Bali and it was not until October 1842 that he first traveled to Lombok. The Commissioner had tried to convince both himself and the Governor-General that contracts binding upon the Balinese rajas would be binding also upon Lombok, the presumed dependency of the Raja of Karangasem, himself the presumed vassal of the Dewa Agung of Klungkung. Recent events had made it apparent, however, that all such assumptions were ill-founded. Huskus Koopman had suggested to the Governor-General that if Lombok objected to this reading of the contracts, the Dutch might spare themselves much money and blood by backstopping the Balinese invasion and reconquest of Lombok which the Dewa Agung, the Raja of Buleleng and the Raja of Karangasem could, in fact, only with difficulty be restrained from mounting. But Dutch official priorities, as established in The Hague and Batavia, called for documentation first, conquest later, hence Koopman's somewhat tardy visit.

Huskus Koopman arrived in Lombok in October 1842 on board the corvette *Argo*, whose captain, Den Berger, faithfully followed his detailed instructions about firing off salutes when the Commissioner landed, staging dress parades ashore and otherwise making of the visit a state occasion. Koopman negotiated not with the Raja of Mataram himself but with his vigorous and quite ambitious brother, the Raja of Selaparang, who was already clearly self-elected as successor. The Raja acceded to the terms which Koopman proposed with regard to reef rights. The same provisions obtained as for Bali: authorization of payment of 15 to 50 percent of the value of the cargo to any legitimate salvager, the exact amount and all other relevant matters to be determined by a three-man arbitration board representing the Dutch, the Raja and the owner. The surprising part of the agreement was Huskus Koopman's nominee as Dutch representative on any future salvage commission—George Pocock King, who, he reported, seemed to have mellowed. The young Raja, having amiably agreed to salvage, refused categorically to accept any suggestion with regard to sovereignty.

In 1843 Huskus Koopman was back in Lombok with a very carefully drafted letter from the Governor-General stating that he wished to clear away any misunderstanding. The contracts already negotiated with the Balinese rajas, he said, were assumed to be binding also upon Lombok, which had been a dependency of Bali. But in view of the fact that Lombok had separated itself from Bali, the Raja's own acknowledgment of the validity of the contracts was now necessary, otherwise the Dutch would "find themselves obliged in safeguarding their own rights to support those of the Balinese and to make them operative." The somewhat clouded implication, which Huskus Koopman was perhaps indelicate enough to clarify, was that the Dutch might unleash another Balinese invasion. On June 7 the Raja yielded and in July 1843 he sent a mission to Batavia bearing gifts of a *kris* and a lance as tokens of submission.

Huskus Koopman, who had now repeatedly persuaded the rajas to agree to whatever contract concepts the Governor-General contrived and longed to rest from his arduous travels, was delighted to hear himself warmly commended and to be proposed for award of the Order of the Netherlands Lion. He was shocked, however, to discover that his labors were not yet finished. Somehow it had escaped everyone's attention that the contract concepts drawn up for the Raja of Lombok did not contain a clause whereby the Raja undertook thereafter to cherish and protect Dutch traders. The necessary addenda were incorporated into the new contract concept, which the Governor-General signed and sealed in advance and confided to Huskus Koopman to deliver. In September 1843 the contract maker was back in Lombok. The Raja promptly signed and sealed his copy (September 23). Perhaps by inadvertence, he attached it to the Governor-General's original and sent both of them back to Batavia, thus perhaps clearing his files of business which he preferred to forget. As it turned out, he was the only one of the rajas actually to ratify the contracts without the necessity for a military expedition. The Dutch conquest of Lombok could thus be postponed for almost exactly half a century.

Princes of Lombok in Power in Bali

The Raja of Selaparang, with whom Huskus Koopman negotiated, was the youngest of three brothers who became joint rulers of Lombok after the triumph of Mataram over Karangasem. The new Raja of Mataram seems to have preferred to share, dilute and obscure the lines of power, and his brothers, especially the younger, were more than willing to oblige him. In 1870 Gusti Ngurah Gede Karangasem, the Raja of Selaparang, succeeded the eldest brother, the Raja of Mataram, as paramount ruler. Commonly known as the Raja of Lombok, he ruled until he was deposed and exiled by the Dutch at the end of the Lombok War of 1894. He was mainly responsible for the military assistance which Lombok provided the Dutch in the course of the Dutch–Balinese wars of 1846–9. By helping to make certain that the Balinese were never again to be in a position to invade Lombok, he made it equally certain that the Dutch would eventually do so. The second brother, a dissolute but nevertheless engaging prince, wisely refrained from disputing the throne. He fathered two sons, however, who succeeded respectively to the thrones of Buleleng and Karangasem in Bali. His third son was Gusti Ketut Jelantik, the hero of the Dutch–Balinese wars. All three perished in 1849. A fourth son was executed for "desecration of caste" (incest?). A fifth was exiled to Negara, Bali, for attempting to usurp the throne of Karangasem.

CHAPTER 6

PUNITIVE EXPEDITIONS (1846-1849)

 orthern Princes' Defiance of the Dutch; Gusti Ketut Jelantik

Once the impetuous young Gusti Ketut Jelantik said "Let the *kris* decide," both the Dutch and the Balinese knew that war was not far off. Emboldened by Jelantik, the Raja of Buleleng remained disinclined to meet Dutch demands. In 1845 J. T. T. Maijor, the Resident of Besuki, East Java, traveled to Buleleng to convey the Governor-General's protests. He received no greater satisfaction than had his predecessor. The Dutch therefore began making ready an expeditionary force, which assembled at Besuki to sail to Bali on the east monsoon of the following year. Jelantik meanwhile began building fortifications, raising troops and acquiring arms, relying, as the Dutch correctly surmised, upon certain enterprising Singapore merchants for large shipments of weapons. Balinese–Dutch relations were rapidly moving into a new and altogether tragic phase.

Balinese military preparations centered upon the northern rajadom of Buleleng. The ruler, Gusti Ngurah Made Karangasem, was the elder brother of Gusti Gede Ngurah Karangsem, the Raja of Karangasem (not to be confused with Gusti Ngurah Ketut Karangasem, the Raja of Lombok, a close relative and bitter enemy). Buleleng and Karangasem, the two most powerful rajadoms of the island and long-time

A view of the old palace of Buleleng, showing the pavilion-style buildings with thatched roofs. A wall encircles the entire compound.

rivals, were now closely allied in opposing the political and military aims of the Dutch. They had the blessing of the Dewa Agung of Klung-kung, who was in no position to provide much more than his bless-ing but at least did not withhold it. The Raja of Badung in the south, who wished to preserve the profits of trade and was no friend of the turbulent northerners, sought to remain detached from the com-ing conflict and exercised his not inconsiderable influence upon his friendly neighbor, the Raja of Tabanan, to do likewise. The other states—Gianyar, Mengwi and Bangli, in south-central Bali, and Jem-brana in the west—were allied rather tenuously with Klungkung but were also attentive to Badung. They were not disposed to become involved and, unlike Buleleng and Karangasem, they had no military tradition to uphold. Bangli, in particular, was determined to remain neutral and did so until the end. With local lines of allegiance thus confused, it periodically served the purposes of the rajas themselves to claim that they could not act without the prior consent of the Dewa

Agung. Similarly, it sometimes suited the Dutch to hold that the Dewa Agung, whom they knew to be all but impotent, ruled as Susuhunan (Emperor) over a united Bali. In fact, everyone acted on the basis of his own best estimate of his own best interests. Dutch self-interest, it was quite apparent, dictated a show of force. Once the Dutch set themselves to subdue Bali, the ultimate outcome was not in doubt. But it took three campaigns to shatter the Balinese defences and morale, campaigns in which the Dutch did not always by any means achieve either victory or glory.

First Dutch Military Expedition (1846); Success and Stalemate

The First Dutch Military Expedition against Bali (1846) seemed a formidable enough force to cope with any Balinese resistance. The invasion fleet was made up of two frigates with a total of 34 guns, four steamships, four schooner-brigs, twelve schooners and 40 small craft. The sea force numbered 1,280 men and the land force 1,700, the latter inclusive of 400 Europeans equipped with 230 pieces of field artillery. As the Dutch fleet prepared to sail, the Danish trader Mads Lange arrived at Besuki from Kuta on his schooner *Venus* to volunteer his own good offices, bringing with him six blacksmiths from Bali to aid the warmakers and five interpreters from Banyu-wangi to aid the peacemakers. The English trader George Pocock King also appeared, coming from Lombok with offers of aid from the Raja, who was eager not to be left out of any expedition against the Raja of Karangasem, his sworn enemy.

The Dutch invasion force was under the joint command of General Rochussen and Rear Admiral E. B. van Bosch with J. T. T. Maijor, the Resident of Besuki and Commissioner for Bali and Lombok as civilian representative. The fleet arrived off the Buleleng coast on June 22, 1846.

Maijor immediately sent ashore an ultimatum denouncing the Rajas of Buleleng, Karangasem and Klungkung for not observing the terms of the 1841–3 agreements and demanding that they undertake to do so forthwith. He also required the Rajas to pay the costs of the expedition and admit a Dutch garrison both to collect the payments and to guarantee the peace. Heer Maijor entrusted his ultimatum to the Chinese trader-captain of a junk from Bangkok, who delivered it to the Chinese harbormaster, who dared not hand so rude a message directly to the Raja. The princes, nevertheless, were quickly apprised of the content.

The two Rajas, inspired by Gusti Jelantik, whom the Dutch conceded to be a man of military genius, had made unexpectedly systematic preparations for resistance. The town of Buleleng was ringed with barricades three to ten feet thick and over twenty feet high in places, constructed of stone and clay packed between tree trunks, with sharpened bamboo stakes set in the sides and top, and some fifty cannons artfully placed and disguised. On both sides of the barricades had been dug deep pits and trenches, and all about were treacherous little traps of pointed slivers of bamboo. Jelantik had not only supervised the building of defence works but had raised and trained an army, a total of some 10,000 soldiers stationed in Buleleng itself and thousands more outside of the town. Many if not most of the recruits were mere youths armed with bamboo spears, but others were stout warriors equipped with European weapons.

Heer Maijor's ultimatum allowed the Balinese rulers "three times twenty-four hours" to comply with Dutch demands. The Raja sent the reply that he needed ten days to consult with his brother, the Raja of Karangasem, and also with the Dewa Agung. Maijor granted an extension of twenty-four hours. The Raja and Jelantik thereupon disappeared from the town, but the troops ostentatiously busied themselves strengthening the defences. A Dutch officer was sent ashore to protest. When the Balinese shouted abuse and threats, the Dutch fired off an admonitory salvo which killed one soldier. The Balinese forces then withdrew from the waterfront, which the Dutch, fearing a ruse, refrained just yet from occupying.

At dawn on June 28, the time limit for compliance with the ultimatum having expired several days earlier, the Dutch frigates laid down a bombardment, and a few hours later the troops landed. They fought their way through fierce resistance into the town of Buleleng, which they captured, pillaged and burned. The next day they subjected the adjacent royal capital of Singaraja to the same treatment. The greatly depleted Balinese forces withdrew inland to the strong defensive positions prepared by Jelantik at the town of Jagaraga, ten miles to the east and five miles from the coast.

The Dutch had won a swift victory at little cost to themselves (18 dead, 47 wounded), whereas the Balinese suffered immense losses of life and property. The Dutch victory was empty, however, unless they could enforce their will upon the rajas, who were firmly entrenched in the nearby hills. Not knowing the country and not having made provision for supply lines extending any distance from the coast, the Dutch were afraid to push inland.

Lange's Intermediation and the Peace Settlement

At this moment of apparent but deceptive victory and defeat, Mads Lange volunteered to mediate. He proposed to travel by horseback from Buleleng to Jagaraga to negotiate with the rajas, taking with him only his Balinese assistant and one servant. The Dutch accepted the offer, thinking it most unlikely that he could get through to Jagaraga or, if he did, that he could return. Contrary to their expectations, Lange made the trip swiftly and safely and brought back the report that the Balinese were willing to participate in a peace conference. The Raja of Buleleng, he said, would not himself appear—he had told Lange, with a laugh, that he was much too ill; nor would Jelantik who feigned a foot injury. Although neither was willing to entrust himself to the Dutch, it was agreed that the Raja's younger brother, the Raja of Karangasem, would represent them.

On July 5, the Raja of Karangasem appeared at Dutch headquarters to make submission. To the surprise and gratification of the Dutch he was followed shortly afterwards by the Raja of Buleleng. On July 9 both rajas formally accepted the Dutch terms. They undertook to abide by the 1841–3 contracts. They would bear the costs of the expedition (fl. 225,000 from Buleleng, fl. 75,000 from Karangasem), the

total to be paid within ten years; they would dismantle their own fortifications and build no more; they would accept a Dutch garrison,
build a fort for it and supply it with provisions; finally, they would accept a Dutch official as regular visitor or as resident representative.
The Dutch were jubilant. The Governor-General and the First Admiral of the Fleet came from Batavia to stage a splendid banquet at
which the two rajas and Jelantik were the guests of honor. The expeditionary force then sailed triumphantly back to Java, leaving behind
a garrison of 150–200 men to maintain the Dutch presence and collect
reparations. The garrison was installed in a newly built fortification on
the coast at Pabean.

Celebrations of peace and victory proved to be premature. The
rajas failed to pay even the first installment on reparations; they re-
fused to provision the Dutch garrison, which was, in fact, so boycot-
ted and harassed that some of the soldiers deserted to join the
Balinese, who gave them a very cordial reception. The irrepressible
Gusti Jelantik traveled throughout the island radiating defiance of the
Dutch. He inspired the Dewa Agung to send protest after protest to
Batavia regarding the Dutch interpretation of the peace terms. The
various rajas resumed the practices which were certain to fetch the
Dutch back again in force, not hesitating, for instance, to exercise reef
rights in the case of an English flagship out of Singapore and a Dutch
flagship out of Batavia, which were wrecked off the south coast.

Second Expedition (1848); Dutch Débacle at Jagaraga

The Second Dutch Military Expedition against Bali (1848) followed
inevitably upon the first. It was one of the strongest military forces as
yet employed against any of the princes of the Indies. The commander, Major General Jhr. C. van der Wijck, was one of the most distinguished colonial soldiers. He demanded and got more ships, troops
and artillery than had been deemed necessary two years before. The
invasion fleet was made up of four steam vessels, five schooners,
eleven transports and miscellaneous small craft. It was manned by
740 sailors and provided with 72 cannons. The land force consisted

of 2,400 men (including Madurese, Javanese and one company of Africans) with a support corps of 500 coolies to maintain a supply line to points distant from the coast. Some 775 members of the land force, 109 of them officers, were Europeans. The cavalry was well represented and it brought with it 156 horses.

Before fully committing themselves to this troublesome new expedition, the Dutch had magnanimously offered the rajas (Buleleng, Karangasem and Klungkung) the opportunity to repent, to send a mission to Batavia to implore the forgiveness of the Governor-General and to hand over Jelantik as a hostage. The rajas ignored the invitation. The force therefore rendezvoused on schedule in early June off the Buleleng coast. Lange was there again on the *Venus*. King was also among those present. The stage was set and the cast was reassembled for a repetition of the 1846 performance.

The operation began on May 7, when the frigates shelled the small port town of Sangsit. It continued the next day with the landing of troops, who succeeded very quickly in establishing a base on shore at the cost of only eight casualties. As a matter of fact, Sangsit itself had been sufficiently subdued a week earlier. The advance patrol craft *Argo* had discovered unexpectedly strong defences and had virtually demolished the town with a midday rain of shells which caught everyone by surprise—men, women and playing children. The demoralizing effect of the *Argo* bombardment was still further extended that same night when a sudden and extraordinarily violent volcanic eruption in Java produced light and sound effects which the population mistook for another attack further down the coast.

General van der Wijck was much gratified by his early successes, even when he discovered that the Balinese defenders had again withdrawn to Jagaraga, where they had greatly strengthened their fortifications and had dug a wide, deep trench barring the approach to the town. On the morning of May 9 the Dutch began confidently to march upon the Balinese stronghold. At first it was an almost effortless advance over gradually rising, mostly arid and treeless terrain which the Balinese made almost no effort to defend. As it soon turned out, they had a better plan. They had laid traps and built road blocks further on, and they had as their ally the blazing tropical sun. The Dutch began to tire and to take casualties, but they pushed doggedly forward. They captured the first of the major Balinese redoubts without too much difficulty and advanced upon the second. But the Balinese, boldly and brilliantly led by Jelantik, had installed 25 cannons and mustered 16,000 men—1,500 equipped with firearms, the others with lances and spears which they used to their advantage. They fought off three Dutch attacks and then began harassing the enemy from the sides and the rear, inflicting numerous casualties.

By midday the Dutch were in serious trouble. They had already expended most of the 100,000 rounds of ammunition which they had thought sufficient for any eventuality. They were stunned by the unexpected strength of the resistance and the size of their own losses. They were also wilted by the heat, parched with thirst and madly tantalized by the sight of cool shade and shimmering water just beyond the Balinese lines. Their supply lines were also breaking down, and the bearers were suffering almost as badly as the troops from heat and thirst. They sank in exhaustion when drafted to carry off soldiers who had collapsed with sunstroke. Led by Jelantik, the Balinese pushed their advantage by launching a strong counter-attack. General van Wijck had no choice but to call a retreat. It swiftly turned into a rout. The Dutch abandoned their equipment and supplies and made for their ships. The Balinese almost succeeded in cutting off their line of retreat and challenged all weary, footsore stragglers to hand-to-hand combat with spear against sword.

That day the Dutch counted 264 dead, including 14 officers. It was small comfort that they thought the Balinese had lost 2,000, including 200 chiefs. From safe sanctuary on shipboard the Dutch petitioned Batavia to send reinforcements, mentioning two battalions of infantry and 1,000 porters. Batavia, instead of complying, ordered the whole forlorn expedition back to Java. There, while conducting an acrimonious inquiry into the reasons for the failure of their second expedition, the Dutch began readying a third.

Bali enjoyed a brief respite which no one expected to last. Mads Lange, who had hoped again to serve as mediator but had found no occasion to do so, returned to Kuta. His business was suffering and he sought to safeguard himself against further losses. George Pocock King returned to Lombok. There he counseled the Raja to prepare to intervene in the new disorders which he knew would soon break out. Jelantik flung himself with furious energy into reminding the Balinese rajas and people of their exploits, reminding them also, however, that for being twice worsted, the Dutch were all the less likely to forget and forgo their claims to sovereignty.

Third Expedition (1849); Theatrics of Conciliation

As was now becoming habitual, the Third Dutch Military Expedition against Bali (1849) arrived off Buleleng with the east monsoon (late March). The commander, General A. Michiels, had prudently reconnoitered the whole of the northern coast in mid-November. The General was convinced it would be a quick and decisive campaign and he would soon be back in Java. His fleet had over 100 vessels—heavily armed frigates, steamships, schooners and scores of large and small auxiliary craft manned in all by some 3,000 sailors. The land forces were made up of 5,000 Dutch and indigenous troops, the former more numerous than the latter, under command of 187 European officers. There were some 400 pieces of field artillery and 273 horses for the cavalry. There was also a support force of 3,293 coolies.

On March 31, encountering almost no resistance, the Dutch landed 700 men at Sangsit and marched into Buleleng and Singaraja, where the General made his headquarters in the Raja's palace. Within the next several days the rest of the expedition disembarked, still meeting with no opposition. The Balinese had withdrawn to Jagaraga, where they had decided to take their decisive stand. From there they sent emissaries to sound out the Dutch intentions, professing themselves loyal to their pledges and dismayed by Dutch hostility. General Michiels received several messengers and several messages, then announced that he would treat only with the Raja and Jelantik in person.

It was arranged, therefore, that the General and the princes should meet on April 4 in the Raja's palace and, said the General, in response to questioning, the princes could bring with them as many of their followers as they saw fit.

On the morning of April 4 the Dutch deployed their troops in full dress uniform in parade formation within and around the palace, on the main street of Singaraja, and out along the road to Jagaraga. At 1:00 p.m. there appeared a small but alert, well-armed party of Balinese, followed at 2:00 p.m. by a force of 3,000 picked warriors. At 3:00 p.m. came the main body of some 9,000 men followed by the Raja of Karangasem and Gusti Ketut Jelantik.

The Balinese troops were dressed in their most splendid costumes, as if prepared not for battle but for the Baris (warrior dance). They carried themselves haughtily, struck theatrical stances and fingered their weapons suggestively—many of these weapons obviously being those captured from the Dutch a year before. They eyed the Dutch with suspicion and hostility and were clearly ready on signal from their leaders to rush to attack.

The Raja and Jelantik were especially magnificent in brilliant red sarongs nattily gathered up to display short tight trousers, below and above which gleamed bare, bronze skin. Their waists were nipped in by golden girdles in which, at the back, each displayed a huge jeweled *kris*, the ornate handles extending above shoulder height for quick, dramatic draw. Their thick, flowing black hair was bound by white headcloths in which were inserted, in the case of the Raja, a green sprig, and in the case of Jelantik, a crimson flower.

The Raja himself was a slim young man of thirty, aristocratic in face and figure, but not, it seemed to the Dutch observers, an especially decisive or dynamic person, being, in fact, almost without animation or expression. But Jelantik, a striking young man of the same age and build, they described as "a very handsome fellow," with fine oval face, straight, thin nose, piercing eyes and highly mobile features, obviously a man of fierce passion and courage. One Dutch military historian, paid him this tribute: "mind fertile with resources, character energetic, heart ardent with patriotism, one of those adversaries who is difficult but glorious to vanquish."

The princes were accompanied by other royalty and by the high priests, some almost as richly dressed and proud in carriage as were the two chief figures. The Raja of Buleleng was not one of the participants. This time his excuse was that he was much too old and frail to risk the exertion and the excitement. In fact, he deemed it certain misfortune to enter his own palace on sufferance of another.

The encounter, which started as a triumph of Dutch and Balinese showmanship, deteriorated into a miserable failure of statesmanship. The Dutch brusquely reiterated their familiar and expected demands except that this time there was no talk either of reparations or of hostages. The Balinese listened politely and seemed to concur but with no very visible display of conviction, the bare points of their spears signaling to those who knew Balinese custom, as the General and his staff did not, that they remained defiant. The General explained that he expected the Balinese to return to Jagaraga to dismantle their fortifications and prepare for peaceful takeover by the Dutch two days later. The Raja, the prince, and their numerous following staged an impressive processional exit and returned to Jagaraga to reconsolidate their position.

Jagaraga Defence and Dutch Seizure

The next ten days were filled with tentative little maneuvers on the side of both the Dutch and the Balinese. The Dutch were testing out the road to Jagaraga, which proved to be impassable without major effort to remove barriers and subdue forts. The Balinese were trying to determine exactly how willing the Dutch might be either to fight or to compromise. On August 13 there occurred yet another staged encounter between the princes and the intruders. The Balinese once more made a show both of splendor and power, this time with much clearer intimation than before that they were quite prepared to fight to the death. Again they talked of yielding Jagaraga peacefully, but they then retired to the hills not to remove the road blocks but to install

AUX INDES NÉERLANDAISES
Le Rajah de Boeleleng, dans l'île de Bali, se suicide avec quatre cents de ses sujets

A contemporary illustration from the French newspaper *Le Petit Journal* depicting the *puputan* of the Raja of Buleleng.

more. At Jagaraga itself, as the Dutch had already been advised by informers, the barricades were even more imposing than those in Buleleng in 1846. Other fortified positions radiated out from the town in all directions and a wide flooded trench twenty-six feet deep cut off the approach from the road.

General Michiels decided to attack without further delay. The Dutch troops marched on Jagaraga early in the morning of August 15, overcoming all resistance along the way until they arrived in front of the town itself and its impressive defences. Within the town Jelantik had massed an army of some 15,000 men, of whom 2,000 to 3,000 were armed with rifles and the others with lances 15 to 20 feet in length. After making several costly probing attempts, the General decided not to risk a frontal attack. Instead, during the night, he dispatched a strong detachment of troops on a flanking maneuver. Early the next morning these troops succeeded in breaching the westernmost defence position and entering the town from the rear. At 11:00 a.m. on August 16 a salvo of 21 cannon shots signaled that the Dutch had seized control of Jagaraga and the Dutch flag was raised over the fortress. But Jelantik, the rajas and most of the troops made their escape and withdrew in good order in the direction of Karangasem and Klungkung.

The Dutch casualties in the battle for Jagaraga totaled 33 dead and 148 wounded, but the Balinese lost thousands. Among the victims, according to some reports, was the wife of Jelantik and a party of high-born ladies whom she led in the rite of the *puputan*, advancing in a state of near trance directly into the line of Dutch fire in a deliberate act of self-destruction.

Once again the war had scarcely started before it was suddenly stalemated. The Dutch were neither ready nor willing to risk an overland advance beyond Jagaraga. General Michiels decided to leave garrison forces in Buleleng but to shift the main theater of operations to the south, where he could conduct a campaign against Karangasem and Klungkung in the coastal region without having to run the risk of maintaining long lines of communication from the ships. Direct action against the Dewa Agung, he thought, would result in quick Balinese capitulation. So he ordered the troops back to the transports and the fleet sailed off.

Transfer of Operations to the South; Lombok Intervention

Mads Lange, who had counseled against a wider war, went back to Kuta to prepare for the apparently inevitable spread of violence. The Raja of Badung was already engaged in a conflict with Mengwi and Lange feared that an injection of Dutch troops into the already incendiary situation in the south could only mean widespread and long-continued disorders. George Pocock King returned to Lombok. From the Raja of Lombok the Dutch immediately received assurances that he would gladly provide troops to help the Dutch discipline Karangasem and any other Balinese principalities of their choice. Jelantik circulated from rajadom to rajadom, rallying, or attempting to rally, all Bali to repel the Dutch aggressors. The Raja of Karangasem returned to his palace to deal with long neglected affairs of state which suddenly became enormously complicated by reason of the agents of the Raja of Lombok, who were stirring up insurrection. The Dewa Agung merely waited while others came to his defence.

On May 12 the Dutch fleet reassembled in the bay of Teluk Amok and troops landed at Padang Bai to attack Klungkung and, if necessary, also Karangasem. Encountering fierce resistance, the Dutch pushed westward along the coast toward the especially strategic and sacred temple town of Kusamba, which, on May 24, they seized and virtually demolished. In this operation they had the very efficient aid of some 4,000 troops from Lombok, whose special function it was to infiltrate the countryside behind the battle lines and create disorders which contributed to the Lombok-inspired insurrection against Karangasem. The Raja himself, despairing at news of the insurrection and of the Kusamba battle, killed his children, his wives and himself. The Raja of Buleleng and Gusti Ketut Jelantik prepared to continue the war from the capital town of Klungkung, which the Dutch were determined to seize.

In Klungkung the Dewa Agung's protectors had assembled a force of some 33,000 men, but their arms were inferior, their defence works were rudimentary and their chances of victory in any pitched battle were exceedingly dim. But then the Dutch, who seemed on the point of decisive victory, were yet once again betrayed by the tropics. This time it was an epidemic of dysentery which did them in, virtually all of the invaders being seized with the most excruciating cramps of the bowels. Before they had a chance to recover, the Dewa Agung's redoubtable sister, the Dewa Agung Isteri, with her ally, the Raja of Gianyar, staged a surprise night-time raid on their camp at Kusamba. The Dutch suffered heavy casualties. General Michiels himself was critically wounded and died the next day. Lt. Col. van Swieten, who succeeded to the command, ordered the troops, along with the work coolies, to retreat to the ships. He also petitioned Batavia for reinforcements. What had looked like victory for the Dutch and defeat for the Balinese had suddenly turned into disaster for both. And then, just as suddenly, came mutual reprieve, but not without prior reversals.

The fluctuating fortunes of war were dramatically signaled by the commander of the Lombok forces, who visited Lt. Col. van Swieten on shipboard and displayed to him three especially valuable and significant prizes. The first was the *kris* of the Raja of Karangasem, signifying that the Raja was dead and the kingdom had fallen. The second was the *kris* of the Raja of Buleleng, and the third that of Gusti Ketut Jelantik. The Raja of Buleleng and Jelantik had been ambushed by the wily troops from Lombok. The Raja had been killed on the spot. Jelantik, seeing no escape, had taken poison.

Victories, Disasters and Reversals

With Jelantik and the two Rajas dead, with the Dewa Agung and his surviving protectors deeply grieved and dismayed, the Balinese resistance was in a state of complete disarray. The Dutch, decimated though they were by disease, could scarcely even have blundered into defeat. Lt. Col. van Swieten still hoped, however, to avoid the hazards of battle. On June 1 he was reassured to receive a message from Klungkung stating that the Dewa Agung was prepared to make peace. On June 2 he received similar messages from Mengwi and Gianyar, which had both come openly and vigorously to the defence of Klungkung, thus compensating somewhat for the disasters which had overtaken Buleleng and Karangasem. Then came subsequent messages indicating that the Dewa Agung was willing to make peace only on the unthinkable condition that the Dutch send a mission humbly to ask forgiveness for the desecration of Kusamba. If the Dutch failed to do so—and perhaps even if they did—the Dewa Agung, it seemed, planned not to surrender but to attack. Van Swieten gloomily decided to renew hostilities. On the morning of June 8 he gave the command and the badly depleted and demoralized Dutch forces began a weary march toward Klungkung.

Just when the climactic conflict seemed unavoidable, Mads Lange again emerged as the worker of miracles. Lange had prevailed upon his special friend, the Raja of Badung, who had been threatened with attack from Mengwi, an ally of Klungkung, to persuade the Raja of Tabanan to join him in a bold maneuver. The two rajas raised a force of 16,000 men and marched into Klungkung. There they negotiated or intimidated or otherwise dissuaded the Dewa Agung and his surviving allies from offering any further resistance. Mads Lange himself had accompanied the rajas by land. He had dispatched his assistant, L. V. Helms, to travel by sea to inform Colonel van Swieten, who thought Helms and Lange quite mad and disregarded the message. But just as his unwilling troops began their arduous march, van Swieten saw advancing toward them a small contingent of Balinese led by a European. It was Mads Lange and his bodyguard. They had come to report that the main body of the 16,000 Badung-Tabanan troops remained in Klungkung, where, in case of attack, they would fight a holy war in defence of the Dewa Agung, but that the Dewa Agung himself was now willing to make an honorable peace. The Dutch column turned back toward the ships and in due course it was agreed that Klungkung need not be taken.

The Dutch and the Balinese were almost equally happy that hostilities were at an end. Both were disposed to engage at once in the peace-making ceremonies which serve to dispel old animosities. In a grand gesture of reconciliation, the Dutch announced that they would bring in Hertog Bernard von Saksen Weimar Eisenach, the new German commander of the Dutch colonial army, who was, in fact, already on his way to Bali with the reinforcements which van Swieten had requested. The Dewa Agung and the other rajas were pleased to learn that they were to deal directly with genuine European nobility and the Dewa Agung ordered that the Hertog was to be received as befitted his station. The two sides had little difficulty in agreeing upon the venue of the preliminary peace negotiations. It would be Mads Lange's factory at Kuta. The final solemn formalities, which most of the surviving royalty of the island would attend, would be held, symbolically, at Kusamba.

Peace Conference and Celebration

The negotiations took place July 10–15, with Mads Lange playing the genial and lavish host. He entertained not only the Dutch and the Balinese dignitaries but virtually the whole of the Balinese army—some 20,000 men, according to the estimate of the Dutch, 40,000 according to Helms. This time the Dutch made no attempt to tot up a tradesman-like bill for the invasions. They insisted, to be sure, upon a treaty based upon their own reading of the 1841–3 contracts with regard to such matters as sovereignty, slavery and salvage, but they promised not to occupy the kingdoms and not to interfere in internal affairs. They insisted also upon the right to station permanent Dutch representatives in the island, and they dictated certain very significant arrangements with regard to redistribution of territories and re-establishment of royal families. They rewarded Lombok for its wartime collaboration by putting rajaless Karangasem under its rule. To Bangli they gave Buleleng, first detaching Jembrana, recently a Buleleng dependency, and making it a separate kingdom. They rewarded the Raja of Badung merely by giving him a bronze cannon to display in his palace alongside the one he had received from the NHM as the price of his consent to the 1838 compact which led to all subsequent agreements and disagreements. The Dutch were destined to recover custody of both these weapons in 1906, when, as a prelude to the *puputan* in Denpasar, they seized the Puri Kesiman nearby. In it they discovered two bronze cannons of which nobody, it seemed, knew the origin. One, ornamented with an elaborate Napoleonic N, especially puzzled them. In all probability it was the cannon, already an outmoded relic of the Daendels era, which they had offloaded onto the Raja as a token of gratitude in 1849.

For the time being at least, the Balinese leaders seemed relatively little concerned about wearisome reformulation of old or new contract concepts which they obviously had no other choice than to accept. They devoted themselves with characteristic enthusiasm, however, to the preparations for the forthcoming ceremonies, which were scheduled for July 5. With the Hertog and many Dutch officers in attendance, also the Rajas of Badung, Bangli and Gianyar, but not the Dewa Agung, who was quite old and also genuinely ill, the occasion proved almost as splendid and as festive as anyone could have wished. Two weeks earlier the main Dutch expeditionary force had already returned to Java. The Hertog and his entourage soon followed, leaving the Balinese to reorder their badly shaken kingdoms. It was a difficult task which involved the installation of several new rulers, the redefinition of overlord–vassal relationships and also, of course, a whole new Balinese–Dutch modus vivendi.

CHAPTER 7

SAGA OF A DANISH TRADER (1834-1856)

Arrival in Lombok of Mads Lange and His Brothers
The Danish trader Mads Lange, who lived in Kuta from 1839 until 1856 and made his appearance at critical times and places in Balinese history, was fortunate in having sympathetic witnesses and biographers. In the accounts left by these writers, Lange appears as the courageous and loyal friend of the Balinese rajas and people, deliberately cushioning the shock of their early encounters with the outside world. Had the record been less full and factual, Lange might have the reputation today of the betrayer of the Balinese rajas to the Dutch builders of empire.

The best known account of Lange's role in Bali, or, to be more precise, the least unknown, was written by L. V. Helms, a versatile Danish adventurer who served as one of Lange's assistants in the Kuta factory from early April 1847 until June 21, 1848 and made a nostalgic return visit not long after Lange's death in 1856. Helms went on to seek and to find his own later fortunes in Borneo with Rajah Brooke, in California and Australia with the gold miners, and in Lapland as a prospector and speculator in Arctic mineral deposits. He eventually found the leisure in which to write his memoirs, *Pioneering in the Far East* (London, 1882), in which he included several chapters on the life and times of Mads Lange as reflected, naturally, in his own engrossing experiences.

Lange emerges through Helms' reminiscences as a man of enormous energy and agreeable personality. This report is supported by the observations of certain distinguished visitors who enjoyed Lange's generous hospitality for more or less extended periods in his Kuta establishment. Among them were the German philologist R. H. Th. Friederich, the Swiss botanist Z. H. Zollinger and the Dutch ethnographer Baron van Hoevell, who grouped themselves about Lange as though his factory were a Kuta salon. A popular Danish writer of the early twentieth century, Aage Karaup Nielson, searched out the more readily available records of Mads Lange, inclusive of comments by these guests, and wrote a lively biography, *Leven en Avonturen van een Oostinjevaarder op Bali* (Amsterdam, 1928). Nielson's account, which was brought out both in Dutch and in Danish, reached an appreciative Dutch and Danish audience but it has never, unfortunately, been published in English. Nor has it been published in Indonesian or in Balinese, although the graves of Mads Lange and his brother at Kuta lead people to ask questions which very few can answer.

Lange as Syahbandar and Merchant in Ampenan

As noted in an earlier chapter, Mads Lange (1807–56) began his South Seas adventures in 1834 when he established a factory (trading post) in Lombok in partnership with Captain John Burd, a Scottish seaman closely associated with the Danish East India Company. Lange's three younger brothers, Hans, Karl Emilius and Hans Henrik, were junior members of the firm from the first. His nephew Christian later joined them. John Burd established business contacts in Singapore, Macau, Canton, Batavia and later Hong Kong, and on his own ship, *de Zuid*, frequently visited Lombok and later Bali. The younger Lange brothers and the nephew captained some of the growing fleet of sailing vessels which the senior partners acquired. Mads Lange himself became Syahbandar (harbormaster, meaning also customs collector, a valuable post for which he paid an annual fee) to the Raja of Karangasem-Lombok. He built a shipyard adjacent to his factory at Tanjung Karang, close to Ampenan town on Ampenan Bay. Soon he became a man of great wealth and influence but vulnerable nevertheless to the whims of Asian rulers. In order to achieve his position he allied himself with Gusti Gede Ngurah Lanang, who had recently had to flee from Karangasem-Bali to Karangasem-Lombok to escape retribution for various atrocities, and also with the Raja's sister, the Cokorda, who actually ruled the kingdom as regent together with an incestuous consort. He associated himself commercially from time to time with George Pocock King, the English trader. King aspired to displace and replace Lange as Syahbandar, and in order to do so he attached himself to a junior ruler, the Raja of Mataram, who, in turn, aimed to depose and succeed the Cokorda.

The involuted dynastic rivalries of the Balinese princes of Lombok and the intrigues in which the princes of Bali itself were always eager to share, plus the commercial rivalries of Lange and King, both of whom had arms to sell, signaled certain trouble. War broke out in early 1838 between the rajadoms of Karangasem and Mataram, with King providing the latter with arms, men and advice, and Lange coming to the aid of the former. The more vigorous new house of Mataram (also of Balinese origin) prevailed over the decadent old house of Karangasem, and King prevailed over Lange, who boarded his yacht *Venus* and sailed off to Bali.

Kuta Factory and Kuta Town in 1839

Arriving in Bali in mid-1839, after five years of exposure to the hazardous life of the trader in the Indies, Lange had just been despoiled of most of his personal property. He was in debt to Chinese merchants in Singapore and Canton for something like 30,000 silver dollars and he had little except his own quite extraordinary experiences and abilities to rely upon as his trading capital. He assumed personal command of a little trading post at Kuta, one which may have been opened by King as early as 1831 and seems for a time to have operated as a

King–Lange joint enterprise under the occasional supervision of an Englishmen named Pace from Surabaya. The scale of operations of the Kuta post had formerly been quite minute, but under Lange's personal direction the enterprise suddenly flourished. Lange soon achieved even greater means and influence than before.

In settling at Kuta, Mads Lange gave new impetus both to Balinese trade in general and to the shift of the center of trade from the traditional market of Buleleng in the north to the rajadom of Badung in the south. Gusti Ngurah Gede Kasiman, the ruler of Badung, was much better disposed than were the rajas elsewhere to the establishment of systematic contacts with the outside world. The Dutch themselves had already perceived the possibilities of Gusti Ngurah Gede Kasiman's little port town of Kuta. They had established a factory there in 1826 but had built up no trade and had therefore allowed it to lapse in 1831. They returned in mid-1839, at just the time that Lange was starting up business. The new Dutch venture was as inauspicious as the former, and in 1844 the Dutch were to close it and to write off a cumulative loss of fl. 172,194.39. By that time Mads Lange had made himself a fortune.

The town of Kuta, so profitless to the Dutch and so productive for the Dane, was (and is) located on an isthmus one to two miles wide and five miles long which connects the southern headlands of the Bukit peninsula (Dutch Tafelhoek on the older maps) to the Bali mainland. With easy access to sandy beaches and sheltered anchorages both to the east and to the west, Kuta enjoyed a major advantage over the northern port of Buleleng in being accessible from one direction or the other no matter which way the monsoon might be blowing. Given ordinary skill and luck, ships' captains could find passage through the coral reefs and put in reasonably close to shore for loading and offloading. The town itself was built along a small stream, the Dawan, which flowed by 39 leisurely bends into the sea near Tuban and was navigable at high tide to small boats. On the edge of Kuta town and on the bank of the stream was located the original factory which Lange expanded into a large compound filled with storerooms and living quarters.

The Kuta site was favorable to trade but the town itself had an evil reputation. It was thought to be populated almost exclusively by scoundrels and ruffians and to be conducive not only to death by violence but to almost equally lethal chills and fevers. Whether guided by knowledge or instinct, Mads Lange chose a well-drained site for his factory and worked such far-reaching improvements that his frequent visitors never echoed the complaints of the early traders that the spot was all but uninhabitable. He also established cordial relations with the townspeople, who seem either to have been grossly maligned by earlier visitors or to have changed quite recently and rapidly for the better. Dutch restraints upon the traditional practices of piracy and slavery may have exerted a tranquilizing influence.

The nearby Bukit peninsula, just south of Kuta, with its high sea cliffs and its dangerous coral reefs, had played the natural role in times past of luring and wrecking incautious seafarers. The people of Kuta, acting upon the belief that whatever the seas cast up was for them to take possession of for themselves, their rulers and the gods, had made a good thing of the frequent shipwrecks. The Kuta market, in which looted cargo and enslaved sailors were often put up for sale, was also the market in which the rajas themselves could conveniently and profitably dispose of such worrisome people as criminals and paupers, who might make good slaves. The buyers were Chinese and Bugis dealers, who gladly paid fl. 100–150 per head, the handsome and accomplished Balinese being much in demand in overseas markets. Prospering as it did on looting and slavery, Kuta had become the home of various unamiable characters, the most infamous of whom was Gusti Ngurah Ketut, the ruling local prince. Gusti Ketut's personal 40-man gang terrorized local residents and visitors alike, but not quite to the extent of inhibiting the growth of the town. At the time that Mads Lange arrived, Kuta had a population of several thousand people, including local fishermen (100 families), Chinese and Bugis dealers in slaves, opium and other merchandise (30 families each), and assorted Balinese refugees and renegades who had found it expedient to vanish from other island kingdoms and resettle in Badung.

Raja Kasiman and the Badung Dynasty

The town and the district of Kuta, which the widely detested Gusti Ngurah Ketut ruled as local overlord, was part of the rich rice grow- ing state of Badung, over which ruled Gusti Ngurah Gede Kasiman. When Lange first encountered him in 1839, Raja Kasiman was already a venerable white-haired gentleman of fifty who had been ruler for the past ten years and was destined to remain on the throne until 1861. He was the son of Gusti Ngurah Made Pemecutan, the founder of the modern rajadom of Badung. Gusti Pemecutan had thrown off the overlordship of Mengwi, conquered Jembrana and made himself the first raja of the south whom the more warlike Rajas of Buleleng and Karangasem respected and feared. His exploits in building his king- dom—and in building his family, which consisted of 500 wives who bore him 800 sons and uncounted daughters, were commonly attrib- uted to his possession of a marvelously potent magical *kris*. His *kris* did not protect him from one of his own sons, to whom he forfeited the throne in 1810. Nor did it preserve the successor, who died in 1813, or endow another of his sons, Raja Kasiman, with sexual prowess to match his politics. For all of his own 80 wives, Raja Kasiman, to his great grief, fathered only one child, and that not a son but a daughter.

Raja Kasiman, as Lange knew him, was a benign and jovial old au- tocrat, six feet tall and heavy set, who bore himself regally on state oc- casions but could relax happily over food, wine, music and dancing, and was especially given to collecting firearms, not for battle but for display, or possibly as fetishes. But Raja Kasiman, who sometimes seemed a little simple-minded and in the late 1850s became child- ish, could be both crafty and cruel, as his earlier record quite plainly showed. Upon the death of his father, Gusti Ngurah Made Pemecu- tan, who had greatly confused matters by fathering so many sons and assigning them small semi-autonomous regions to rule, the rajadom proper passed to his eldest son, who died in 1813, leaving the king- dom to be disputed by many claimants, among whom Raja Kasiman eventually prevailed. Raja Ngurah's second successor was a young prince, Gusti Gede Pemecutan, who died in 1817 and was followed by his sister's son, Gusti Ngurah Pemecutan, a very weak and short-lived ruler. It was widely believed in Badung that the untimely demise of these two rulers was not unrelated to Kasiman's own aspirations to the throne and that he had quite certainly supplied the second with excessive quantities of opium. He had further strengthened his own position by marrying the widow of another of the princes, whose claim to the throne was stronger than his own and whose death occurred under suspicious circumstances. The widow, a strong-willed woman who preferred to enter Kasiman's harem rather than perform the rite of suttee, was eager to gain status as a raja's consort. When the next raja, the son of Gusti Ngurah Pemecutan, also conveniently died, Kasiman possessed himself of the sacred royal regalia, without which the heir apparent could not establish his legitimacy but with which Kasiman could and did successfully demand that the priests proclaim him raja. Nevertheless, Raja Kasiman ruled over only about 6,000 of the 10,000 households of the rajadom, the others remaining under the control of some 15 minor princes, one of them his nephew, the infamous Gusti Ngurah Ketut of Kuta. These quarrelsome princes came together occasionally in royal council, which, for some thirty years, Kasiman successfully steered.

This annotated royal genealogy goes to show that in resettling himself at Kuta, Lange required all of the acute political and commercial instinct which he had had an opportunity to develop in Lombok. He was to deal with the devious Raja of Badung as he had previously had to deal with the dubious Raja of Karangasem-Lombok, and at the same time he had to cope with the NHM, a business rival much more formidable than George Pocock King. The Raja and the Dane seem to have developed mutual affection and confidence, and the NHM, after competing with Lange, was soon to co-opt him as its own agent. The Raja, who may well have mellowed with years and profited—or suffered—from Lange's guidance, played a conciliatory rather than an inflammatory role in the Balinese–Dutch conflict which soon ensued after he granted trade and other privileges to the Westerners.

Kuta Factory as Home and Trading Post

At Kuta Lange built up his new factory as a commercial and residential complex placed in a spacious Balinese-style compound surrounded by high walls and approached through an ornamental stone gateway. Just inside the gate were installed brass cannons, not for protection but for signaling ships. Several large *pendopo* (open pillared halls) provided public rooms and offices, and many little *bale* (closed pavilions) served as private quarters for the staff. The resident and transient population of the factory came to number at least a hundred people. It included Lange himself, his brothers, visiting ships' captains, his English doctor, his wives (one Chinese, one Balinese), and his numerous retinue of servants and slaves. Much to the amazement and gratification of visitors, some of whom stayed for months as Lange's pampered guests, the establishment manifested some of the aspects of a gentlemen's club in the West. One of the *pendopo* served as a music room where staff and the visitors might be called upon in the evening to perform. Mads Lange himself played the violin, one of his brothers the flute, another the cello and the third the piano. Resident talent was not lacking and musically inclined visitors received and earned an especially cordial welcome. Lange also had a billiards room and somewhere, above or below ground, a cellar well stocked with European wines and liquors as well as other drinks, among them the very agreeable Balinese *brem* and *arak*. Cooks trained in Balinese, Chinese and European cuisine prepared a memorable table, for which fish, flesh and fowl, fruits, vegetables and spices were all abundantly available. A visit to Lange's factory was a revelation with regard to the degree of refinement and luxury to which a European in the East could then aspire.

The factory was as well arranged for efficient business as for gracious living. Certain of the *pendopo* served as market halls where imported goods and local produce could be displayed and sold. Beyond the *pendopo* were warehouses in which could be stored many hundreds of tons of rice and great quantities of other goods. Alongside the warehouses was an oil press, especially imported at great cost from Europe, for the extraction of coconut oil intended both for local sale and for export. Outside the compound were pens for cattle, pigs and poultry. Beyond were rich farm lands, which Lange himself gradually acquired in order to produce rice and coconuts to augment his purchases. Stretching both eastward and westward from the compound to the seashore ran roadways, over which Lange traveled in style in a fine carriage. It was the only such vehicle on the island, and it was drawn by high-stepping Makassar horses which dwarfed the ponies of the Balinese. Inevitably, Lange came to invite comparison with certain other White Rajas: naturally, with George Pocock King, the new White Raja of Lombok, but also with the great Rajah Brooke of Sarawak. Their impact upon the East, like the impact of the East upon them, served in still not especially well understood ways to illustrate the Victorian concept of the white man's burden.

Riches from Rice, Gambier, Kopeng and Ships Servicing

Lange's business was built originally on rice. The Balinese produced high quality rice in such superabundance that the grain sold on the local market for no more than one half of what it would fetch in Java, Singapore or China. Lange exported rice in 1,000 ton quantities and on the quick, easy profits of rice he built up a commercial fleet of a dozen or more schooners, brigs and barks which the brothers and various other Westerners captained. To pay for the rice he imported whole shiploads of commodities for which the Balinese demand seemed insatiable, especially gambier from Singapore and Chinese coins.

The gambier was intended for use with betel nut. In Lange's day and much later, Balinese men, women and older children were almost universally addicted to betel chewing, a practice which did nothing to enhance their physical appearance or the general surroundings. The plug of betel, which was chewed with lime and gambier to soften the nut and bring out the flavor, distorted the lips and jaw and stained the teeth. The red spittle dyed the ground around all the homes and market places. Betel nut, which possesses mild narcotic qualities, was no doubt less harmful and expensive than the opium which the wealthy Balinese also fancied. A case can be made for betel as somewhat preferable to marijuana, which was also known and used. But the practice of betel chewing, which never had much to recommend it, did not begin to die out until long after Lange's time.

The Chinese coins which Lange imported along with gambier served purposes which were at once utilitarian and aesthetic. Stamped with Chinese characters, perforated with a square hole which permitted them to be strung into convenient loops of several hundred each, these brass coins, then and now widely known as *kopeng* or "cash," constituted Bali's basic currency. Commodity prices might be quoted in the market place in Indian rupees, Dutch rijksdaalder or Singapore dollars, but cash transactions were generally in "cash" and it was sometimes a matter of nearly equivalent weights of coins and purchases. According to Helms, Lange bought "cash" in China at the rate of 1,400 to the Singapore dollar and sold them in Bali at the rate of 700 to 1, thus realizing a neat 100 percent net on the transaction. Greatly increasing quantities of these "cash" were absorbed by the Balinese market, which was just then moving out of the long sustained barter phase. Because of their intrinsic and ornamental value, the coins were also used in preparation of many of the offerings which were taken on all festive occasions to the palaces and temples. *Kopeng*, therefore, became an important element in certain Balinese arts and crafts. In constituting himself the principal supplier, Lange made himself in effect both the national banker and a leading patron of the arts.

Mads Lange's specialization in rice, gambier and *kopeng* did not deter him from dealing in any other commodity in which he might make a profit, and in Bali the opportunities were dazzling. Lange imported English and Indian textiles; Western firearms of all descriptions and the bullets, lead and powder to keep them functioning; porcelains, particularly celadons, and silks from China. It must be mentioned also that he brought in opium from Calcutta and Singapore, some of it for local consumption, much of it to be smuggled over to Java in contravention of the Dutch monopoly. On behalf of the rajas, always his best local customers, Lange held himself ready to undertake special commissions. These included the acquisition of precious stones, Chinese and Western medicines and various novelties and curiosities such as European clocks and chandeliers, engravings and paintings.

Lange's purchases in Bali for his own account or on behalf of the captains of trading and whaling vessels, for whom he served as comprador, included the full range of local products. He acquired large quantities of cattle, pigs, dried meat, hides, ducks, chickens, coffee, tea, sugar, coconuts, tobacco, fruits and vegetables, much of which went to provision ships' crews and the rest to be sold on the Singapore market. He bought these commodities from Balinese traders, mainly from certain extremely enterprising females. These ladies, some of them from the royal families, handled most of the market goods, the men deigning to deal only in rice or cattle. On signal from Lange that he needed supplies for a whaler or a trading ship, the women would converge upon Kuta with processions of ox carts and pack trains of ponies, fetching him—all neatly done up in wicker baskets—live pigs and fowls, fresh fruits and vegetables, and whatever else they might wish to offer for sale. Lange would often buy much more than he actually needed at the moment, for he was reluctant to disappoint these cheerful tradeswomen. He knew that he had only to wait a few days for another ship's captain to call for cargo and provisions.

At the peak of his career in the mid-1840s, Lange's factory at Kuta was doing a million guilders' worth of business per year with Java alone. The trade with Singapore and China must have been even greater. Lange's own fleet of ships, some in the 800 to 1,500 ton range, came to number between ten and fifteen, all very profitably employed. His favorite craft, the *Venus*, served him as a yacht for his frequent trips to East Java and various coastal towns of Bali where he maintained warehouses.

NHM Competition and Concession of Defeat

During his early days at Kuta, while his operations were still tentative, Lange was kept under close scrutiny by the Dutch, who also provided him with what might have seemed like almost prohibitive competition. Heer Schuurman, the agent for the NHM, together with one or two Dutch assistants, set out to monopolize the Bali trade, but the rajas preferred always to deal with Lange, as did the common people. The Balinese preference was so unanimous that the Dutch were convinced at first that Lange was using his influence with his special friend, the Raja of Badung, to effect a boycott of their interests. But then, after an interval of regarding him as a dangerous and unscrupulous competitor, they decided that he might better be treated as a useful partner. Schuurman began to make regular recommendations to Batavia that rather than compete with Lange at Kuta, the NHM would be better advised to appoint him as its own commercial agent.

Schuurman's own mode of life and manner of doing business sharply pointed up the contrast between the Dane and the Dutch. Lange chose to build in the Balinese manner and to make his factory and himself easily accessible. Schuurman put up a solid Dutch-style building surrounded by forbiddingly thick, high walls on which he mounted a row of cannons so conspicuous that the Balinese found it difficult to believe he intended to use them, as Lange did his, merely for signaling. Schuurman and his assistants deported themselves as though they anticipated siege rather than trade and for months at a time lived lonely, morose lives, isolated from Bali and the Balinese. Just how much Schuurman's personal distaste for Bali influenced his views regarding prospects for Dutch trade and the reliability of his Danish competitor as potential colleague it is impossible to determine. But his recommendations carried weight with Batavia. In 1844 the NHM wrote off its heavy losses (for which it was to be compensated by the government), closed down its Kuta factory (which Lange bought for the bargain price of fl. 3,095.83), ordered the staff back to Java and appointed Lange to represent it. Already in 1843, for services performed or anticipated, the Batavia government had granted him *burger rechts* (right of residence). In 1849 The Hague conferred the Order of the Netherlands Lion upon him in appreciation for his services during the Dutch–Balinese wars of 1846, 1848 and 1849.

Lange's Political Role; His Later Years and Death

The decade of 1839–49, in the course of which Lange built up his business success at Kuta and his reputation as a peacemaker accept-able to both sides in the Dutch–Balinese wars, was the period of his greatest prosperity and influence. After 1849 his career went into gradual decline, a circumstance which reflected deteriorating condi-tions in Bali itself and the uncertain and unhappy state of his friends, the rajas. After the war and the peace of 1849 Bali did not enjoy the prosperity and progress which the beginnings of the process of mod-ernization might have been assumed to bring. Distressing new trends were readily discernible in the market place, and Lange was one of the first to feel the effects.

Lange had expected that the end of the wars and the lifting of the partial Dutch blockade would result in the quick revival of agricultural production and commercial activity. His expectations were swiftly and bitterly disappointed. Bali experienced a series of droughts and bad harvests—sure omens of divine displeasure. Produce was far from plentiful, and people murmured that worse was yet to come. Rather than exporting rice in the same huge quantities as before, Lange found it necessary at times to import from Lombok in order to satisfy Bali's own requirements. He took less profit or pleasure in such a trade. The royal courts, furthermore, were not soon again in a position to make lavish outlay on ceremonies and on the luxury goods which royal pomp required. It was clear that the day of the independent or semi-independent Western trader was passing. With the appearance of the steamship, the big Batavian concerns became even more aggressive-ly monopolistic than before, and only the Chinese, with their clan loyalty and organization, were really able to compete. Even Lange's ship provisioning service very sharply declined. The whalers, which had come to be his best customers, were now following the whales into other and distant waters. And even though he was only in his early forties, Lange was beginning to show the strains of an extremely eventful life.

The true spirit of Mads Lange, just as his powers passed their peak, comes through best in the affectionate description by Helms:

The protracted blockade which [the Dutch] had maintained during their languid operations against the Balinese had destroyed the trade of the island, and caused him losses which he never recovered. He could not adapt himself to the altered circumstances in which the Dutch expeditions had left him; and he was not the man to retrieve his position by long continued thrift and prudence. There was more of the bold Viking than the prudent trader in his nature. He delighted in tossing about in a gale in his little yacht, the *Venus*, which he loved as though it were a living thing. He knew every rope and spar in his considerable fleet, and no laggard captain would return from a needlessly protracted voyage with impunity. He delighted in overcoming all difficulties save those of commercial life. He was not a skillful rider, yet so bold a one, that I have seen him break in obstinate and vicious horses by sheer force of will. He was a power in the country, and the Balinese feared, yet liked and admired him, and, in truth, though severe, he was generous even to a fault, and loyal to his trust, without thinking of the consequences to himself.

In the early 1850s Lange toyed with the idea of revisiting Denmark. He had not seen his native country since 1833, but he had relatives and friends with whom he had kept occasionally in touch, including a childhood sweetheart whom he may all along have intended eventually to marry. With thoughts of return in mind he built and outfitted a new brig, planning to load it with local produce and to captain it himself on the voyage to Europe. But he delayed too long. On May 13, 1856, he died. He had just written but not yet dispatched a farewell letter to his long-time friend, the Raja of Tabanan. This letter, inscribed on *lontar* (strips of palm leaf) in the Malay language in Balinese script, was carried to Denmark by one of his ship captains and turned up eventually in the National Museum along with various specimens of Balinese arts and artifacts which also came directly or indirectly from Lange. It is a touching document:

> In several days I shall undertake the journey to my homeland. Since I do not feel well, I cannot take my farewell in person but rather in this manner. I find it difficult to speak of all that my eyes have seen but there is no one in Bali to whom my feelings are as well known as to the King. Of my return I cannot speak. The King shall have news of me from the other side of the earth. As the King will be so good as to have his royal name engraved upon a goblet and send it to me. As I have always in all that I have done been my brother's friend, so shall I always live.

Subsequent Fortunes of Factory and Family

Lange's sudden death, at age 49, gave rise to reports, as was inevitable given the time and the place, that he had been poisoned and that good fortune had deserted his heretofore remarkably lucky establishment. The latter part of the report was confirmed by immediately subsequent events. The factory passed to his brother Hans, who was not especially gifted in commerce and survived him by only a year or two. On Hans' death it passed to the nephew Christian, who quarreled with the Balinese rulers and had little knack for dealing with ships' captains. The property began to look badly run down, the oil mill was abandoned and trading activities languished. Christian had brought out a bride from Denmark just about a year before Mads Lange's death. There had been much celebration when she bore him a child and Mads Lange had dreamed of establishing a family concern which would last for generations. But two of his brothers had preceded him in death—one in a distant shipwreck, the other drowned in the surf before his eyes on return to Bali after a long voyage. Now both Mads and Hans were buried in adjoining graves in a coconut grove not far distant from the factory. Christian decided to abandon the enterprise, including the lands and buildings, to which he could convey no clear title. He sold what goods he could, loaded all other portable belongings, his wife and his child onto his one remaining ship, and sailed off to Denmark, where, in 1872, he died.

Several of the local princes and some of the Kuta Chinese competed to acquire possession of the factory, the rice fields and the coconut groves which Mads Lange had built or acquired. Theoretically, any abandoned property fell to the raja, but a crafty Chinese, Lauw Ho Sen, persuaded Raja Kasiman's successor that the Lange property would bring him bad luck and he himself assumed the proprietorship. Gradually the property was divided and passed into other hands. But the graves of Mads and Hans were faithfully maintained by another Chinese, Ong Po Hien, who seems to have been a business associate of Lange's and also—to introduce the long delayed element of romance—a relative of Lange's Chinese wife.

In the course of his seventeen years in Bali, Mads Lange took two wives, one Balinese, one Chinese, but very little is known about either. By the Balinese wife, who may have been the first and certainly preceded Lange in death, he had two sons. The first, William Peter, died as a child in Singapore, where he had evidently been sent to school. The second, Andreas Emil (later known as Henrik) was also sent to study in Singapore at Raffles Institution. He remained abroad after his father's death save for one quick trip back to Bali in 1906 in an unsuccessful effort to claim his father's property. By his Chinese wife Teh Sang Nio, who survived him and inherited a comfortable home in Banyuwangi, Java, Lange had a daughter, Cecilia Catherina. Cecilia was educated in a Singapore convent and remained abroad after her father's death, making one trip back to Bali in 1859 to visit his grave. Lange attempted to make long-term financial provision for his children, leaving each of them fl. 10,000 by an early will (fl. 7,000 in a later one), but his will was never honored. Christian neglected to share the proceeds with his cousins when he sold off the remaining possessions in Bali and set out for Europe.

Andreas Emil (or Henrik) was somehow able to complete his education in Singapore and he found employment (perhaps through L. V. Helms), which was at once most implausible and most appropriate. He went to Borneo to work with Rajah Brooke of Sarawak. In Sarawak he married a local girl, who eventually bore him nine children. The family presently backtracked from Sarawak to Singapore, where descendants still live, but never, save for the one disappointing trip of the father, did any of the family return to the island of Bali. If Andreas Emil's destiny was dramatically fitting, Cecilia's was sensational: she became the Sultana of the important Malay state of Johor.

After her father's death, Cecilia was befriended by an English family, who took her to live for a time in India, then to England and France, and later brought her back to the East. On her return to Singapore, where she attended school in a convent, she met Abu Bakar, the Sultan of Johor, who fell in love with her and after an impetuous courtship made her his Sultana. Since Sultan Abu Bakar, unlike his peers, remained officially monogamous, the Sultana Cecilia enjoyed an especially honored position in his court. She eventually bore him two children: a daughter, who was to become the first wife of the Sultan of Pahang; and a son who was to succeed his father (d. 1895) and rule in Johor as Sultan Ibrahim.

A man of most extraordinary vitality, Sultan Ibrahim constantly amazed and shocked the conservative colonial British by behavior which they deemed outrageous. He gave almost equally grave affront, for instance, by denying the colonial officials the use of the palace golf links and by taking many wives and mistresses, European women among them in both categories, including a certain British woman in Singapore and his official Sultana, a Hungarian. Sultan Ibrahim was an avid sportsman, an indefatigable hunter of tigers, leopards and elephants. He was also a shrewd businessman who built up a vast fortune in rubber plantations and other enterprises. Despite British disapproval of what would now be termed his lifestyle, which caused them to put a 6:00 p.m. curfew on his visits to Singapore, Sultan Ibrahim was an Anglophile. He presented the British

Royal Family with valuable gifts and the Royal Navy with warships to help, naturally, in the defence of his own prosperous little state, which was overrun nevertheless by the Japanese. He even forgave such affronts as the postwar occupation of his favorite palaces in Singapore and Johor by the British High Commissioner—from his point of view, a squatter on royal domain.

Sultan Ibrahim, in short, was a feudal aristocrat in the grand tradition, a ruler who seemed in many respects closely akin to the Balinese rajas of his grandfather's day, yet a progressive cosmopolitan. When he died in London in 1959 he was genuinely mourned both by his Malay subjects and his British associates. His European, Chinese and Malay heritage combined to make him one of the commanding figures of early twentieth-century Southeast Asian history.

The dowager Sultana, née Cecilia Catherina Lange, lived on in a secluded palace in Johor until about the year 1930, rarely appearing in public but occasionally receiving a European visitor. On one occasion she was called upon by her father's Danish biographer, Mr Nielson. The Sultana, said Nielson, was an animated little lady with white hair, blue eyes and aristocratic features, who reminisced happily about her father and her childhood in Bali. She remembered a little Danish and sang for him several of the songs which the brothers Lange had sung in Kuta. She had already had his book about her father translated into English for her personal pleasure and she supplied certain supplementary information regarding, for instance, the shabby treatment she had received from her cousin Christian.

The visitor to Bali today can still find the Lange graves and the site of the Lange factory at the edge of the town of Kuta. Nearby stands a Chinese temple—a reminder that Kuta is still an important center of Bali's Chinese community.

CHAPTER 8

EVOLUTION OF THE COLONIAL EMPIRE (1849-1900)

Resident and Controleurs; Regent and Punggawa
As a result of the military expeditions of 1846, 1848 and 1849, and of certain subsequent disorders, in 1854 the Dutch began to exercise a rapidly increasing degree of direct control over northern Bali and to interfere more and more frequently and vigorously in Balinese domestic affairs. In the 1849 peace settlement, they placed big Buleleng under the rule of little Bangli and isolated Jembrana under a new raja whose claim to the throne was obscure. These arrangements could not and did not last. In 1854 Buleleng rebelled against Bangli, whose raja appealed to Batavia for help. The Dutch assumed direct control and Buleleng became the first of the Balinese principalities to fall under overt Dutch administration. In 1855 the Raja of Jembrana, finding himself quite unable to assert his presumed authority, relinquished that kingdom also to the Dutch. In the case of both Buleleng and Jembrana the Dutch adopted the administrative device which they had found to be effective in Java. They appointed a member of the royal family as regent and assigned him a Dutch Controleur who, as the title clearly implied, controlled both the regent and the kingdom. Thus, as of the mid-1850s, the Dutch found themselves in the posi-

tion of actually beginning to exercise the sovereign power which they had long claimed, or at least they were openly exercising it over northern and western Bali. Half a century later they ruled the entire island.

Patterns of Dutch Rule and Its Extension

The transfer of authority from the traditional rulers to the colonial officials was gradual but conclusive. The ceremonial investiture of a new regent or of a raja as regent, accompanied by his formal re-affirmation of existing treaty terms and perhaps acceptance of new ones, made it unmistakably clear that he ruled thereafter as much by Dutch sanction as by destiny. To assist each regent, or, more precisely, to guide and direct him, there was always the Controleur, a man of many departmental trades who was sometimes amazingly accomplished and effective. Presently there were assistants to the Resident and the Controleurs, who also exercised de facto authority over the indigenous *punggawa*, or district heads, technically the subordinates of the regents. Thus there developed an interlocking Dutch–Balinese administrative bureaucracy which eventually worked out remarkably well. Resident and Controleur, Raja-Regent and *punggawa* made up the composite constellation of dignitaries by whom and about whom Balinese affairs were ordered.

The colonial administration in Bali remained centered in the port town of Buleleng and the adjoining royal capital of Singaraja, with Sub-Regency offices after 1906 in Denpasar in the south. The first resident Dutch official was Heer P. L. van Bloemen Waanders, who, like certain of his successors, was to become a serious and sympathetic student of Balinese life and customs. Bloemen Waanders settled in Buleleng in 1855 with the rank of Controleur as the administrative subordinate of the Resident of Banyuwangi under whose jurisdiction fell both Bali and Lombok. His counterpart for Jembrana, Controleur Schalk, arrived in 1856. In 1860 Bloemen Waanders was promoted to rank of Assistant Resident (still assigned technically to Banyuwangi), provided with one assistant as Controleur and given responsibility not only for administering Buleleng and overseeing Jembrana but

Gusti Ketut Jelantik, Raja of Buleleng, north Bali, with his scribe, 1865.

also for observing and reporting developments in all other parts of the island. In 1882 Bali, together with Lombok, was constituted a separate Residency with headquarters in Buleleng and varying degrees of control over the various rajadoms.

The expansion of the Dutch colonial service and the definition and extension of its functions proceeded by logical stages. In 1861–2 Batavia drew up an elaborate set of regulations to guide all routine administrative practices. In 1875 it announced new regency procedures (the same as those to be applied thereafter to all other Dutch-ruled areas). In 1894 Karangasem (and all of Lombok) was added to the list of kingdoms under overt but indirect Dutch rule: in 1900 Gianyar; in 1906 Badung and Tabanan, and in 1908 Bangli and Klungkung. The Dutch official presence remained inconspicuous throughout this entire period, never totaling more than a score of people. But peripatetic officials from Buleleng made regular rounds of observation and inspection throughout the island and wrote regular reports to the Resident. Even though they had no official function within a state until it had been formally constituted a Regency within the Residency, they nevertheless offered advice which the rajas generally found it prudent to accept.

Western Studies of Balinese Institutions

After the difficulties of the first few years had been overcome and the Dutch and the Balinese had made certain basic accommodations to each other, for the northern states of Buleleng and Jembrana the latter part of the nineteenth century was a period of reasonably peaceful and satisfactory development. In assuming control of a land and a people about whom they had as yet very little knowledge, the Dutch themselves were gravely handicapped. Fortunately, however, the early officials were men of wide-ranging interest and inquiring intelligence and some became serious scholars. They were able to rely for guidance on the work of R. Friederich, a German Sanskrit scholar who had been sent out in the 1840s to make a study of Bali on behalf of the Batavia Society of Arts and Sciences. Friederich's pioneering effort (published in 1849–50 in a learned journal) gave a remarkably detailed report on the rajas and the rajadoms, the religion and culture, the manners and customs of the people, serving in fact as a basic work of reference. To complement it Controleur Bloemen Waanders published a series of reports with regard to his own investigations of local administration, taxation, agriculture, trade and commerce, and his discerning observations in the course of his official travels throughout the island. Van Eck,

Gusti Ketut Jelantik, Raja of Buleleng, north Bali, with one of his daughters and a slave, 1873.

the pioneer Christian missionary, gave up evangelism for social and cultural research, producing and publishing a series of sketches which illuminated both the more and the less esoteric aspects of Balinese life. Controleur Liefrinck studied and explained the complex system of land rights and the historic circumstances of Dutch colonial penetration. H. Neubronner van der Tuuk produced a basic dictionary and translated important chronicles. There were perhaps half a dozen others of major importance, coming mainly later in the century, but these were the first great names of Balinese scholarship, which has not, in fact, been greatly supplemented since their time on the subjects on which they worked. Nor, unfortunately, have their works been collated, translated (except for Friederich's) or even very much remembered.

The first Dutch officials to live and work in Bali thus had much to learn from their own experiences and mistakes. One of the most difficult lessons they had to master was how to select and supervise the Balinese officials to whom they had to entrust most of the routine. In the early years they made a series of serious blunders. One regent after another had to be removed, exiled and replaced. The Dutch sometimes found it expedient therefore to designate a provisional regent, promising him eventual regent status as reward for good behavior. Or they operated through a state council of whom the leader was given the less elevated rank of Patih (Chief Minister) and thus, they hoped, less lofty pretensions. For a long period of years both Buleleng (1972–82) and Jembrana (1856–82) were rajaless and regentless, the Dutch themselves assuming open responsibility for more and more state affairs. If regents and provisional regents and even *patih* were worrisome, so too were the *punggawa*, who quarreled with one another, conspired against the regent and kept testing how far they dared go in defiance even of the Dutch. It took two decades for a stable system to work itself out. Meanwhile the population of Balinese royalty living in exile in Java assumed impressive proportions, and the Fourth and Fifth Military Expeditions had to be dispatched to put down two potentially serious little insurrections.

The troubles with the regents actually began, as already noted, with the failure of the Raja of Bangli to designate a suitable official who could or would rule Buleleng to the satisfaction of its people, the Dutch or himself. The Dutch then designated Gusti Made Rahe (1851), only to depose him a few years later and ban him from Bali for the numerous offences of which his own people angrily accused him. They next tried a mere youth, Gusti Ketut Jelantik, appointing him as provisional regent with his own father, Gusti Putu Kebon, as his guardian-counselor. They delayed until 1861 in deciding which, if either, of the two to declare regent with the title also of raja. They then chose the younger man, only to have to depose and exile him in 1872 for his cruel and avaricious oppression of his subjects.

In Jembrana, meanwhile, Gusti Putu Ngurah Sloka, whom the Dutch had named regent in 1849, made himself so hated that in 1853 he had to flee to Buleleng. In 1855, to end his conspiracies to regain the throne, the Dutch forced him to abdicate and sent him off to join certain of his compatriots in exile. His son and successor, Gusti Ngurah Made Pasekan, named merely as *patih* and not as regent, also had to take refuge in Buleleng. The next incumbent, Anak Agung Made Rai, proved, according to the Dutch Controleur, to have more the mentality of a coolie than that of a raja. He was removed and exiled in 1866.

Nyoman Gempol Insurrection; Fourth Military Expedition (1858)

It was the *punggawa* rather than the regents who actually gave the Dutch the most trouble, being farther removed from Dutch scrutiny, more secure in position as semi-hereditary chieftains with loyal village followers, and much disturbed by the changes which were being introduced, especially those that affected their own prestige and their revenues. In the mid-1850s one particular *punggawa*, Nyoman Gempol, made himself especially objectionable by spreading reports, whether true or false, of ruthless Dutch exploitation in Java and urging his people to rebel while they still could. The Dutch rushed troops from Java, not even waiting for a military transport but chartering on emergency basis the merchant ship resoundingly and unforgettably named the *Jungheer Meester van der Waf van Puttershoek*. This Fourth Military Expedition (December 10–26, 1858), consisting of 12 officers and 707 infantrymen, swiftly accomplished its mission. It so systematically searched and ransacked the villages in which Gempol's adherents lived that the farmers soon handed over the fugitive *punggawa* in order to be free of the soldiers. He was sentenced, naturally, to exile in Java. Another *punggawa*, Ida Made Rai, was then also giving the Dutch too much trouble. He was banned to Java from whence, in 1864, he returned without permission. Soon he was the leader of a new uprising.

Ida Made Rai Insurrection; Fifth Military Expedition (1868)

Ida Made Rai was a flamboyant character who made himself a folk hero of Buleleng despite the fact that he quite ruthlessly destroyed friends and foes alike. The hereditary *punggawa* of the prosperous and populous district of Banjar, he gained early notoriety for his self-indulgence in opium, cockfighting, love-making and theatrical performances, and later for his murder of a rival in love. When his uncle denounced him for the murder, Ida Made Rai charged the uncle with incest and contrived for him to be condemned to death by the great Kerta Court of the Raja-Regent. Ida Made Rai also feuded for years with a prominent neighbor, Ida Ketut Anom, his rival for the love of a beautiful young girl whom both sought to kidnap (this being the traditional sportive Balinese preliminary to marriage). His own well-practised techniques, which ensured success, and Anom's rather clumsy failure, served only further to inflame the feud.

The Dutch and the Raja, tiring of Ida Made Rai's escapades, exiled him to Java and appointed a new *punggawa* of Banjar. When this incumbent died and was replaced by Ida Ketut Anom, Ida Made Rai returned from exile and devoted himself to stirring up trouble for the *punggawa*, the Raja and the Dutch. He attracted such a large and powerful band of followers, including the chiefs of four villages and other highly placed people, that the Assistant Resident and the Regent precipitately departed from Singaraja to solicit advice and assistance in Banyuwangi. During their absence Ida Made Rai's supporters attacked Singaraja and assassinated the Patih. The Resident himself hurried from Java to Bali and attempted, with no success, to reconcile the conflicting versions of events and the bitterly disputing parties. The case went to the Kerta Court, which found four of Rai's adherents guilty of crimes against the state and sentenced them to 12 years of hard labor. But Ida Made Rai himself remained free, ruling in fact in Banjar like an independent raja. He had driven out Ida Ketut Anom. He had gained the support of the Raja of Bangli and he had surrounded himself, according to common report, with an army of 2,000 well-armed men who were preparing to attack Singaraja with the intent of expelling both the Dutch and the Balinese authorities and declaring their own leader the new raja.

The Resident assembled and dispatched the Fifth Military Expedition (September 19–November 27, 1868). It consisted of 800 men under a certain Major van Heemskerk, a poor second choice as leader, the original head of the expedition having died of cholera just as it was about to set out. Major Heemskerk and his men floundered about rather aimlessly for a full month, badly led and badly supplied. The Major was then replaced by a Colonel de Brabant, who brought with him some 700 reinforcements and made swift work of attacking and subduing the rebellious villages. Ida Made Rai and five of his chief associates tried unsuccessfully to find sanctuary in Jembrana and then fled to Mengwi, but not for long. The local population delivered them over to the Dutch who exiled them to Java. The campaign cost the Dutch the lives of two officers and ten soldiers, but there were no serious disorders thereafter in northern Bali.

Bloemen Waanders as Controleur and Observer

The first resident Dutch official in Bali, Heer van Bloemen Waanders, who arrived in Singaraja on August 12, 1855, settled himself rather uncomfortably into a dingy pavilion in a back court of the Raja's *puri*, hung out the Dutch flag and began to cope as best he could with the problems of a strange land and people. Under Bloemen Waanders and his eventual associates and successors, the northern states of Buleleng and Jembrana began to experience changes of which some at least constituted notable improvements. One of the first official acts of the Dutch, for instance, was to introduce vaccine and vaccinators from Java, where the colonial government had pioneered in the prevention of epidemics. These measures proved so effective that in 1872, when smallpox next struck, Buleleng and Jembrana had few victims whereas in the southern states the death toll was perhaps 15,000. The Dutch also took steps to stop the practice of suttee, which was formally banned in 1859, and to wipe out slavery. They exercised strict controls over the Kerta Court so that it could no longer hand down sentences of death without the Resident's review and approval. Nor could it inflict barbarous punishments, such as maiming and burning alive. They established a Dutch-style court in which Europeans or Chinese would be brought for trial, also such Balinese as committed offences against the government or its representatives.

Dutch Policy on Slavery, Opium, Land; Residency Finances

In dealing with the very delicate problem of slavery, the Dutch announced that all owners must register their slaves, that they could not thereafter claim ownership of anyone not so registered, that the sale of slaves would be prohibited, and that the slaves themselves had the right to buy their freedom They also undertook to persuade the owners voluntarily to free their slaves, the most effective method of persuasion proving to be for the government to pay compensation. In 1876 there were 60 slaves in Jembrana; in 1878 none. In Buleleng the total in 1876 was 800; by 1885 there remained only 500, whom the government then bought free.

The Dutch officials gave their attention from the very earliest days to the improvement of economic conditions, acting on the dual assumption that a more prosperous people would be a more tractable people and a more prosperous state would be a financial asset rather than a liability to the colonial government. They therefore encouraged the extension of the irrigation system for the improvement of the rice crop, the planting of coffee as a cash crop, and the construction of roads, bridges and port facilities for the enhancement of trade, commerce and communications in general, including, of course, official communications. By 1875 northern Bali was already a distinctly profitable colonial enterprise and by 1900 it was paying also for a good part of the administrative expenses of nearby Lombok.

Controleur Bloemen Waanders was largely responsible for putting the state on a paying basis. In an early attempt to analyze its actual and potential revenues, he made the following calculation of the income of the Raja-Regent of Buleleng for the year 1859.

Tax on rice lands	fl. 5,900
Tax on water (for irrigation)	1,500
Trade licences	4,200
Special levies on imports and exports	20
Tax on coconut trees and gardens	40
Tax on salt making	10
Sale of postage stamps	100
Tax on gambling	430
Tax on cockfights	300
Share of court fines (2/3)	300
Proceeds from sale of property of people dying without heirs	50
Proceeds from sale of indigent widows, orphans and other people impressed into slavery	200
Licences for dancing girls	600

The Controleur quickly concluded that revenues could be very greatly increased, and in the course of the next few years he proved to be right. He noted the second largest item of revenue—the trade licences which yielded fl. 4,200. This was the amount paid to the Raja each year by the Chinese Syahbandar and Opiumpachter (opium monopolist) of the seven port towns for the privilege of levying charges upon imports and exports, by far the most important single item of trade being opium. The annual import of opium into Buleleng came then to approximately 300 chests valued at a total of fl. 450,000, of which the Raja, it seemed, was getting less than one percent. So the Dutch themselves assumed the responsibility for licensing and controlling the Opiumpachter and by 1875 the trade was yielding them fl. 217,000. With such sure and sizeable profits from opium, it scarcely seemed necessary to encumber other trade with the assessment of duties. So the Dutch, breaking with their long tradition of monopolistic practices, declared Buleleng a free port. They kept it open even to their formidable rivals, the Singapore merchants, who accounted, in fact, for at least half of its trade, including almost all of its opium. It was one of the special anomalies of the situation in Buleleng that a good half of the opium which was legally imported under the approving eyes of the Dutch officials was promptly smuggled over to Java, where the Dutch monopoly maintained prices so high that smuggling was well worth the risk.

Bloemen Waanders noted that the largest item in the state revenues was the yield from the tax on rice lands, a tax paid either in cash or in kind on the basis of a certain percentage of each harvest. He began surveying the *sawah*, checking on yield, studying the complicated method whereby the taxes were collected and passed from level to level in the Raja's hierarchy. He decided that the Raja was receiving only a small proportion of the tax which was presumably being collected for him, that many fields were escaping the tax in whole or in part, and that merely by instituting a more efficient and honest method of collection he could greatly increase state revenues. He did, but he himself and his successors probably also increased the percentage to be claimed from the farmers. By the end of the century the Buleleng rice fields, by no means the most extensive or productive, were yielding fl. 150,000 annually in taxes.

Not content with sharply rising revenues from opium and rice, the Dutch instructed the *punggawa* and their agents to count and recount every coconut palm and coffee bush and to assess standardized taxes upon them. They also taxed cockfights and games of chance, making the fees much higher than they had been before, on the assumption, probably known to be fallacious, that this would discourage the frivolous Balinese from trifling away their time and substance when they might be productively laboring in the fields.

Bloemen Waanders calculated Buleleng's imports and exports in 1859 as follows (one picul being approximately 132 pounds):

Exports:

30,000	picul rice	fl. 100,000
700	picul tobacco	34,000
10,000	picul beans	30,000
3,000	picul cotton	19,500
300	picul coconut	7,500
1,500	picul coconut oil	22,500
200	kilograms coffee	36,000
100	cattle	18,000
150	horses	4,500
600	pigs	3,600
	TOTAL	275,600

Imports:

300	chests opium	450,000
700	picul gambier	7,350
420	picul iron	9,250
80	cases cotton goods	20,000
10	picul silk	7,500
Other (including gold)		10,000
	TOTAL	540,100

After 1859 Buleleng trade increased quite rapidly. Allowing for the fact that opium remained by far the single most important article of import, accounting generally for at least two-thirds of the total value, and that at least one-half of this opium was re-exported without being recorded in trade statistics, there remained a consistently large excess of exports over imports even as more and more luxury goods began to be brought in for the wealthy. By 1873 imports totaled fl. 3,414,000 in value (of which fl. 2,101,800 was in opium) and recorded exports fl. 2,034,000. Trading capital in Buleleng rose from fl. 800,000 in 1858 to fl. 11,000,000 in 1874. The government itself lent new impetus to trade by starting a monthly shipping service between Buleleng and Java by the officially subsidized *Indische Stoomvaart-Maatschappij*. In 1874 the Singapore Surabaya–Makassar Line began including Buleleng as a port of call, and in 1876 the *Stoomvaart-reederij Banda* started regular service to the eastern islands. In the mid-1870s Buleleng was being visited by an average of about 125 European-style vessels each year and some 1,000 local craft.

Christian Missions; Vroom–Nicodemus Tragedy

The ever-increasing contact between Buleleng and the outside world resulted in attempts to introduce Christian missions. There ensued a protracted and highly charged debate over the appropriateness of such intervention in the area of custom and culture, which in the treaties of the 1840s the Dutch had formally undertaken to respect and protect. The debate had started in fact in about 1830. It continued for well over a hundred years with impassioned dispute whether the Balinese were or were not implacably hostile to conversion and whether the Dutch officials were or were not misguidedly paternalistic and indulgent in trying to shelter hedonistic pagans from missionary morality.

The first mission enterprise in Bali began and ended in early 1838, when as a consequence of Dr Medhurst's report of 1830 a certain Englishman, Rev. Ennis, settled in Buleleng to preach the gospel only to leave forthwith for failure to gain a hearing. The second attempt was in 1865, when the Utrecht Missionary Society sent out Rev. van der Jagt, who experienced the same sense of futility, despaired and departed. In 1866 the Society tried again, this time sending Rev. R. van Eck, a man of many resources. Quickly determining that the exercise of proselytizing among the contentedly Hindu Balinese was likely to be unproductive, he converted himself instead into an authority on Balinese life and thought, diligently studying language, literature, religion, manners and customs—everything which attracted his interest. But Rev. van Eck did score one soul, a certain Gusti Wayang Nurat Karangasem, to whom he taught the Ten Commandments and the Lord's Prayer and then arbitrarily pronounced him a Christian, conferring upon him the baptismal name of Nicodemus. Gusti Wayang seems, in fact, to have been a servant in van Eck's home whose curiosity about foreign rites and whose tractability to his master's wishes deterred him from protesting.

Rev. van Eck enthusiastically reported to his sponsors and supporters that he had converted a Balinese prince. If so, said van Eck's later critics, he was a prince unknown to his peers. He elaborated glowingly upon the opportunities for exporting salvation to an island which, like Houtman before him, he rapturously described as "Young Holland." Van Eck's subsequent reports to Utrecht were curiously empty of statistics on conversion but full of learned discourses on the beauty of the island and the wonders of its culture. The Utrecht congregation, much edified but perhaps equally mystified, decided to send two assistants to perform the ecclesiastical chores which, it was feared, this erudite agent might be somewhat neglecting. In due course there arrived a Rev. K. Wiggelendam and a Rev. J. de Vroom, who took up some of Rev. van Eck's duties in Buleleng and moved also into Mengwi. Rev. van Eck himself presently returned to Holland, where he assumed a professorial post in the Royal Military Academy in Breda, lecturing on the Netherlands East Indies and writing learned articles for Dutch journals.

The position of the inadvertent catechumen, Nicodemus, meanwhile, was becoming quite untenable. De Vroom and Wiggelendam, feeling impelled to demonstrate greater evangelical fervor than had their predecessor, but finding themselves unable to match even his modest record of a single convert, concentrated much of their attention upon Nicodemus himself. Nicodemus was caught between two spiritual fires. On the one hand, his new Dutch mentors were admonishing him that all the punishments of hell awaited him if, feeling himself saved, he failed to win other Balinese to the true faith. On the other hand, his own village priests and such relatives and friends as would associate with him at all—for any apostate from Hinduism was automatically rejected as un-Balinese and to all intents and purposes both physically and spiritually dead—were reminding him of the fate of those who ventured into the hereafter without benefit of Hindu rites. His family, they pointed out, would certainly not provide him with cremation, without which he would be reincarnated, if at all, as a serpent or demon. The pressures upon Nicodemus became so intolerable that he attempted to run away. But de Vroom pursued him and either persuaded or forced him to return. Shortly thereafter Nicodemus once again disappeared, returning, it seems, to his original home in Mengwi.

In early June 1881 Rev. de Vroom was found dead, brutally murdered by unknown assailants. Two household servants—I Klana, a Balinese from Karangasem, and Udin, a Javanese from Madura—were suspected of the crime and soon confessed. But the instigator, they said, was Nicodemus, who had paid them 35 pieces of silver and persuaded them to make away with the missionary. His motive, it seems, was to free himself from all ties to an alien faith. Nicodemus himself was apprehended in Mengwi and more or less freely confessed. He was sentenced to be encaged in a bamboo basket and exhibited throughout Buleleng and neighboring rajadoms as a criminal apostate, then to be executed. The shocking fate of the intense Rev. de Vroom and his unbalanced disciple Nicodemus moved the Resident to notify the Utrecht Missionary Society to recall Rev. Wiggelendam at once and to send no replacement.

The de Vroom–Nicodemus tragedy demonstrated to the Dutch administrators very early in the colonial history of Bali the danger inherent in tampering with a well-adjusted social system. This one experience was to a remarkable degree responsible for developing within the Dutch establishment in Buleleng the conviction that if changes were to be introduced they should be initiated only by the competent authorities. In the short term this signified an artificial limitation upon social contacts, corresponding to the economic and political monopoly which always weighed heavily in the Dutch colonial mentality. In the long term it meant the development of a policy of benevolent paternalism which, in the case of the Bali administration, became remarkably enlightened.

CHAPTER 9

DISINTEGRATION OF THE DEWA AGUNG'S EMPIRE (1832-1908)

P atterns of Conflict among States of the South

For the northern states of Bali the latter part of the nineteenth century was a period of not especially easy adjustment to Dutch rule, but on the other hand, except for the brief insurrections of Nyoman Gempol and Ida Made Rai, one of relative calm. For the southern states it was an era of great turbulence induced by the disintegration of the long declining empire of the Dewa Agung, a process to which the Dutch military expeditions of 1846, 1848 and 1849 gave fatal impetus.

Dewa Agung Putra was old and ill at the time of the wars and lacked either the inclination or the capacity to make more than feeble pretence to past glories. He died in 1849, leaving the throne to Dewa Agung Sakti, his son not by a noble but a commoner wife, the succession thus still further diminishing the much depleted authority of the royal line. Dewa Agung Sakti ruled for only about one year before he too died. Sakti was succeeded by a brother, Dewa Agung Gede Putra, who tried to enhance his position by marrying princesses of Bangli, Mengwi and Badung. Putra succeeded in reviving the rather tenuous allegiance of Bangli and Mengwi and the tolerance of Badung, but in counting upon the very limited support which they were prepared to offer, he began to play power politics without reliable strength upon which to fall back.

Power, such as it was in Klungkung itself, had long since passed from the male ruler to the female members of the royal household. Dewa Agung Gede Putra's father had been completely dominated by one of his many wives, a formidable princess of Karangasem who had dared even to contrive the murder of a rival, a princess of Badung, and had then boldly defied all accusers, a set of circumstances which had done nothing, naturally, to improve the already badly frayed Klungkung–Badung relations. Dewa Agung Gede Putra's half-sister, the daughter of the infamous Karangasem princess, who had arrogated to herself the title Dewa Agung Istri (a distinction traditionally reserved for the first wife of the ruler) lorded it over the court of her own day. She gained fame as the heroine of one of the great Balinese exploits in the war of 1849, when she planned and led the surprise night-time attack upon the Dutch camp at Kusamba, a Balinese victory which cost the Dutch many lives, including that of their commanding general. But momentary glory could not disguise the fact that Klungkung was now virtually a matriarchal monarchy, a sure sign to the Balinese that it was both decadent and decayed.

In the 1850s and later, despite his effort to revive dead loyalties by numerous marriages, the Dewa Agung was unable to command much respect, let alone obedience. He could put no more than about 10,000 soldiers into the field, as contrasted with the 25,000 which the neighboring and especially defiant state of Gianyar could at times muster.

Emergence of Gianyar; Quarrels with Its Neighbors

The Raja of Gianyar, whose usual title, that of Dewa Manggis, suggested that he aspired to achieve status comparable to that of the Dewa Agung, proved to be the most disruptive influence of the times in the southern region. The Dewa Manggis seemed almost always to be embroiled in conflict either with his peers of the other rajadoms or else with his own *punggawa*, of whom there were 35, each with aspirations and grievances and conspiracies of his own. The first Dewa Manggis had emerged as ruler of a distinct new state only in the latter part of the eighteenth century, the very fact that his was the newest of the royal houses signifying an abundance—his neighbors thought an excess—of energy and ambition. In his early years he had been the commander of a small 200-man garrison of the village of Gianyar, then a mere subdistrict under the *punggawa* of Sukawati, one of the most important district heads of the Dewa Agung. He was never much admired by his contemporaries or even by his progeny. According to the report of the German scholar Dr Friederich, who collected historical information in Bali (1845–6) from the royal families themselves:

By deceit, violence and poison he gained the mastery over those *punggawa*, and conquered from Mengwi to the country of Kramas. On account of his infamous deeds, his poisonings, etc., he is said to have changed after death into a serpent, which was kept for a long time in the palace at Gianyar, but disappeared in the last few years. His success in all his undertakings was probably owing to the fact that he began in a time when Klungkung was defeated by Karangasem, and deprived of all power. Gianyar, however, has submitted to the Dewa Agung as the supreme ruler, and sends him numerous presents, which cause him to forget that his nearest relatives are disgracefully oppressed—for the former *punggawa* are still living in Gianyar.

The late nineteenth-century descendants of the Dewa Manggis were more amiable by far than their forebears, impressing Dutch visitors always with their cultivated manner and the relative enlightenment of their administration. They were usually preoccupied, nevertheless, with feuds against their neighbors, especially the Dewa Agung. Gianyar's relations with the nearby rajadoms, complicated as they were, provide the clearest thread of continuity in the chain of events in southern Bali between 1840 and 1900, events which were opaque to the outside observer and have since been embellished by Balinese fantasy.

The Raja of Gianyar and his *punggawa* in the front courtyard of the palace at Gianyar, ca. 1900.

Beginning in the 1840s, when south Bali waged several small conflicts of its own before, during or in between the Dutch military campaigns, the countryside was never altogether at peace. For the most part these conflicts meant only occasional pitched battles involving a few score troops. But numerous little bands of mendicant soldiers constantly roved the landscape, burning, looting and killing when they met with any opposition to their requisition of provisions, shelter and valuables. The quarrels between and among the rajas, to whom these freebooters were more or less formally attached, were occasioned by disputes over land and water rights, or collection of tolls on roads and bridges, or runaway slaves, fugitive wives and broken pledges. Gianyar being the newest of the states, and one created by seizure of land from the others, became the focus of rancorous claims and counterclaims to legitimate control of its rich *subak*—rice-growing villages lying within a given irrigation system which might draw water from one district for land in another. Gianyar not infrequently found itself pitted simultaneously against all of its neighbors—Klungkung, Bangli, Mengwi, Tabanan and Badung. It survived only because these states were, in turn, inimical to one another, Mengwi being generally hostile to Tabanan and Bangli to Badung, so that there emerged at times a rather fragile alliance between Gianyar and any one, two or even three of its customary enemies.

War on Payangan (1843); Gianyar Provocation

The chain of circumstances which led to the final upset of equilibrium among the southern states and their complete control by the Dutch began in 1843. The Dewa Manggis then allied himself with nearby Klungkung and Mengwi, also the large northern states of Karangasem and Buleleng, to make war upon Payangan, a virtually autonomous district of Bangli which was often regarded as a separate rajadom. The ruler of Payangan, taking advantage of his strategic position across the main route between the north and the south, had been conducting himself quite arrogantly and barbarously. At one point, for instance, he seized six men from Buleleng who had given him some offence, put out their eyes and left them to fend for themselves in the forest. The Gianyar–Klungkung–Mengwi–Buleleng–Karangasem coalition forces, under command of Gusti Ketut Jelantik (who was to be the hero of the Balinese–Dutch wars of 1846–9), swiftly conquered the whole of Payangan. The victors deposed and killed the troublesome *punggawa* and as a compromise measure with regard to the disposition of his land, they offered it to the Dewa Agung to distribute. The Dewa Agung assigned the major part of the conquered territory to the royal family of Bangli. The new ruler apparent, knowing that the imposition of authority would not be easy, applied to Gianyar for support. Gianyar, instead, seized the greater part of the territory for its own. The Dewa Manggis thus so outraged the other rajas that they would no doubt have launched a concerted campaign against him had the wars of 1846–9 not intervened. He himself died in 1847, to be succeeded by Gusti Gede Ngurah Pahang, who died in 1856 and was succeeded by Dewa Manggis VII, who found himself, not unsurprisingly, surrounded by enemies.

Dewa Manggis VII was almost immediately involved in open warfare with the Dewa Agung, who succeeded in 1860 in seizing and
holding the region of Gunung Rata on the Gianyar side of the strategic ravine, which presumably constituted the boundary between the
two states. The Dewa Manggis consequently did not trouble himself
to acknowledge, let alone to accept, an invitation, i.e. command, to
attend upon the Dewa Agung in his wedding journey from Klungkung to Badung, where, in 1861 he was to be married to a daughter
of the Raja. The Dewa Agung could not forgive such lese majesty,
especially when the Dewa Manggis dared add ridicule to insult. He refused to chastise—perhaps because he had, in fact, inspired—two of
his close friends who perpetrated an outrage which almost everyone
conceded to have been in rather bad taste. A pair of commoner brothers, Made and Ketut Pasek, who consorted with royalty because they
were prosperous dealers in opium and hence very influential citizens,
had caused a ludicrous straw effigy of the Dewa Agung to be placed
in the public square in front of the Gianyar *puri* and had invited pass-
ersby to kick it and spit upon it.

Despite these several offences, and in part because the Dutch Resident himself several times intervened to settle certain quarrels in the
south, Gianyar enjoyed a period of relative calm during the 1870s and
did not again find itself in really serious trouble until the early 1880s.
Then, suddenly, everyone seemed to be fighting everyone else. Mengwi
was fighting Tabanan, Badung and Gianyar; Bangli was fighting Gianyar
and Mengwi. The Dewa Manggis was even fighting some of his own
punggawa, who had broken away to ally themselves with various of
his enemies and were receiving as strong support from the Dewa
Agung as he could then provide. The situation was further complicated by the fact that the Dewa Agung himself ruled, presumably, over
four scattered enclaves within Tabanan and Gianyar, greater in total
area than Klungkung proper, and these enclaves constituted cells of intrigue and villainy almost as vexatious to the Dewa Agung himself as
to the neighboring rajas. Furthermore, Karangasem, the big eastern
state, which normally held itself aloof from the south, was beginning

to aspire to slices of southern territory. It was being incited by its own overlord, the Raja of Lombok, to help to dismember the empire of his long-time enemy, the Dewa Agung.

Feud with Klungkung; Seizure of Gianyar Royal Family

In 1882, in the interest of sheer self-preservation, seeking maximum insurance at minimum risk, the Dewa Manggis made certain rather unconvincing professions of renewal of allegiance to the Dewa Agung, even going so far as to imply willingness for Gianyar to merge with Klungkung. In 1885, as a measure of last resort when his many enemies were still pressing in upon him, the Dewa Manggis and all his family and his court journeyed to Klungkung to perform the ceremony of homage. They also sought the Dewa Agung's intervention with the two states still reasonably loyal to him, Mengwi and Bangli, which were Gianyar's two most dangerous enemies. The Dewa Agung, deftly matching treachery to expediency, caused the whole company to be seized and detained. He sentenced the Dewa Manggis and his sons to lifelong internment under vigilant guard in a nearby village. He then assigned the state of Gianyar to one of his own sons to rule as regent. When the son was forced to flee from his new subjects, who immediately rose up against him, the Dewa Agung partitioned the state between Klungkung and Bangli and called upon Bangli to make the arrangement work. The partition of Gianyar so outraged the Raja of Karangasem, who had certain rather dubious claims of his own to assert, that with the support of 500 soldiers shipped over to him by the Raja of Lombok, he prepared to launch an invasion.

The Dewa Agung called upon Mengwi to make itself master of Gianyar and thus to forestall Karangasem. But the Mengwi attack miscarried, and presently many armies were moving confusedly in many directions. Badung attacked Mengwi. So too did Tabanan. Badung captured the capital of Mengwi and killed the Raja but was unable to subdue the state as a whole. Karangasem tried to march through Klungkung to participate either in the reconstitution or the dismemberment of Mengwi, as might seem the more expedient, but encountered unexpectedly strong opposition from the Dewa Agung's own forces. Karangasem succeeded briefly in besieging the Klungkung *puri* but suffered such heavy losses that it had to withdraw to the east. Klungkung, meanwhile, had called upon Bangli for aid, and Bangli again occupied most of Gianyar. Badung and Tabanan partitioned Mengwi, prudently allotting some of the remoter border area to Karangasem. A son of the late Raja of Mengwi escaped from exile in Badung to raise a Mengwi insurrection. Tabanan and Bangli allied themselves with Badung to put down the insurrection and repartition the state. There were other complications too numerous to recite.

Dewa Gede Raka and Gianyar's Revival; Regency Status (1900)

In the midst of all these alarms and excursions, two sons of the Dewa Manggis had made their escape from Klungkung (1889) and returned to Gianyar. The second of these sons, Dewa Gede Raka, succeeded in enlisting the aid of Cokorda Sukawati, the powerful *punggawa* of Ubud, who rallied some of the other *punggawa*, raised a new army and began a war for the reconstitution of the state. In 1892 Dewa Gede Raka gained recognition as Raja by most of the Gianyar *punggawa* but not from the other rulers. He then devoted himself to the delicate and dangerous task of impressing his personal authority over those other *punggawa* who still wavered and persuading all of them to share with him such revenues as they were still able to collect, the Raja himself being impoverished and the *puri*, the symbol of royal prestige, being only very shabbily restored as yet after having been sacked by the men of Klungkung a decade earlier. But his royal neighbors were still implacably hostile to him and his own state was still in disarray. With the support of Cokorda Sukawati, Dewa Gede Raka convinced the other *punggawa* that there was only one way to preserve the rajadom—to place it under the protection of the Dutch.

In 1898 Dewa Gede Raka, the new Dewa Manggis, began negotiating with the Dutch Resident to accept the rajadom as a protectorate, a move which the Dutch were hesitant to make for fear of provoking the Dewa Agung and the other southern rulers. The Dewa Manggis solicited the good offices of the ruler of Karangasem, who enjoyed the special confidence of the Dutch. He also sent his most distinguished *punggawa*, Cokorda Sukawati, to consult with the Resident personally in Buleleng. The Resident referred the decision to Batavia and on February 28, 1900 received the historic telegram from the Governor-General authorizing him to name the Dewa Manggis as Dutch-designated and protected Stedehouder, or Viceroy, a more elevated rank than that of Regent, which was conferred upon the rulers of the other states, except only Karangasem, where the Raja also was entitled Stedehouder. The Dutch thereby extended their overt control from northern into southern Bali.

On March 8, 1900 Raja Dewa Gede Raka was duly installed as Stedehouder, the occasion being celebrated in Puri Gianyar by eight days of feasting and entertainment with the Dutch Resident and all of the *punggawa* in attendance. The Dewa Agung immediately protested that Gianyar belonged to Klungkung and could not be alienated without his consent, a claim which Bangli, Badung and Tabanan were easily persuaded to endorse. The Dutch replied at their leisure to the general effect that the new status quo in Gianyar was already a fait accompli. The newly appointed Dutch Controleur, Heer Schwarz, had already taken up his post, having occupied a pavilion within the *puri* itself in order to be close to the Raja. According to the Controleur's own account, the Raja sought him out eagerly by night as well as by day in order to elicit advice. With Schwarz's appearance, the Raja's position vis-à-vis the Dutch and his own *punggawa* was greatly strengthened and the turbulence which had beset the state for the better part of the last half century began rapidly to subside.

Controleur Schwarz and Modern Progress; *Sri Kumala* Incident (1904)

Thus, in 1900 the Dutch presence began to make itself clearly felt in south Bali just as it had almost half a century earlier in the north. With Controleur Schwarz at hand to guide the Raja, Gianyar went through much the same transformation as that which had occurred decades earlier in Buleleng under the influence of Controleur Bloemen Waanders. The administrative system was regularized; taxes were more efficiently collected and more wisely used; roads and bridges and irrigation systems were improved; other public works were built; health and educational services were introduced, and the system of justice was reformed. The whole state experienced such unaccustomed security and tranquility that the Dutch hailed it as a model of colonial achievement in pacification and development. The model was not one which pleased its neighbors. As the Dutch tactlessly pointed out, Gianyar in the south, like Buleleng earlier in the north, became a sanctuary for refugees from the tyranny of the other rajadoms, such refugees including runaway slaves and people falsely accused of crimes.

The Dewa Agung, in particular, could not be reconciled to the presence of a Dutch Controleur within only a few miles of the sacred Puri Klungkung. He determined to assert his customary authority and he strongly advised Bangli, Badung and Tabanan to do likewise. In his defiance of the Dutch he elected Gianyar as the surrogate object of his attentions. He therefore tolerated if he did not actually instigate the practice of certain of the farmers in the Klungkung–Gianyar border area, who took to planting sharpened bamboo splints in their fields in order to impede the work of the surveyors attempting to determine exact state and property lines. He provided shelter for fugitive criminals and tolerated trade in stolen or smuggled merchandise and committed other minor nuisances far too numerous even for the meticulous Dutch to catalog. The Dutch attempted to deal with the Dewa Agung by sending officials to lodge formal protest and by deploying warships in maneuvers offshore as they did so, but he persisted in his intransigence. It was widely assumed, therefore, that there would soon occur some especially outrageous incident which would launch another Dutch expeditionary force.

The incident happened on May 27, 1904. The *Sri Kumala*, a Chinese-owned schooner out of Banjarmasin, Borneo, struck the reef near Sanur close to the Badung–Gianyar border, and was allegedly plundered by the people with the approval of the rajas. The Chinese owner of the craft gave an altogether implausible account of his misfortune and demanded an altogether fanciful indemnity for the cargo, to the original itemization of which he added as a curious afterthought large quantities of silver and gold. The Dutch scaled down his claims to a mere fl. 7,500 ($2,500) and presented the bill to the Raja of Badung, who flatly refused to pay. The Dewa Agung backed him in his defiance and so too did the Raja of Tabanan, who happened also to be involved just then in a crisis over a recent ceremony of suttee which he had permitted despite Dutch protest. So in June of 1906 the Dutch blockaded the coasts of Badung and Tabanan while they drew up and presented certain ultimata and assembled a military expedition.

Sixth Military Expedition (1906); Puputan in Denpasar

The Sixth Military Expedition, under the command of General Ross van Tonningen, consisted of three battalions of infantry and a detachment of cavalry, two batteries of artillery and strong naval support. It arrived off the southern coast of Bali in early September. On September 12 the General sent a final ultimatum, which the Raja of Badung rejected. On September 14 the Dutch landed their troops on Sanur beach. In the course of the next few days, without meeting any significant resistance, the forces proceeded inland. On September 20, early in the morning, they moved into the town of Kesiman, the seat of a minor ruler, also titled Raja, who administered the district on behalf of the Raja of Badung. They discovered that the aged, half-crazed Raja had been killed by his own high priest for refusal to lead a resistance, that the *puri* was in flames and that the people had deserted both the *puri* and the town. Having little to detain them in Kesiman, they continued their march toward Denpasar, expecting the action to be more of a dress parade than a pitched battle.

The Dutch troops, marching in orderly ranks along a long roadway walled on either side, which led to the royal palace, were not surprised to find the town apparently deserted and flames and smoke rising over the *puri*, the most disquieting factor being the sound of the wild beating of drums within the palace walls. As they drew closer, they observed a strange, silent procession emerging from the main gate of the *puri*. It was led by the Raja himself, seated in his state palanquin carried by four bearers, dressed in white cremation garments but splendidly bejeweled and armed with a magnificent *kris*. The Raja was followed by the officials of his court, the armed guards, the priests, his wives, his children and his retainers, likewise dressed in white, flowers in their hair, many of them almost as richly ornamented and as splendidly armed as the Raja himself.

One hundred paces from the startled Dutch, the Raja halted his bearers, stepped from his palanquin, gave the signal and the ghastly ceremony began. A priest plunged his dagger into the Raja's breast, and others of the company began turning their daggers upon themselves or upon one another. The Dutch troops, startled into action by a stray gunshot and reacting to attack by lance and spear, directed rifle and even artillery fire into the surging crowd. Some of the women mockingly threw jewels and gold coins to the soldiers, and as more and more people kept emerging from the palace gate, the mounds of corpses rose higher and higher. Soon to the scene of carnage was added the spectacle of looting as the soldiers stripped the valuables from the corpses and then set themselves to sacking the palace ruins. It was a slaughter and self-slaughter of the innocents and a plundering of the dead made all the more appalling by reason of its recurrence that same afternoon in nearby Pemecutan, a minor appendage of Badung. There the frail old Raja and his terrified court, having heard what had already happened in Denpasar, elected the same fate. When the victorious Dutch troops marched from Denpasar to Pemecutan, the Raja and his retainers were ready to enact yet once again the grisly rites of the *puputan*. This time the Dutch were prepared to refrain from participation if not from profit.

Wesatia (1904) and Suicide (1906) of Tabanan Royalty

Equally moving scenes occurred in adjacent Tabanan both shortly before and shortly after the Badung spectacle, first despite and later because of Dutch intervention. The venerable Raja Ngurah Agung, who had come to the throne in the year 1844 and was the last well-known survivor of the stirring events of the mid-nineteenth century, died on March 3, 1903, and his cremation, scheduled to be held seven months later, was a signal for a reunion of royalty from all of the other rajadoms. It quickly became known throughout Bali—and in Batavia as well—that two of the Raja's aged widows intended to follow their husband in death by performing the rite of *wesatia*, or suttee. The Resident advised the old Raja's son and successor that he expected him to prevent this sacrifice. The new Raja replied that he knew of no clause in the famous contracts in which *wesatia* was even mentioned, let alone proscribed, and that the Dutch themselves had, in fact, undertaken not to interfere in internal affairs of the rajadom, especially those which related to *adat* (tradition). He added, in a more placatory tone, that this Tabanan ceremony would no doubt be the last of its kind and that he himself could not and would not deny the wishes of the grieving widows. The Dutch sent two warships to cruise suggestively close off the Tabanan coast and assumed that this would suffice to dampen traditional ardor. But the Raja's pride and prestige were at stake, and on October 20 the ceremonies of cremation and suttee occurred exactly on schedule. The Dutch press, public and administration in Batavia and The Hague debated for weeks what, if anything, should be done about this "barbarous" or "sacred" custom and Tabanan's defiance of civilized norms and Dutch wishes. The Resident of Bali finally drew up a contract (1904) in which suttee was explicitly prohibited and the Controleurs were instructed to make quite certain that no subsequent crises arose with obstinate rajas and determined widows, and none did.

Seventh Military Expedition (1908); Puputan in Klungkung

Very soon after the Tabanan suttee, men of Tabanan were implicated, along with those of Badung, in plundering the shipwrecked *Sri Kumala*. The Dutch expeditionary force which arrived subsequently, having dealt conclusively with Badung, marched next upon Tabanan. The new Raja and the Crown Prince, who rejected the advice of certain of

The Raja of Gianyar greeting Lt Schutsal of the Sixth Dutch Military Expedition, 1906.

their priests and courtiers that they had no choice but to resort to the *puputan*, fled from the *puri* together with some of their more timorous followers and sent emissaries to bargain with the rapidly advancing Dutch. They offered peacefully to accept regency status, which was about to be imposed upon Badung, but they sought some reassurance that they themselves would not be exiled, as seemed all too likely. They were required to present themselves in Denpasar as humble petitioners, as they hastened to do, only to be detained, interrogated and abruptly informed that exile to Madura or Lombok was indeed to be their well-deserved punishment. The Raja and the Prince preferred suicide in their Denpasar prison. For lack of a *kris*, the Raja plunged a *sirih* knife into his throat and the Crown Prince took poison. Their closest relatives were exiled to Lombok. Their palace, the finest in all of Bali, was plundered and razed, and Tabanan followed Badung into the Dutch sphere, itself to be followed, in 1908, by Bangli and Klungkung.

As a side excursion to their invasion of Tabanan, the Dutch made a show of force in Klungkung. They hoped thereby either to prevent or perhaps to provoke a show of resistance by the Dewa Agung, for there were certain of the military who thought the time was opportune quite definitively to pacify and occupy the whole of southern Bali. But the Dewa Agung was either cowed or prudent. He resisted the urgings of the Punggawa of Gelgel, the one real firebrand in the state, and declined his offer to man and lead an attack. He even went so far as to command his own small palace guard to ring the Punggawa's *puri* to prevent him from taking any rash action on his own authority. The Dutch presently withdrew, some of them predicting that they would soon be back.

For the time being the Dutch contented themselves with presenting the Dewa Agung with a whole new set of agreements almost indistinguishable from ultimata, all of which he accepted virtually at sight. The Dewa Agung was required to dismantle all fortifications, to deliver all firearms, to renounce all levies upon imports and exports and to cede to Gianyar and Tabanan certain remaining Klungkung-ruled enclaves within their territory. In compensation for his loss of revenues from customs, the Dutch granted him an apparently generous annual pension of fl. 7,117. But opium, by far the most important item of trade, was soon yielding the Dutch themselves much more than that amount under their new opium monopoly.

Everyone knew that the next move would be Dutch imposition upon Klungkung of the same sort of general administrative guidance which their Controleurs provided in other states and that any small incident would provoke it. Disorders duly broke out, especially in the town of Gelgel. Some of the Punggawa's men intimidated and attacked certain agents of the opium monopoly, the incident resulting in the death of the Gelgel shop manager and two of his assistants and the subsequent looting of the stock. The Dutch brought in warships and landed a small party of troops which marched into Gelgel to seek out and to punish the Punggawa. The Punggawa and his supporters offered resistance and a sharp engagement ensued in which 180 Balinese were killed and so many of the Dutch soldiers were injured that the detachment had to withdraw to the sea coast. The Punggawa sought shelter in Klungkung where the Dewa Agung, correctly antic-

A self-sacrifice ceremony (*wesatia*), from Ludvig Verner Helms, *Pioneering in the Far East*, London, 1882.

ipating naval bombardment and land maneuvers, had already authorized certain measures of defence. The weak little Klungkung defence force reintensified its rather forlorn efforts to contrive shelters against shells, to buttress the *puri* walls, to dig protective pits and ditches and to plant bamboo spikes and sharpened bamboo splints where they might do the expected attackers the greatest damage. The bombardment swiftly followed, virtually demolishing the guilty town of Gelgel and working great destruction upon innocent Klungkung. Then came the troops with their field pieces, which they deployed in the square in front of the *puri* at a distance of little more than 500 feet from the main gate and began firing admonitory salvos.

The Dewa Agung ordered the gongs to sound the call to the *puputan*. He himself led a procession of some two hundred people who emerged from the *puri* to confront the Dutch soldiers. Clad all in white, he carried in one hand a ceremonial lance with a golden tip and in the other his ancestral *kris*, magically and mystically the most potent item of the royal regalia. Pausing about three hundred feet from the momentarily silent cannon, he bent over and with an imperious gesture thrust the *kris* blade into the ground. Thus, if the prophecy of his high priest came true, he would create a great chasm in which would swallow up all of his enemies. As he straightened, he received a gunshot in the knee, and before he could even crumple he was killed outright by another. Six of his wives knelt around him and solemnly drove their *kris* blades into their own hearts. The whole company, men, women and children alike, engaged in ritualistic self-immolation or sacrificed one another while murderous cannon and gunfire contributed to the mayhem.

There were very few royal or other survivors of the Klungkung *puputan*, but nineteen of them were exiled to Lombok. The *puri* was razed, except for one gateway which led to a barracks and a prison. What little had remained of Klungkung's ancient glory had vanished, but the last bright blaze of martyrdom had burnt away many stains. Thus, on April 18, 1908, after 600 years of rule in Bali, the lineal descendants of the Majapahit emperors were decimated, the ritualistic victims of relentless Western intrusion.

CHAPTER 10

TRAGEDY IN LOMBOK (1891-1894)

Origin in Bali and Lombok of Sasak Insurrections
The chain of events which culminated so disastrously in Bali proper with *the puputan* in Denpasar (1906) and Klungkung (1908) had, in fact, already led in 1894 to a penultimate climax in Lombok which was in certain respects even more shocking and horrible. The Lombok tragedy of 1894 clearly signaled the fate of the Dewa Agung and those of his vassals who objected to the active exercise of the Dutch sovereignty which they had long since acknowledged but never fully accepted. This catastrophe on the nearby island was directly related to the late nineteenth-century turbulence in Bali itself. In playing a minor role in the dissolution of the Dewa Agung's empire, the state of Karangasem, a dependency of the Balinese Raja of Lombok, triggered a crisis which destroyed the Lombok rajadom.

Lombok and Karangasem enjoyed almost half a century of peace and obscurity between the troubles of the earlier part of the century and those which broke out in the 1890s. At the end of the Balinese–Dutch War of 1849, the Dutch rewarded the Raja of Lombok, who provided the troops which conquered Karangasem, by recognizing his claim to the state and permitting him to rule it through his own regent. Neither Karangasem nor Lombok gave the Dutch any special trouble for decades thereafter. In 1870 Lombok came under the rule of Raja Ratu Agung Gede Ngurah, who proved to be extraordinarily capable and durable. In Karangasem a Balinese prince of Lombok, Gusti Gede Putu, was Regent, but his half-brother, Gusti Gede Jelantik, had become the actual ruler.

Gusti Gede Jelantik; His Career in Bali and Lombok

Gusti Gede Jelantik, one of the most controversial figures in Balinese history, was a prince of the Balinese royal house of Karangasem who was born and brought up in Lombok and was treated by his uncle, the reigning Raja, as a prime favorite. In his early youth he fell in love with his uncle's daughter whose caste (Brahman) was higher than his own (Wesya). When the affair resulted in accusations of defilement of caste, an offence for which the death penalty was mandatory, Gusti Jelantik was suddenly forced to flee to Bali, doing so, it seems, with the connivance of his uncle and his half-brother.

In Bali, very soon after his arrival, he all but openly ruled Karangasem. His domination of the state was so complete that when the Regent's son committed the same offence of which he, Gusti Jelantik, had been guilty in Lombok, he prevailed upon the father to cause the son to fall by the *kris*. His influence over the Regent and his obvious intention to clear the way for his own succession aroused intense resentment among various members of the Karangasem court. But at just that time Karangasem was being pressured by Lombok to intervene in the wars in the southern Balinese states, and Gusti Jelantik was the obvious choice for command of the joint Karangasem–Lombok forces then assembling. His subsequent campaign in Klungkung ended in disaster, especially for the Lombok soldiers, who were poorly armed, clothed and provisioned and suffered frightful losses. These Lombok troops were reluctant recruits drafted from the native Sasak population into the service of their Balinese rulers. Their decimation in Klungkung combined with efforts to impress and send replacements precipitated outright Sasak rebellion at home. Gusti Jelantik, who had so recently been fighting a war for Lombok in Bali, was suddenly called upon to lead a Balinese expeditionary force of 1,500 men to go to the aid of the Raja of Lombok. Jelantik and his army crossed from Bali to Lombok on November 29, 1891, and there, for the next year, he himself was deeply involved in the tangled affairs of the Lombok rulers.

Royal Family of Lombok; the Raja; Gusti Made; Gusti Ketut

In 1891 Raja Ratu Agung Gede Ngurah was already long since past his prime, frail, deaf and at times childish. He was given to unpredictable displays of the alert intelligence for which he had been famous but also to studied or unstudied senility and stupidity. He had placed the affairs of the realm largely in the hands of his eldest son, Anak Agung Made, or Gusti Made, the son not of a noble wife but of a low caste concubine. According to conflicting accounts, Gusti Made was possessed of enormous capability and courage or of almost infinite craftiness and cruelty. As his heir apparent, the old Raja had designated his eldest son by a noble wife, Anak Agung Ketut, or Gusti Ketut, a youth who seemed to the Dutch to be moronic. Since the Raja had dozens of wives, scores of children and hundreds of royal relatives holding high positions at court, the rajadom was riddled with intrigue. The three closely adjacent towns of Ampenan (the port), Mataram (the seat of the Crown Prince) two and a half miles away, and Cakranegara (the seat of the Raja) a mile further distant, were Balinese-Hindu enclaves in an island where 95 percent of the people were resentful and rebellious Sasak Muslims. The Sasak complained, and were able to cite convincing evidence, that the Balinese rulers, especially Gusti Made, oppressed, exploited and terrorized them, in fact brazenly robbed and murdered, and might be planning a war of extermination of Muslims as a counter measure to Sasak rebellion. Such was the stage setting for the reappearance of Gusti Jelantik together with his force of 1,500 Balinese warriors at the court of the old Raja, with whom he swiftly re-established himself as favorite.

Sasak Petitions; Raja's Appeal to the Dutch and the English

Both the Raja and the Sasak rebels had addressed themselves frequently to the Dutch, the Raja seeking aid in putting down the rebellion, the

Sasak requesting a Dutch punitive expedition against the Balinese leaders and promising to join it. The Dutch were cool to the Raja's advances, being much preoccupied at the time with a long and costly war in Aceh, Sumatra, and indisposed to open a distant second front. They sententiously reminded the Raja of their recently redefined colonial policy of "abstinence," signifying non-intervention in local disputes. The Raja turned to Singapore, seeking to buy arms and charter ships and to invite the colonial British to intervene. He employed as his intermediary Said Abdullah, an Ampenan merchant who belonged to a wealthy and influential Singapore Arab family and held the post of Syahbandar which had once been occupied by Mads Lange and George Pocock King. Said Abdullah and his sons were murdered not long afterwards, presumably because they served also as intermediaries for the Sasak, who turned to them as co-religionists and potential confederates.

The Raja, it might seem, could have caused no greater dismay to the Dutch than to appeal to their British rivals, but he managed to compound his offence in an objectionable manner and thus to destroy the possibility that they would espouse his cause. When Dutch agents journeyed to Lombok to investigate the Sasak complaints—first and several times later a Controleur, once the Resident himself—the Raja refused on one flimsy pretext or another to receive them. The Dutch dignitaries indignantly departed to report unanimously that they had confirmed the worst of the Sasak charges and to recommend firm measures against the insolent and cruel Balinese. They had laboriously drafted a letter which was not exactly an accusation or an ultimatum but included nicely calculated nuances of both. They were especially annoyed that they were never able to deliver it.

Ultimatum and Military Expedition of 1894

In June 1894, when the Aceh war seemed to be won and troops could be released for other operations, the Governor-General drew up an ultimatum in which he made four demands, to which, later on, another three were appended. From the Raja he required: (1) sincere repentance for his disrespectful behavior; (2) solemn assurance of future compliance with Dutch wishes; (3) immediate banishment of the evil Gusti Made; (4) acceptance of Dutch mediation to restore peace between the Balinese and the Sasak; and later, (5) abdication in favor of the Crown Prince; (6) declaration of willingness to conclude new treaties; (7) payment of indemnity. The Raja rejected the ultimatum. The Dutch launched the Lombok Expedition.

The Lombok Expedition of 1894 was assembled in Batavia and Surabaya out of elements hastily withdrawn from Aceh and was placed under the command of Major-General J. A. Vetter with Major-General P. P. H. van Ham as his deputy. The designation of these two highly respected and experienced officers to joint command signified the importance which the Dutch attached to the new enterprise and the high regard in which they held Balinese warriors. The expeditionary fleet consisted of four warships and eleven transports. The land forces consisted of 107 Dutch officers, 1,320 European soldiers (including 175 cavalry), 948 indigenous troops (mainly Ambonese), 216 servants, 64 overseers and 1,718 convict laborers.

The invasion fleet arrived off Lombok on July 5 and the Generals at once sent the Raja another ultimatum which would expire at sunrise the following morning. The Raja sent back a messenger requesting three days' delay, but the Dutch held to the original deadline and at 6:30 a.m. on July 6 they began landing their troops. They encountered no resistance whatever. The whole expedition was ashore by mid-afternoon and scouting parties were sent out into the countryside, where all seemed to be quiet. On July 8 a strong reconnoitering force set out in the direction of Mataram and Cakranegara with Generals Vetter and van Ham in the lead and Controleur Liefrinck accompanying them as representative of the Resident of Bali and Lombok and expert adviser on matters of local psychology and politics. The party very soon encountered Gusti Jelantik who had come, in fact, to intercept it and report to it on conditions at court. Gusti Jelantik engaged in a long and friendly conversation with the Dutch officials and promised to meet them again the next day after first conferring with the Raja and Gusti Made. He kept his July 9 appointment and informed the Dutch that the Raja accepted virtually all of their conditions. His report was confirmed the following day by a letter from the Raja requesting modification only of the provision with regard to Gusti Made, suggesting that arbitrary banishment might incense the people. He would prefer that the Dutch first conduct an on-the-spot inquiry into his alleged offences. The Commander replied that the prince must be surrendered to him at once or else the expedition would march upon Cakranegara as, on July 11, it did, no reply having yet been received.

The march on Cakranegara had barely begun before messengers arrived with a letter saying that the Raja had given Gusti Made the choice between exile and suicide. A second messenger followed hard upon the first to announce that, in fact, the prince had committed suicide and that his wife had joined him in death. The Dutch were skeptical but accepted the messenger's suggestion that they send someone actually to view the bodies. The assignment fell to Controleur Liefrinck, who was personally acquainted with the people in question. Arriving in Cakranegara without incident, Liefrinck was admitted at once to the *puri*, which seemed to be virtually deserted, but was then subjected to a long wait. Eventually, he demanded to see Gusti Jelantik, who presently appeared, asked him to wait just a little longer, then vanished. After another long delay, Liefrinck again demanded to see Jelantik. The prince returned and escorted the Controleur into an interior courtyard in which lay two bodies clothed all in white. Liefrinck recognized one as that of Gusti Made, who just at that moment drew his last labored breath.

The Dutch never determined to their own satisfaction, and Gusti Jelantik never confided in them, exactly what had been the circumstances of the prince's death. He had plunged his *kris* into his own heart, just as the old Raja had said, was the official version of the incident. Most people thought Gusti Jelantik had guided his hand. Others held that the old Raja had condemned him to death just then in expiation of the crime of incest and that the high priest had been the executioner. Whatever the true explanation, Gusti Made, whom the Dutch regarded as the evil genius behind the Lombok troubles, was undeniably and opportunely removed from the scene and there seemed to be no further obstacle to peaceful relations. The troops marched into Mataram and Cakranegara that same day through what appeared to be a friendly countryside. Seemingly cheerful spectators lined the roadways and the town markets remained open with stall keepers and buyers alike apparently unconcerned about any danger. Everybody, in fact, seemed much diverted by the military parade and delighted with the martial music.

General Vetter, General van Ham and Controleur Liefrinck took up residence in comfortable compounds requisitioned from the nobility. They adopted Gusti Jelantik as their confidant and intermediary in their relations with the local people. The troops settled themselves into bivouac areas on the outskirts of Cakranegara, Mataram and Ampenan, with the largest contingents in Cakranegara, and prepared to enjoy an agreeable stretch of not very strenuous occupation duty. The old Raja abdicated, the Crown Prince succeeded him and exchanged ceremonial calls with the Generals and the Controleur. Negotiations began for fulfilment of Dutch conditions, most of which the young Raja seemed to accept with such compliance and indeed indifference that the Dutch suspected, and Gusti Jelantik confirmed, that he really did not comprehend except when it came to payment of indemnity. The Dutch demanded fl. 1,000,000 and the prince quickly paid over the first three installments—200,000, 250,000 and 250,000 in silver coins—but not without evidence of anguish. The only real trouble the Dutch encountered came not from the Balinese but from the Sasak. It was part of the Dutch mission to reconcile the Sasak to Balinese rule, but it was not until they promised to station permanent Dutch representatives in Lombok to look out for Sasak interests that the Sasak leaders became receptive to Dutch suggestions.

The Generals were elated by their bloodless victory. The Controleur was delighted with progress in treaty-making and the troops were so relaxed in their bivouac areas that they neglected to take the most elementary precautions against trouble. They drilled and paraded and staged concerts of band music for great crowds of admiring, respectful spectators, among whom were many Balinese soldiers. It seemed only mildly curious that Gusti Jelantik's own army of some 1,500 men from Bali proper still remained in Lombok, even though it had been several times scheduled to return home. Then in late August there were certain danger signals.

The Balinese soldiers became less respectful and, in fact, occasionally provocative, one of them, for instance, throwing a bottle at soldiers who were counting the coins in the latest installment of indemnity payment. One morning the market places were almost deserted and the population of both Mataram and Cakranegara seemed strangely diminished. Then came an informer on August 24 to report that the Balinese were planning a surprise attack upon Cakranegara for that same night. The Dutch sought to consult their trusted friend, Gusti Jelantik, and also the simple-minded young Raja. Both were much too ill, it seemed, to be visited. They sent a military doctor to diagnose Gusti Jelantik's sudden seizure. He pronounced it a stupor induced by opium. It was already much too late in the day to stage an orderly withdrawal from Cakranegara, and to retreat in great haste, said Controleur Liefrinck, would only make the Dutch appear cowardly and ridiculous in the eyes of the bold, proud Balinese warriors. So they called a special alert and posted a heavy guard and the night passed without incident. They learned only much later that the Balinese had suddenly discovered that the horoscope readings were inauspicious for an August 24 attack. Next day the Dutch roused Jelantik from his torpor long enough to get him to swear that he had absolutely no knowledge of any conspiracy. That night, at 11:15, just as they were congratulating themselves that danger was quite certainly past, the attack came.

The camp in Cakranegara was suddenly surrounded by hundreds, perhaps thousands, of Balinese warriors, firing off rifles with deadly aim, their battle cries as blood-curdling as their attack was furious, massacring Dutch soldiers who had no place to take shelter. The attack continued all night. At 7:00 a.m. on August 26 the Dutch withdrew in reasonably good order to a nearby temple in which they would have stone walls to protect them. But they were without food, water or adequate ammunition, and the Balinese soon began boring holes through the walls and firing into the closely packed masses of troops in the restricted and sweltering compound. At 3:00 p.m. the Cakranegara forces began to retreat toward Mataram.

General van Ham himself was fatally wounded just after he emerged from the temple gateway. The troops suffered frightful losses as they moved from Cakranegara into and through the town of Mataram. The Balinese could and did take shelter behind thick stone walls in order to fire with quite devastating effect upon the confused Dutch ranks, especially at one point where the road made a right-angle turn. When the retreating troops reached the Mataram bivouac area, they discovered that the Mataram garrison had been subjected to equally strong attack and had already withdrawn toward the coast. The next day the Cakranegara forces also retreated to the port town of Ampenan, suffering losses all along the way but not as severe as on August 25–26. By final official report, once all the scattered detachments were accounted for, including several which had been dispatched to the interior and one which was captured—and freed—by the Balinese, the Dutch casualties on August 25–27 totaled 98 dead and 272 injured. The dead were 60 Europeans (nine officers) and 38 members of the Ambonese and other indigenous auxiliary forces. The injured were 121 Europeans (17 officers) and 151 indigenous auxiliaries.

General Vetter's own telegraphic summation of the events of these dreadful days by which his career was irretrievably ruined warrants at least the following partial citation as a moving historical document:

Cakra attacked on the night of 25th. Firing continued all day. Losses in course of 26th are 14 killed and 85 wounded. No water, foraging impossible, losses increasing; at 3 p.m. retreated to Mataram. Baggage left behind so as to carry wounded in wagons. Heavy losses on the road. Situation Mataram worse. Camp deserted. Eight in the evening Bijlevelt's column from the interior arrived, also heavy losses. Provisions failed, could not reach bivouac, communication with Ampenan interrupted, hemmed in between Cakra and Mataram; impossible to take offensive. Situation untenable on account of numbers wounded, on morning 27th retreated Ampenan in southerly direction, losses were comparatively small. Killed: four officers, 63 soldiers; Wounded: 12 officers, 153 soldiers; Missing: six officers, 143 soldiers. Four field guns left behind at Mataram. Nothing known of Van Lawick's column in the interior.

"Treachery" of August 25–27; Puputan at Mataram and Sasari

The August 25–27 Battle of Cakranegara and Mataram entered Dutch colonial history as "The Lombok Betrayal" or "The Lombok Treachery." When telegraphic word reached Batavia and the Netherlands, the wrath of the government and the people could only be assuaged by the immediate assembly and launching of a new expedition to reinforce the remnants of the old and to carry the battle back to its starting point. The reinforcements began arriving in Lombok in early September, eventually totaling at least another 1,000 officers and men, among them a higher percentage of Europeans than before. There were also large detachments of convict laborers—650 of them at first with more to follow.

The Dutch took every possible precaution against being surprised and advanced only very deliberately through the countryside in which every village proved to be strongly defended. Since each village was a maze of compounds with thick stone walls, the seizure of any one of them was no easy tactical maneuver. The Dutch resorted to virtual demolition, first laying down such heavy artillery fire that the walls began to crumble, and then, upon occupying a village, moving in the convict laborers to level the walls in order to preclude any possibility of reoccupation by the Balinese forces. Relentlessly they advanced upon Mataram, which they seized on September 29 and systematically razed, an enterprise which occupied them for the next several weeks. It was not until November 18 that they reached Cakranegara and not until November 19 that they actually occupied the whole of the city, subjecting it afterwards to the same treatment as Mataram.

In Mataram the defenders took up their final stand in the *puri* of the young Raja, who seems to have roused himself from his habitual torpor to lead them in the final act of defiance, which was the performance of the rite of the *puputan*. The Dutch finally broke into the *puri* over mounds of bodies which piled up without and within as the defenders performed the *puputan*. Among the corpses they discovered and with some difficulty identified that of the young Raja, so hideously mutilated that they later declined to show it to his grieving father. In Cakranegara, after a day of hard fighting, the Dutch next morning captured a deserted *puri*. The old Raja and his court had fled during the night to the nearby town of Sasari.

On November 20 the Dutch marched upon Sasari and demanded immediate surrender. The old Raja delayed for two hours, then, dressed all in yellow, seated in a palanquin carried by four slaves, accompanied by escorts who carried two golden parasols—all that remained of royal splendor—he caused himself and a grandson to be carried to the Dutch lines. The Dutch refused him his last request, that he be carried by his own bearers to whatever destination they chose. They assigned him convict bearers, who carried him to Ampenan, where he was held until he could be sent to Batavia. But the rest of the court refused to yield. There was therefore enacted yet once again the appalling rite of the *puputan* as men, women and children emerged as in a trance from the village and if they did not die by the *kris,* they rushed headlong into the fire of the troops. By Dutch count there perished that day at Sasari ten of the highest-ranking noblemen of the kingdom and 50 of their wives and children. Even this was not the finale. More and more people reported themselves to surrender, but others, including the next heir apparent, Anak Agung Nengah Karang, fled to a village still further distance, where, on November 26, occurred the last attack and *puputan*.

Before they razed the *puri* in Mataram and Cakranegara the Dutch afforded both the native and the European troops opportunity to ransack and loot while officers sequestered the treasure which they found in the royal storerooms. In Mataram they found 1,000 pounds of gold and 6,996 pounds of silver, and that was only a part of the booty. In Cakranegara they discovered to their amazement a room fifty feet square in which silver coins were heaped six feet high. Other valuables such as *kris* and ceremonial vessels of sold and silver were piled upon the money. Together with fl. 450,000 of indemnity which the Dutch sent out from Cakranegara before the surprise attack or else carried with them in their retreat, the proceeds of the Lombok War much more than offset the total expenditures, which, according to announcement in Parliament, came to exactly fl. 2,658,917.

Fate of the Raja, Lombok and Gusti Gede Jelantik

The Dutch thus swiftly and to their own satisfaction wound up the Lombok campaign. The deposed Raja was sent off to exile in Batavia, where his arrival and transit from the port of Tanjung Priok to the residence which the Dutch made available to him on Tanah Abang created a momentary public sensation. He died on May 20 of the following year, then all but forgotten and unattended, most of his own people having repudiated him for not having led the *puputan*.

As for Gusti Jelantik, who vanished from Lombok and reappeared in Bali well before the seizure of Mataram and Cakranegara, the Dutch debated just how to reward or punish what had been, according to variant versions, his singular services or deceptions. They decided at last to make him Regent of Karangasem. Although he experienced grave difficulties at first with his own subjects and aroused profound misgivings on the part of the Controleurs, he proved, in fact, to be a loyal and effective ruler. In Lombok itself the Dutch established direct rule through an Assistant Resident and three Controleurs, dividing the state into 24 districts, 12 of them presided over by Balinese and 12 by Sasak chieftains. Lombok began almost immediately to prosper again and so too did Karangasem. Nevertheless, the events in Lombok in 1894 left deep scars upon the Balinese soul and the Dutch conscience.

CHAPTER 11

TURN OF CENTURY TOUR (1902)

Kol's Grand Tour and His Published Account

K ol's Grand Tour and His Published Account
The first tourist in Bali was a member of the Dutch parliament, Heer H. van Kol. He was a tourist, that is, in the sense that he visited the island on his own volition and at his own expense, not by reason of official assignment, and he traveled extensively while there as much for his own pleasure as for any other profit. He was atypical of the genre in that he briefed himself tirelessly before, during and after his trip and visited also Sumatra, Java and the eastern islands. He had the built-in advantage, furthermore, of previous acquaintance with the area, having served in the 1880s as a civil engineer in the colonial government. It did no damage that he entertained a certain ulterior motive for what proved to be his extremely arduous but also informative and enjoyable travels. As a member of the Second Chamber of the Dutch Estates General, he sought to inform himself, his colleagues and his constituents about conditions in the Dutch East Indies and to influence colonial policy with regard to which he was disposed to be critical, especially in Java, but not, in 1902, in Bali. He also sought to bring back as a trophy, as he did, a travel book which would both inform and sell.

Notwithstanding such political and utilitarian objectives, Heer van Kol was first of all a discriminating traveler, as is evident from his serendipitist outlook upon all strange adventures and misadventures. He was secondarily a journalist, forgoing no opportunity to investigate recent events, to interview important personages and to explore unknown regions. He made himself something of a scholar, reading Dutch official and unofficial reports, of which certain extensive collections could be discovered by the diligent searcher in some of the dustier archives. Undeniably, however, he was also a junketing parliamentary fact-finder, never hesitating to use official credentials and personal pressure to overcome Dutch bureaucratic obstruction and Balinese royal indifference. He traveled, all the same, in the already anachronistic manner of the underprivileged nineteenth-century politician. He made do without any staff assistants, although he did generally move about with a Controleur pressed into service as companion and guide, and with an explorer's retinue of servants and porters. He conducted his own inquiries, wrote up his own observations and experiences and relied much more upon his own than upon any sifted, strained and systematized official intelligence.

Heer van Kol's *Uit Onze Kolonien* (Out of Our Colonies), published in Leiden in 1902, is a massive 826-page travel account which includes 123 pages of closely packed information about Bali. It deserves to have been published in some other language than Dutch in order to have commanded a larger audience in its day than the very restricted Dutch reading public, and greater celebrity today than small-type listing in the catalogs of rare book dealers. The early twentieth-century panoramic view of the island of Bali which Heer van Kol so admirably presents would seem to be of some intrinsic interest to the more perceptive modern visitor or would-be visitor, affording as it does, a multi-dimensional perspective. What follows, therefore, is a selective summation of Kol's report, with emphasis upon what is supplementary rather than duplicative of materials from other sources in the foregoing or the following pages, with resort, as seems appropriate, to direct quotes and bracketed editorial interpolation.

Reception in Karangasem; Impressions of Raja Jelantik

On the morning of July 4, 1902, traveling on the government steamer *de Zwaluw*, Kol arrived in Labuan Bay on the southwest coast of Bali. He was met on shipboard by Heer Schwarz, the Dutch Controleur for Gianyar, who was assigned to him as escort and was by all odds the most knowledgeable European with regard to the southern part of the island. Kol made the trip to shore, not in the ship's boat as he had expected but in a little Balinese outrigger. It was an exhilarating transition from Dutch to Balinese ambiance, made on board a fragile and lovely craft skimming the high waves and the barely covered coral reefs into an enchanting bay. From the moment he set eyes on the sea coast and skyline of southern Bali and encountered the handsome and animated Balinese in their own milieu, Kol, like many a Dutchman and other Westerners before and since, fell, or rather prostrated himself under the spell of what was already becoming known as *l'île sans pareil*.

Controleur Schwarz, it immediately developed, was accustomed to asserting his dignity by riding a high-spirited horse decked out with saddle and bridle brightly ornamented with silver, preceded and followed by a procession of splendidly uniformed lance and banner bearers. The Controleur graciously provided Kol with a similar mount and together they went cantering off toward the royal capital of Karangasem, their dress parade attracting an excited crowd of children and being eyed with deferential admiration by all wayfarers. Thus they passed through bustling market towns, lush rice fields and densely grown coconut groves, crossed precipitous ravines through which flowed rushing streams, with the blue-green sea sometimes within view and the majestic Mt Agung rising above them. It was a romantic ride on a bright sunny day in a superbly scenic South Seas island. If Kol was not irrevocably spellbound when he set out, all resistance wilted when he arrived in Karangasem. There the Raja himself, Gusti Gede Jelantik, regally dressed, met them ceremoniously at the *puri* gateway and made them welcome.

Raja Jelantik escorted his two visitors through grotesquely ornamented monumental gateways and then through courtyard after courtyard until he showed them into the most elaborate section of all—his own private quarters which he had vacated in order to make them available to his honored guests. The Raja then discreetly withdrew, and Kol explored his accommodations with growing amazement. It was a large walled pavilion opening off a deep gallery, all very serene save for the rather startling interior decor. The doors were intricately carved and brightly painted and gilded in the Balinese manner, as were the windows and beams, but the furnishings were exclusively European. In the center of the room stood a huge brass bedstead overhung by a richly worked canopy, provided with silken counterpane, cushions and pillows. There were marble-top tables, carved and gilded chairs and mirrors and hanging lamps with crystal pendants— all in purest rococo, including an especially fanciful music box. But there were also some dismaying omissions. On the toilet table there was no water basin but rather an ornate soup tureen. In the pitcher there was only a little water, which, upon being shaken up, became muddy. And there was no visible evidence whatever of any toilet facilities except for the garden. Close to his quarters Kol found a pond filled with fish (carp and gurame) which would come at the sound of a gong. [The fish pond probably was the toilet, such installations serving such purpose in rural Bali and other parts today.]

The entire furnishings, Kol discovered, had been the gift of the Dutch Queen in return for the Raja's own presentation of fl. 20,000 on the recent occasion of her birthday.

The Controleur and Kol were no sooner well settled than servants began arriving in relays. They fetched in great silver dishes loaded with fruits and other foodstuffs and great quantities of flowers, the gifts from the Raja and various of the princes, always duplicate gifts, one for Kol, another for the Controleur. Soon the Raja himself appeared again, accompanied by a large retinue of officials and servants, and the formal part of the visit, which was to include much speech-making, feasting and dramatic performances, began to get under way. Thus, in Puri Karangasem, Kol was initiated into the traditional life of a Balinese court, which was also, in many significant respects, the life of the people. He began to accumulate the detailed information which he later included in his travel account with regard to religion, art, agriculture and many other aspects of Balinese life, not neglecting matters of such lasting concern to the Dutch and to others as slavery and suttee, cremation, taxation and public administration.

Kol engaged in several long conversations with the Raja, one of the most important and controversial of the leading Balinese personages. The Raja often adroitly converted these conversations into occasions for extracting highly miscellaneous information from his guest with regard, for instance, to the Dutch royal family, the cities of The Hague and Amsterdam, the uses of railways and telephones. The Raja also wanted to hear Kol's report on conditions in Lombok, but he was reluctant to speak of his own role in the events of the early 1890s.

After the Dutch conquest of Lombok, they had appointed Gusti Jelantik Regent of Karangasem, the decision being immediately challenged both by Dutchmen and by Balinese, many of whom, albeit for quite different reasons, regarded him as a traitor. Certain of his own *punggawa* aroused the people to surround the *puri* and shout threats upon his life. He was saved by the guile of one of his followers, who challenged the crowds, if they were so bold, to storm the palace at once and get on with their wicked business, thus shaming them into disbanding. The Raja then retired to a sacred spot in the mountains, there to spend his time in prayer and meditation until he was visited by a delegation of *punggawa* inviting him to resume the throne. Since that time he had enjoyed the confidence of his own people and of the Dutch officials and had proven himself a shrewd ruler.

One evidence of the Raja's shrewdness—and of Dutch official blundering—was his way of handling his own investiture as Regent. Instead of making a great ceremony of it, as did the Raja of Gianyar later on, he received the Controleur in private audience, accepted the letter of confirmation of authority, then sped the Dutchman on his way again before his people knew what had happened. It was a change of

status of which even yet very few of his subjects were more than faintly aware. Thus Gusti Gede Jelantik maintained his own authority and
made it more difficult for the Dutch to assert theirs.

Kol admitted that it was not easy to appraise the true character and
capability of the Raja, but, after weighing all of the arguments he came
to the conclusion that his conduct in Lombok had been "correct"
and that his rule in Karangasem was just. His conduct had been "correct" in that he had answered the call to come to the defence of his
overlord. It had been no act of disloyalty to depart when the Raja of
Lombok, under the evil influence of his Regent and advisors, broke his
own pledged word to the Dutch. "More of him men could not ask,"
wrote Kol. "It was too much to require him and his army to range
themselves on our side—he, who had no reason to trust us, quite
the contrary, witness the lesson of history." His rule was both firm and
beneficial, and his state was obviously prospering in spite of certain
very serious shortcomings.

The rajadom of Karangasem, said Kol, was critically overpopulat-
ed. It could no longer grow sufficient rice to feed its people, and there
was no possibility of developing new land or water resources. Great
quantities of rice had to be imported from neighboring states. Other
crops, such as coffee, which would grow in the high mountains, had
recently been introduced and would help to pay for the rice, but
coffee would not suffice as a new economic base. The rajadom also
produced and exported superior fruits, especially oranges, and significant numbers of fine fat pigs, sleek beautiful cattle and sturdy little
ponies. Forging and pottery-making offered promise, as did spinning
and weaving of cotton thread. But real economic opportunity lay elsewhere, perhaps in distant, underpopulated Jembrana. The people of
Karangasem would like to migrate to Jembrana, and some did in fact
migrate to Buleleng, but the Dutch had as yet to establish any policy
of deliberate and effective support.

The Raja seemed to understand the problems of his state and to be
willing to accept advice. But when the Controleur suggested that he
send an intelligent young prince, his nephew and heir apparent, Gusti

Bagus Jelantik, to attend school in Buleleng, the Raja pleaded that he could not afford the expense. His private revenue, Kol calculated, was approximately fl. 30,000 per year, derived mainly from taxes upon rice lands, licence fees for cockfights and duties on imports.

At the time of Kol's visit, Raja Gusti Gede Jelantik was a man of well over sixty but still robust and active. He had once apparently been quite handsome and was certainly intelligent, but there was about him also an air of furtiveness which, Kol thought, scarcely befitted his reputation for forthrightness. Kol was especially disturbed by the sight of the Raja's constant companion, a malevolent-looking prince named Anak Agung Ketut Jelantik, who had inspired the early uprising against him and still quite clearly aspired to succeed to the throne or to usurp it. Perhaps it was merely elementary prudence which prompted the Raja to keep this prince always within his sight, and since the young man himself seemed rather extravagantly fond of women, cockfighting and the theater, the matter might resolve itself. The young Gusti Bagus promised much better and Kol hoped he would be chosen as heir, as in fact happened.

Kol's conversations with the Raja, which, as noted, often seemed more like the Raja's interrogations of Kol, were conducted under no little difficulty occasioned by the interruptions of others and the Raja's own rather inconsecutive physical and intellectual maneuvers. The Raja never sat still. He was on his chair and off again within moments, catching his visitor's hand in his own, then dropping it, drawing his visitor close to him, then moving away. He leaped quickly from subject to subject and answered only those questions which he chose to deal with. Although he evaded any mention of the Lombok war, his eyes lighted up and his voice grew vibrant when he talked of his exploits in the Karangasem invasion of Klungkung in 1891. His troops had besieged the *puri* of the Dewa Agung and had had to withdraw, he said, only because the Raja of Lombok recalled his auxiliaries and the Dutch threatened to intervene. The Raja grew even more animated when he spoke of cockfighting. He would roll his headdress up into a tight knot in his hands and talk excitedly of his champions and his wagers, but then his eyes would begin to wander and his voice to drift off and it seemed almost as though he were going into a trance. He was always the generous and thoughtful host, however, and he especially pleased his guests with his farewell speech: "We shall dedicate ourselves to ruling wisely; we must always stand by our white friends."

Rigors and Pleasures of Travel; Roads and Accommodations

For Heer van Kol, his subsequent visits to other parts of Bali, even those areas usually regarded as more scenic and cultured, could scarcely be expected to surpass or even to match the introductory exposure in Karangasem and, in fact, none did. He traveled indefatigably, however, visiting successively the rajadoms of Bangli, Gianyar, Klungkung, Badung, Tabanan and Buleleng, missing only Jembrana, which he had already visited briefly in 1877 while serving with the colonial government. He called not only upon the rajas but upon the more important *punggawa*. He attended feasts and entertainments, religious ceremonies and court celebrations. He collected information about agriculture, industry and administration, religion, manners and traditions, taking notes of memorabilia and trivia such as few other visitors to Bali at the time either discovered or mentioned. After the luxury of Karangasem, he found conditions of transportation, lodging and provisioning elsewhere in Bali a challenge both to ingenuity and endurance.

For travel in Bali, Kol noted, one needed first of all a *laissez passer* attainable only through the good offices of the Resident, who would have to approve any request in person and then advise the local rulers and get their concurrence. The process might consume many days if not many weeks or months and only rarely was it even attempted. He had set the wheels in motion by calling briefly in Buleleng on his way to visit Lombok. Upon arrival in Karangasem he was delighted to take delivery from Controleur Schwarz of the coveted passport. It was a great four-fold document on heavy paper impressively inscribed in Dutch and Balinese and even more impressively sealed.

One needed next to assemble and outfit an expedition, meaning riding horses and pack ponies; porters, interpreters and servants; furnishings, such as a bed, or at least a mat; and equipment for preparing, cooking and serving food and drinks, not to mention miscellaneous provisions, since local supplies were likely to be bacteria-laden. In the course of any given journey one must expect the porters to lose part of the baggage, the saddle of the riding horse to be a torture, the stirrups to be too small for Western feet and the leather straps on the pack horses to break. Roads, trails and pathways were certain to be either rocky and dusty or muddy and slippery; ascents and descents were frequent and treacherous; bridges were likely to give way and apparently shallow fords to prove bottomless. Lodgings were almost always stifling, filthy, vermin-ridden and stained with betel nut spittle. Disinfectant soap was a necessity and a tough skin the best protection against mosquitoes. Visits to rajas and other dignitaries had to be timed to correspond to the brief intervals between their sorties to patronize cockfights and their self-seclusion to smoke opium. "But I am ashamed of myself to speak of all this," he added, "when for all of these miseries my desire to repeat the journey is so very ardent."

Visit to Gianyar; Controleur Schwarz at Work

It was in the rajadom of Gianyar that Kol came closest to recapturing the first fine exhilaration of Karangasem. In Gianyar he called upon Raja Dewa Gede Raka, who had just recently (1900) been made Dutch Viceroy and whose state, thanks to his own efforts and those of the new Dutch Controleur, Heer Schwarz, was beginning to recover from decades of disorders. The Raja received him in state with his high priest beside him and his *punggawa* gathered around. He replied patiently to questioning and provided a great deal of information, but more about the turbulent recent history than about immediate circumstances. Yet Kol could observe for himself that the *sawah* were now being planted with fine rice, new homes were being built, work was in progress on roads and irrigation canals, and the state was quite certainly not the scene of terror and desolation it had so recently been. And he had Controleur Schwarz to brief him regarding all that he, Schwarz, had learned since his arrival and to pose for him as the model Controleur performing his multiple and startlingly variegated tasks.

For the enlightenment of those who had never observed a Controleur at work, Kol recorded a few of the more or less urgent items of business of a typical day. "It was 7 July in Gianyar," he wrote, "in the course of our stop at the *pasangrahan* [government rest house for officials and other visitors] and two very wearisome trips to and from Ubud." Controleur Schwarz had to cope with the following:

1. A question with regard to *sawah* boundaries disputed by Klungkung.
2. Protest from Klungkung with regard to the recent incident of Gianyar citizens casting the body of a deceased Klungkung citizen into a ravine instead of allowing it decent burial.
3. The complaint of a *punggawa* with regard to his runaway wife.
4. The protest of a Chinese market woman with regard to the confiscation of her possessions.
5. A dispute with regard to the extradition of criminals from Bangli.
6. The Raja's perplexity with regard to appropriate action to take against one *punggawa* who imposed illegal assessment upon coffee and another who withheld certain tax monies.
7. Preparation of proposals for improvement in the state financial administration in order to prevent Chinese merchants from evasion of taxes.
8. Prevention of certain rash actions which would have stirred up trouble with Klungkung.
9. Consideration of plans for improvement of water distribution in a certain rice-growing area.
10. Clarification to the Raja of a certain recent property settlement and explanation with regard to punishment of misdemeanors.
11. Consideration of methods to combat the use of false weights by Chinese coffee buyers.

Dutch cavalry at Sanur.

A religious service for Dutch troops inside a Balinese temple.

12. Consideration of the proper route for a new roadway.
13. Escort for a certain *punggawa* who feared being intercepted by agents of the Dewa Agung.
14. Rescue of a woman who had been guilty of breach of *adat* (customary law) and had fled to Buleleng, only to return and be threatened with punishment by death.

At the end of the day, he concluded his inventory, "A Gusti (warrior) came to complain that one of the *punggawa* was neglecting his sister, a report which brought a smile to our lips and provides good evidence of the boundless confidence which Schwarz inspires in the breasts of the people, great and small."

Kol acquired from Schwarz certain statistics with regard to the Gianyar population. Before the troubles started in the 1880s, the population was 150,000, inclusive of 900 Brahman, 8,000 Satria, and 1,500 Wesya. During the period when most able-bodied men had been recruited into military service and bands of enemy soldiers had wandered through the land doing damage when and as they could, there had been great loss of life, but by the year 1900 the population figure was up to 190,000. Controleur Schwarz could not provide much precise information about production and revenues, such facts remaining still to be accumulated. But he did mention that the normal tax on rice amounted to about 4 percent in kind, which the Raja shared with the *punggawa*.

With regard to Dutch policy in Gianyar, evidently well coached by the Controleur, Kol wrote:

We remain true here to the well-proven tactics of our colonial policy and to this we owe our greatness. We grant the raja self-rule and we permit the people to observe their ancient laws and customs. We remove abuses, and those which remain will yet disappear. The rule of the raja replaces that of the *punggawa*, who are concerned only with their private satisfactions. The position of the once powerful *punggawa* is now reduced, as it should be, to that of servant of the raja under our watchful supervision ... we have brought law and order.

Conflict with the Dewa Agung

Kol's great disappointment on his journey was his visit to Klungkung to meet the Dewa Agung. The Dewa Agung ignored him. The Dewa Agung, in fact, was deliberately making himself difficult and in so far as possible also inaccessible to the Dutch. It was his intention, said Kol, thus to assert his great power and prestige, which, in fact, had all but vanished. The position of the Dewa Agung and his claim to being Susuhunan (Emperor) of all of Bali, Kol added, was now sustained not by his own vain pretensions or the meager tribute and homage of his presumed vassals but only by the tolerance of the Dutch themselves. The Dutch had recognized him as Emperor in negotiating their mid-nineteenth century treaties, and in continuing to show special deference they provided what little substance there was to his claim to hegemony. The Dewa Agung himself seemed most ungrateful for Dutch support. He consistently delayed for a month or more in replying to any communication from the Resident and in his own messages to him assumed an air of arrogance. When a mere Controleur came to call, the Dewa Agung habitually feigned illness so sudden and severe as to be intentionally unconvincing. His realm, the smallest and poorest of the Balinese states, had a population of a mere 36,000 people, many of whom actually lived not in Klungkung proper but in widely scattered enclaves within adjacent states. The entire rajadom was obviously impoverished and retarded in comparison, especially, with the Dutch-dominated areas. Kol hoped that the example of prosperity and progress elsewhere would exercise a sobering influence upon the Dewa Agung, but he placed more confidence in the salutary effects of Dutch official firmness and tactfulness, which had not recently been much in evidence.

An audience with the Dewa Agung being out of the question, Kol contented himself with an "eye-witness account" of an audience which the Dewa Agung and the Crown Prince had recently deigned to grant the Resident and the Controleur. The Resident arrived on a warship, which cruised ominously offshore. He traveled to Klung-kung with a marine guard, which was obviously tough, and he spared no other stage effects which would make it very clear that he was not to be trifled with. The Dewa Agung Putera, aged about 50 but still notably vigorous and handsome, richly dressed and with much of his regalia on display, languidly received his visitors, leaving it to the Crown Prince, equally elegant and striking in appearance, to do most of the talking, as he did with great eloquence and at times at great length. During the intervals when the Dutchmen were speaking, the two princes chewed betel nut, smoked tobacco, toyed with their jewels and otherwise deported themselves as though the performance were exceedingly wearisome. The court interpreters and secretaries tediously clarified and transcribed in quite excessive detail just what it was the Resident had on his mind. What the Resident and the Controleur had on their minds and on their agenda was a long catalog of offences and affronts for which they were resolved to get immediate satisfaction.

The Resident made formal charges that the Dewa Agung had deliberately obstructed the work of surveyors sent to determine boundaries and engineers sent to repair waterways; he had violated the land and water rights of his neighbors; he had harbored criminals and debtors and other fugitives from Dutch-controlled states and had received stolen property which he refused to restore, etc, etc. If Klung-kung did not make amends within fourteen days, announced the Resident, the Dutch would blockade its sea coast and reduce the state to submission. There had been no blockade and the Dewa Agung had neither repented nor reformed. He still had the effrontery, in fact, to demand that the Dutch themselves return—or purchase—the *puri* slaves who sought shelter and freedom in other states, and to make other equally outrageous proposals, doing so, the Dutch were certain, only to annoy.

Imports and Exports; Receipts and Expenditures

Kol proceeded from Klungkung through the states of Badung, Tabanan and Buleleng, where he accumulated, among other information, the most recent figures on receipts and expenditures of the Residency. These statistics, which relate mainly to Buleleng and Jembrana, the only two states which had already been for any considerable period of time under full Dutch control, were as follows:

Receipts

Tax on *sawah*	fl. 149,600
Opium monopoly	102,200
Tax on dry fields	33,300
Trade tax	12,800
Posts	8,000
Tax on slaughter of beef	5,000
Sea passages	3,700
Tax on home grounds	3,500
Tax on houses	3,300
TOTAL	333,000

Expenditures

Administrative services	139,200
Public works	65,200
Justice	32,600
Finance	7,100
Marine service (ports)	7,000
Education	5,000
TOTAL	233,000

In making mention that the stated items do not add up to the stated totals, it seems appropriate to point out certain other facts upon which Kol did not comment: (1) The largest source of revenue in the north was the tax on rice lands, calculated at about 12 percent of the crop value, whereas in the newly controlled state of Gianyar the Raja's tax was only about 4 percent. (2) Opium, the second largest source of revenue, brought in over fl. 100,000. (3) The outlay on education was a minute fl. 5,000, but, in fact, the government had already opened at least one primary school in Buleleng and an expanded educational program was clearly in prospect.

Admonitions and Predictions

Kol's experiences and findings in all of the states except Klungkung seemed reasonably reassuring. He wound up his trip to Bali convinced of the general efficacy of Dutch rule and the benefits which the Balinese derived from it. It was a conclusion which contrasted quite sharply with his categorical declaration with regard to Java, where, he said, the Javanese were being repressed, exploited and impoverished. "In Bali," he wrote, "there is great and noble work to be done, and hail to the Dutch if we proceed with this beautiful task in a spirit of dedication and selflessness!"

The melancholy postscript to Kol's carefully conditioned prophecy should be his own. Kol returned to Bali in 1910 to resurvey the situation after what he regarded as a fair test period of Dutch rule over the island in its entirety. He was saddened to have to report that in this "Hellas under a tropical sun" his countrymen had created grave political, economic and social problems. He concluded, less confidently but more oracularly than before, "It is our sacred duty so to conduct ourselves that the results of our rule will be beneficial to the people, as will happen only if we are guided by humanitarian rather than selfish motives. Then, sooner perhaps than many people think, the time will come when our own task will be completed, our own pledges will be fulfilled and the Balinese will regain their freedom. May the Dutch in Bali work toward this end."

CHAPTER 12

ETHICAL INTERLUDE (1908-1930)

Re-examination and Reformulation of Colonial Policy

The punitive expeditions against Bali in the late 1840s passed almost unnoticed in the outside world except among the Dutch themselves, who were as greatly upset by their own reverses as they were gratified by their eventual victories. The Lombok Expedition and the *puputan* somewhat troubled the better informed and more compassionate sectors of the world public of the 1890s. Then came reports of the *puputan* of 1906 in Badung and that of 1908 in Klungkung. Certain private citizens, religious groups and even official agencies in Batavia and The Hague were deeply disturbed by the massacres and the looting, and shock waves spread to London, Paris and even, ever so faintly, to New York. Protests poured into the colonial office with regard to Dutch reprisals wildly disproportionate to any known Balinese offences. The Dutch, who were under pressure also with regard to their policies in Java, Sumatra and the eastern islands, resolved to make amends. In fact, since 1901 a so-called Ethical Policy was already supposed to underpin Dutch rule across the East Indies. From 1908 it informed their approach in Bali too.

Before, during and after their open conversion to colonial ethicalism, the Dutch in Bali showed themselves to be genuinely in earnest about redefining and discharging their colonial responsibilities. Some of them became amateurs of professional quality in the new field of Bali studies, and upon these pioneering ethnologists, philologists, archaeologists and others almost equally receptive, Bali worked its native magic. There grew up a whole new generation of Residency administrators who regarded themselves not only as the agents of modernization in education, health and administrative services but as the protectors of Bali's own traditional culture. It was a matter of at least equal significance that there grew up also a whole new generation of Balinese, among whom there were significant numbers of people who were disposed to make the transition from a medieval to a modern society. What did not emerge, then or later, was a new Balinese way of life compatible with a new century.

Traditional Ruler as Raja and Regent; Role of Controleur

The Governor-General in Batavia continued to treat Bali along with Lombok as a separate Residency administered under a Resident and his staff in Buleleng in the north with a southern sub-office in Denpasar. Each of the eight rajadoms had its Controleur, who personally embodied Dutch dignity and authority immediately alongside the throne. The Balinese ruler himself played the dual role of Raja and Regent, the rather subtle distinctions being at times lost upon both the incumbent and his subjects. The ruler, as Raja, retained most of the traditional responsibilities and perquisites insofar at least as those did not interfere with the proper functioning of the new Dutch Residency programs. As Raja, he was the venerated head of state, the ultimate authority in matters of *adat* (religion and custom), but an ornamental figurehead in matters relating to modern progress. He continued to perform the vital ceremonial functions upon which the welfare of the state traditionally depended, civil and religious ritual being as important to the Balinese as were protocol and administrative regulations to the Dutch. He lived in his ancestral palace, a complex of scores of more or less imposing and resplendent structures which constituted a walled royal village. Within the *puri* was always at least one *pura* (temple) for private and public ceremonies. There was an archive in

High officials at a formal reading of lontar palm manuscripts in the library at the palace of Buleleng, ca. 1920. Second from left is the Punggawa of Sekaseda. Third from left is the Patih of Buleleng.

The Patih of Buleleng and his family in the Buleleng palace, ca. 1920.

which were kept manuscript copies of literary and religious works engraved on strips of lontar palm, some of them splendidly illustrated and great works of art and literature. There was also a treasure room in which were stored the sacred and magical articles of the royal regalia: lances, kris, rings, betel boxes, parasols and banners, often lavishly ornamented with gold and jewels. The Raja was surrounded by a retinue of dependants and retainers, who might number a hundred or more within the *puri* walls.

The Raja's *puri* was the focus of a civil and religious hierarchy of *punggawa* (chiefs) and *pedanda* (priests), who extended the royal influence into every village and every village temple. *The punggawa* made certain that the agricultural pursuits of the villagers proceeded smoothly; the *pedanda* made certain that all the proper rituals were observed; the *punggawa* and *pedanda* together resolved any serious dispute, perhaps by convening a *kerta* (court) over which the Raja might preside. Besides being the focus of civil and religious authority, the *puri* was also the center of arts and crafts, of which the Raja was always the chief patron. The Raja's *gamelan* (gong orchestra) was generally the finest in the kingdom, the instruments often being part of the royal regalia. The court dancers were the most accomplished, and many of the pretty young dancing girls were destined to become royal concubines. Every *puri* had its craftsmen nearby—sculptors, painters, weavers, silversmiths and goldsmiths—whose products ornamented and enriched the court. The Raja and his family were the owners of large tracts of land from which they received rich revenue. Payment in cash or kind were occasions for visits of officials and farmers as well to the *puri*, so there was always a sense of public participation in *puri* affairs. The Raja was the personal patron of various temples, upon which, particularly at festival time, he lavished gifts which thus constituted return royal tribute not only to the gods but also to the people.

The protocol-conscious Dutch and the *adat*-alert Balinese found it necessary very early on to work out a precise code of conduct for guidance of the Resident and the Regent in their official encounters so that neither would inadvertently give grave offence to the other. In

The Raja of Karangasem, Gusti Bagus Jelantik, and daughter, dressed in rich hand-woven brocades, ca. 1918. In 1937 he took on the hereditary title of Anak Agung Ketut Karangasem.

A Dutch official being received by the Raja (Regent) of Karangasem. Strict protocol governed meetings between the Resident and Regent.

accordance with a formal Residency ruling in which each Raja concurred, the Resident would give two days' notice to the Regent whenever he intended to pay an official call, advising him of the nature of his business, making arrangements for a rendezvous with the Regent's representative at the state boundary, and spelling out his requirements with regard to accommodations. Upon arrival at the state capital, he would notify the Regent of the day and hour he wished to set for an audience. The Regent would send a high court official to conduct the

Resident from his lodgings, usually an official guest house, to the main gate of the *puri,* the Resident clothed in full dress uniform with sword and plumes and walking under the royal golden parasol. The Regent would meet him ceremoniously at the gate, conduct him to the audience *pendopo* (pavilion), seat him to his right—but never on a chair higher or more splendid than his own. At the end of the audience, the Regent would walk with the Resident to the steps of the pavilion, no further. It was necessary then for the Regent to call upon the Resident, who would send an aide to escort him, meet him at the door, seat him to his right and escort him to the door again at the time of his departure. Any breach of this protocol was presumed to be a deliberate affront so serious that one was seldom made.

Much the same procedure applied in the case of the visit of a Controleur, up until the time, that is, that the Controleur took up his residence in the royal capital, when informality began to set in.

The Raja, in short, continued to reign in magnificence. But as Regent he ruled by the consent of the Resident and the Controleur, the latter of whom prompted his important decisions and relieved him of much routine by exercising control also over the *punggawa.* The Controleur very soon introduced the engineer who built the public works, the doctor who opened a clinic, the teacher who established a school and eventually the military officer who recruited and trained a few soldiers. Perhaps as many as three or four Dutchmen settled into a given rajadom. But most of the Dutch officials lived in Buleleng or Denpasar in little Dutch enclaves, populated by about 50 and 25 official families, respectively. One of the most important of the officials was the fiscal officer, who raised more revenue than the Residency in fact spent, his main sources being the opium monopoly and land taxes. With these revenues, and with enormous resources of unpaid labor, the Residency achieved an almost miraculous proliferation of roads, bridges and dams, and also a few schools, clinics and other modern facilities. Visitors to Bali very soon began to report that the island was just about the prettiest little exhibit in the whole of the Indies of Dutch efficiency and enlightenment.

The Raja of Karangasem and his wife flanked by the Dutch Resident of Bali and Lombok and his wife, with various Dutch and Balinese colonial officials, the district heads of Karangasem (front left) and court priests (front right), ca. 1920s.

European and Chinese Business Interests

Not the least of the evidence of ethical Dutch behavior and Balinese benefit therefrom was the absence of any conspicuous colony of Western residents. From the very beginning the Residency opposed all efforts of Dutch big business firms to open up rubber or tea plantations or sugar or tobacco estates such as flourished in Java. Only a very few Dutch business interests therefore found it either expedient or profitable to open up offices in Bali. The few that appeared were to be found in Buleleng and Denpasar. The most conspicuous was the KPM (Koninklijke Paketvaart-Maatschappij), the giant steamship line which linked Bali to Java and the eastern islands and presently began to experiment with tourism. The firm Jacobsen van den Berg opened up an import–export agency, as did Reiss. Afscheep en Commissie Zaak, an affiliate of the NHM (Nederlandsche Handel-Maatschappij, the successor to the defunct VOC), which thus returned to Bali in about 1910, engaged in banking and shipping. Shell opened a Denpasar office. That was the Western business community, which might include at any given time up to ten representatives and their families. There were also a couple of German planters, who had acquired leaseholds in Buleleng or Jembrana, and a few Arab, Armenian, Javanese and Chinese who had similar holdings. These dated from the previous century or from short periods of years in the twentieth century when the Dutch experimented with limited relaxation of their rules against alienation of land. They found themselves flooded with applications, mainly by speculators who somehow induced Balinese to join them in visionary schemes for opening up plantations. Those which existed rarely flourished.

The really important foreign enterprises in Bali were those of the Chinese, who acquired much urban property and a few coffee gardens and coconut groves, holding them generally in the name of a Balinese wife, but were rigorously excluded from acquiring other agricultural land. The Chinese merchant-traders, whose shops were to be found in all the larger towns, collected and shipped local produce and distributed daily necessities and seemed always to make good profits, no matter what restrictive measures the rajas—or the Dutch—adopted against them. They also constituted themselves the money-lenders and thus gained even greater wealth and opprobrium. By readily advancing much more money than the client could possibly pay back at their usurious interest rates, the Chinese burdened many a Balinese of high or low degree with debts which eventually cost him his lands. But these lands normally passed to another Balinese rather than a Chinese owner. Iniquitous as the system was, it did not result in great tracts of Balinese land passing into the possession of non-Balinese.

Usury; Corvée; Taxes; Land; Production; Exports
Protection of the Balinese farmers against the exploitation of foreign merchants and planters and protection of the Balinese culture against sudden and disruptive impact of outside influences constituted the two great achievements of the Dutch colonial administration. There

A street in Denpasar in the 1920s lined with the shops of Chinese merchant-traders. These merchants collected and shipped local produce and sold daily necessities to the local population. Many also acted as money-lenders.

A view of Gianyar in the 1920s. A *pura* (temple) within the walled royal palace complex (*puri*) was the site of private and public ceremonies. From the 1920s high Dutch officials went about their business in motor cars, not on horseback.

were also grave failures both of commission and omission. It is difficult to grade these shortcomings in order of magnitude, but one of the
greatest was certainly the operation of the opium monopoly. Another
was the toleration of the evil system of Chinese usury. Another was the
neglect of education and yet another was the near passivity of the administration in the face of the very clearly analyzed problem of too
many people, too little land and too few job opportunities. Two
shortcomings which attracted remarkably little attention at the time
but loom large in retrospect were the heavy reliance upon obligatory
labor and the sharp increase in the effective rate of taxation. Both help
to explain how the Dutch accomplished so much in so short a time
with so little drain upon their own resources in improving the physical aspect of the island.

The Balinese were accustomed by long tradition to the performance of obligatory labor, which was endowed, indeed, with such
social and religious significance as to seem virtually voluntary. The
Dutch happily accepted and greatly expanded the scope of what
they identified as *heerendienst* (the labor due to a feudal overlord)
but never as corvée. The Balinese of the lowest caste (not of the three
higher castes), which meant 90 to 95 percent of the population, were
subject to call for work on ordinary community projects such as construction and maintenance of temples and palaces. When the Controleur moved in, he quickly discovered that the best and ofttimes the
only way to carry out new public works was to persuade the Raja and
the *punggawa* to call up the farmers.

The new roads, dams and ports, also the new offices and homes
for the Dutch and the new palaces and temples for which the rajas felt
an insatiable craving, required an enormous amount of labor. The
Dutch supplied certain imported materials, but the people were expected to contribute not only their time and energy but also the very
simple tools and materials upon which most of the work depended.
Whereas in former times the people had devoted perhaps 15 days per
year to the community and 15 days to the *pura* or *puri*, they were
called upon to donate at least another 30 days to the colonial govern-

ment. Many of the improvements, of course, were for their own good, but that was not exactly how they viewed it as a few weeks or even a few days of work on a new road could very seriously impair the prospects for their crops. Thirty to thirty-six days of labor per year for the state alone became the new standard, with provision that it should not interfere with harvests or festivals. Occasional little rebellions or threatened rebellions served to indicate that requirements became extremely onerous, but resentment was directed more against the *punggawa* than against the Raja or the Dutch. The *punggawa* often had other offences for which to answer and were suspended or removed from office when they became especially unpopular.

According to the traditional system, the Balinese were subject to various direct and indirect taxes which might add up to about 4 to 6 percent of an independent farmer's income. If he was a tenant farmer, however, the burden of taxation in addition to rent might become as much as 50 percent of his harvest. Few Balinese had been tenant farmers in the past but great numbers became so in the late nineteenth century, when population pressures first began to make themselves seriously felt.

The traditional system of taxation was for the Raja to appoint a Syahbandar, a Pekaseh (crop collector) and an Opiumpachter. The Syahbandar and the Opiumpachter, who were usually Chinese, paid the Raja an annual fee of several thousand guilders or more for the privileges of an office of which he retained most of the proceeds. The Pekaseh, who was almost always a Balinese, collected a portion of the crop for his own, the *punggawa's*, and the Raja's disposition. The Syahbandar, it was generally understood, would collect approximately 2 percent on all imports and exports. He might sometimes make quite extortionate levies and accumulate enormous profits, but he was vulnerable to undermining and overbidding by rivals for the position so that a system of checks and balances came to prevail. The Opiumpachter, whose calling was more dubious and therefore more hazardous, was subject to many pressures from the rulers, the smugglers and the Dutch, and was put out of business in 1908 by the opium monopoly.

The Pekaseh, the Raja's agent who became also the agent of the colonial administration, assessed various fees in various locations for land and water rights. In general, his collections on behalf of the rajas had come to about 4 percent of the crop, the assessment upon rice being by far his most important consideration. But the Pekaseh and his assistants also tapped other sources of income, including the crops from dry fields and from all village agricultural and commercial activity. They might collect a royalty of 1½ to 3½ guilder cents on each coconut tree or coffee bush, 10 guilders for each cockfight, and levy road tolls at the rate of 25 *kopeng* for a loaded pack pony, 8 *kopeng* for a porter carrying two baskets slung from a shoulder pole or 4 *kopeng* for a woman bearing a burden on her head. Under the rajas, in short, the assessment of taxes was well organized and the system was well understood. The tax burden was seldom crushing and seemed on the whole remarkably light.

As the Dutch established and extended their rule, they devoted themselves quite methodically to restructuring the tax system on a basis favorable to the colonial administration. One of their first moves was always to persuade or compel the ruler to relinquish control of customs (i.e. opium), which became a source of colonial rather than royal revenue, although in certain cases the Raja might be compensated by an annual pension. They then set about compiling a register of agricultural lands and a new system of assessment. The very compilation of the land register served, along with the sudden growth of population and consequent shortage of land, profoundly to alter Balinese concepts and practices with regard to land tenure. In early times the land was regarded as the property of the gods who made it available to the farmer for his use in accordance with his needs, his ability and his performance of all the prescribed ceremonies with regard to planting, cultivating and harvesting. Every man had the right to enough land to support himself and his family, and when his requirements for or his utilization of the land changed significantly there might be a reallocation. Certain lands, furthermore, were held in common as community pasture or as fields of which the proceeds would be used for community purposes. The rajas acquired rights to extensive tracts of land by reason of the tradition that all property of a man who died without male heirs was theirs to dispose of, as, in the case of lands, they did by renting to landless people.

In Dutch times population pressure and lack of new lands to be opened up, also the fact that the administration was compiling a very detailed register of who operated exactly what fields and therefore owed exactly how much in taxes, combined to convert rights of land use into rights of ownership and hence also of private transfer and sale. Good rice land (*sawah*) began to be valued at approximately fl. 1,200 per hectare, a price which long prevailed.

The value of *sawah* was directly related to the value of crops and the level of farm income, whether of the owner or the tenant farmer. One hectare of good *sawah* in Bali would produce approximately double the rice crop of a hectare of *sawah* in Java, so rich was the soil and so skilled were the farmers. The commonly accepted crop figure was 150 *ikat* (300 *kati*, or 400 pounds) of rice per harvest, with two harvests each year and a total annual yield of 300 *ikat* valued at fl. 300. On this amount, ten *ikat* per harvest were reserved for taxes, ten for the harvesters, two for other labor and one for seed, leaving the owner-farmer a quantity of rice worth approximately fl. 250. The tenant farmer, after payment of rent in kind, had approximately half that amount. Since the farmer had other sources of income, the normal income per farm family was something well over fl. 250 ($110, i.e. 50 percent higher than the 1976 figure). And the landowner, whose hectare of *sawah* would yield at least fl. 120 after deduction of the Raja's tax and the tenant farmer's share, calculated that it had a sales value of ten times that amount, or fl. 1,200. Such was the tidy arithmetic of Balinese agriculture, at least until the Dutch tax assessor began adding on extras, which presently drove the total tax up to about 12 percent.

The average farm holding in Bali at the turn of the century was about one hectare of good land, irrigated or dry, which would yield crops and income as indicated above, the produce from copra and coffee and other crops being about the equivalent of that from rice. There were many farmers who operated more than one hectare of land and thus earned more than the average income, but there were also an alarming number of tenant farmers. Rich as the rice harvest was, more and more of the population was coming to depend very largely upon other staples, especially sweet potatoes and cassava. But the island had an impressive quantity of rice available for export, to the value annually in the early part of the century of approximately fl. 500,000.

In the early twentieth, as in the nineteenth century, rice was always a major item in Bali's exports, but as the population increased, rice exports dropped. Copra and coffee, cattle and pigs came to surpass rice in importance as earners of export income, upon which the Residency itself realized approximately 3 percent of the value in various duties. Cattle and pigs were of especial importance to the ordinary household economy, almost every family having at least one cow and several pigs which were intended, sooner or later, for sale on the local market and perhaps for export. In the year 1910 the total export of pigs from southern Bali came to 33,400 and the total of cows to 9,500, the pigs fetching approximately fl. 20 each for the owners and the cows fl. 40–50 each.

Trade and commerce were to a serious degree inhibited by anomalous conditions with regard to currency. The money of the people and of the village market place was the *kopeng* or *pitji*, that is, the small brass "cash" originally minted in Canton and later forged in Singapore, which had been introduced into the island by early foreign traders. The Balinese, characteristically, had endowed the *kopeng* with aesthetic as well as monetary significance, distinguishing at least eight types of differing artistic and therefore economic value, reserving one variety exclusively for ornamentation of ceremonial offerings. Large transactions, however, required resort to silver coins, which might mean Singapore dollars, Indian rupees, Spanish or Portuguese pieces-of-eight, Dutch guilders or any other coin of precious metal, preferably attractive in mintage and convincing in pure metallic ring.

The Balinese placed no confidence whatsoever in paper money and consistently refused to accept it. They were not even fully convinced about silver coins, preferring the bulk and reassuring weight of the strings of brass *kopeng*, several pounds of which were required to exchange for the *rijksdaalder* (2½ guilders). And much to the annoyance of the Dutch, they preferred the silver coins of almost any other nation to those of the Netherlands. The Willem II *rijksdaalder*, which the Dutch themselves thought so handsomely embossed with the distinguished features of the King, were known to the irreverent Balinese as the "dollar of the King with the long neck"; the Willem III coin, the pride of the Dutch mint, was disdained as "the dollar of the King with the cowlick." These pieces would not exchange in Bali for their worth in silver, but the Chinese craftily bought up at cut rates all that somehow made their appearance and put counterfeits into circulation in order to ensure continuing lack of enthusiasm for any coin of Dutch provenance.

The *kopeng* were not only difficult to carry or to count, they also fluctuated wildly in value in relation to silver, the usual rate being between 600 and 800 to the Dutch guilder but sometimes touching 2,000. One *kopeng* was enough for a serving of rice, a drink of *arak* or a few pieces of fruit. A loop of *kopeng*, strung through their square holes on cord made of palm fiber, would more than suffice for ordinary marketing, but the more important traders found the Balinese fixation upon the *kopeng* to be extremely awkward. So too did the Dutch administrators, who were frequently embarrassed to discover that no strong box or even strong room ever seemed sufficiently capacious for the safekeeping of petty cash.

The cult of the *kopeng* gave rise to one further cause of confusion and also, frequently, of litigation. Among different states and even adjacent villages, there was no consensus on the exact number of coins which should be strung to constitute a standard loop, to make it easier, presumably, to give and receive payment without the laborious necessity of fingering every coin. In Gianyar the number was commonly 175 and in Karangasem 185 and there were various gradations in between. Certain traders, furthermore, made it their larcenous practice to extract one or more *kopeng* from a loop which was apparently intact. At times people carelessly entered into contracts for payment in a specified number of loops without stipulating exactly which loops and determining the so-called *long*, that is, the exchange rate between the loops of different villages. Disputes over *kopeng* led to such numerous court cases that at times the Raja's *kerta* seemed to be concerning itself with little else. Certain foreign observers were under the distinct impression that the Balinese themselves rather enjoyed all the confusion and litigation and that they regarded deliberate obfuscation with regard to the *long* not as a swindle but as a gamble.

Opium and the Monopoly; Education and Medicine

Neither financial vagaries nor moral scruples ever much inhibited trade in opium, which, almost from the beginning, was a major item in Balinese commerce. Visiting merchants fetched opium to exchange for local produce, and in Balinese markets the standard unit, a ball of raw opium worth fl. 25, circulated as the equivalent of legal tender. The drug commanded a ready retail market among both Chinese and Balinese users, and it was a favorite investment for smugglers, who carried it to Java, Borneo, Sulawesi and other islands in defiance of the Dutch *opiumregie* (opium monopoly).

Opium reached Bali from India, commonly by way of Singapore, packed into chests which could be purchased for fl. 1,550 wholesale to yield at least fl. 2,500 retail. Opium was a major source of revenue to the rajas, who always assessed import duty upon it and licensed the Opiumpachter (opium monopolist), generally a Chinese, who gladly paid a handsome annual fee for what amounted to a local dealership monopoly. Opium consumption by the Balinese themselves was originally confined mainly to the palaces, where court retainers and harem wives had money to spend and time on their hands. But in the late nineteenth century its use increased alarmingly among the common people, especially at festival time, when all manner of self-indulgence was encouraged and novelties were eagerly tested out.

The rajadom of Bangli, which required only two chests of opium in the year 1860, consumed 15 in 1870. In 1873 the reported import of opium in the northern seaport of Buleleng, where the Dutch exercised close control and compiled careful statistics, came to a total value of fl. 2,250,000. The Chinese Opiumpachter of Badung at the turn of the century was paying the Raja fl. 3,600 annually for his privilege and other rajas were realizing even more. But opium addiction was obviously becoming a curse upon the island. The Dutch, who felt that in Bali, as elsewhere in the Indies, outright prohibition of opium would be both unrealistic and profitless, decided to regulate it. While earnestly advising the rajas and the people against its use, they promulgated the *opiumregie* which had already afforded them great moral and financial comfort in Java.

The *opiumregie* went into effect throughout all of Bali on January 1, 1908. It immediately induced certain more or less predictable consequences. In Gelgel, in particular, there occurred a series of disorders and outrages which provoked a punitive expedition which, in turn, resulted in the Klungkung *puputan* of 1908 and the total submission of the last of the states to resist Dutch rule. Government regulations provided that no one under the age of eighteen would be permitted to make purchases and that all adult users must register with one of the hundred official outlets. But opium was packaged in a manner which lent itself to easy and widespread sale to the common people. The popular "two drop" dosage, for instance, retailed for six guilder-cents. Later, when opium prices were increased by 50 percent and more, the "two drop" dosage was largely replaced by the "one-half drop," which sold for a mere three cents, the equivalent, to be sure, of 5 to 10 percent of the daily wage of the manual laborer, who found it a solace. Adult users who failed to make their habitual purchases over any period of a few weeks' duration were subject to a fine for patronage, it was presumed, of an illegal market. Purchase of opium was made especially attractive, furthermore, by acceptance of payment in the popular coin of the people, the brass *kopeng*, at a more favorable rate of exchange against the guilder than that which prevailed in the public market. In the year 1910 the average outlay for purchase of opium throughout the whole of Bali worked out at about fl. 12 per household. This was almost exactly enough for one half-drop daily for every adult male.

In 1908, the first year of operation of the monopoly, when large stocks of pre-monopoly opium were still on hand, the *opiumregie* itself reported the import of stocks valued at fl. 273,000. In 1909 the value was fl. 894,000, of which about 90 percent would be net profit. Sale of opium accounted, in fact, for about 75 percent of the administrative budget and assured the Residency each year of a very gratifying surplus which was often larger than total expenditures.

While actively and profitably marketing opium through the state monopoly, the Dutch were conducting a campaign to combat its use, especially in the royal families where the habit had become a vice which interfered quite seriously with affairs of state. As early as 1870 the Resident himself had persuaded the Dewa Agung and the Dewa Manggis to renounce the use of the drug, at least for the moment. The Dewa Agung, upon pronouncing himself cured, had dispatched his silver opium pipe to the Governor-General as a gift of gratitude, receiving in return a fine Damascene sword. But the use of opium was always especially difficult to combat because many of the Balinese regarded it as a cure-all even more efficacious than the long popular Chinese medicines, of which it might also be an ingredient.

In the year 1910, when the Dutch realized well over fl. 1,000,000 from the sale of opium in Bali, they expended less than fl. 20,000 on schools, increasing their educational budget only very modestly and gradually thereafter. Heer van Kol, the visitor of 1902 and 1910, an outspoken critic of his country's colonial policies, was almost equally censorious with regard to the opium monopoly and educational neglect. He pointed out that the Balinese were avid for learning and that despite the lack of any formal school system in the past, many could read their own language and some were familiar with *kawi*, the archaic language of religion and literature. The ordinary Balinese, it seems, sometimes achieved literacy by understudying the highly trained temple priests and then proudly introduced his friends to his own new accomplishment. The Dutch themselves had begun building *inlandsche schoolen* (primary schools for indigenous children) as early as the 1890s, first in Buleleng (two schools), later one each in Badung, Gianyar, Bangli and Tabanan, the total enrolment being about 600. Kol complained, however, not only that the schools were far too small but also that they were modeled upon those of Java. Rather than teaching Balinese literature and the practice of agriculture, as would have been appropriate, they adhered to a sterile and unimaginative Dutch-prescribed curriculum derived from Dutch texts and taught mechanically by Javanese teachers, even the vacation period corresponding not to any Balinese festival but to the Muslim fasting month. Such schools seemed to Kol to be conducive only to the creation of "imitation Dutchmen" or "bastardized Javanese" who would be supercilious toward other Balinese but incapable of earning a living. Kol urged immediate rethinking as well as expansion of the program, which in fact occurred over the next several decades. Even then only a small minority of Balinese actually achieved even lower primary level education although a select few, the children of royal families, received special attention and were taught in Dutch so that they might, if they chose, continue their education in Java or Holland.

Heer van Kol was more complimentary to his countrymen in Bali when he reported upon the medical services which they provided. The Dutch, he said, had already made great progress in the control of smallpox, cholera, venereal diseases, leprosy and other more or less common maladies. The Residency had established four clinics, all predictably packed with patients, and the offices of the Controleurs were frequently visited by people seeking the simple remedies which they too dispensed. A certain Dr Kroll treated 150 patients each day in the Karangasem clinic and other foreign doctors were soon to be introduced to manage other clinics already built or contemplated. A Chinese "Java Doctor," that is, a trainee of the medical college in Batavia, was in private practice in Denpasar and others were expected. In the decades after Kol's visits, the medical services, like the schools, were to be much expanded and improved, and the Balinese population seemed to later visitors to be notably bright and healthy, as, indeed, it had been before.

Balance of Benefits and Burdens; Kerta Courts

Assuming that it was inevitable that Bali should pass through a colonial period and that it is fruitless to repine, it seems admissible to suggest that the benefits and burdens of Dutch rule almost counterbalanced. The Dutch did grave damage to Balinese political and economic self-sufficiency and also to Balinese pride and self-confidence. But the evils of the colonial era—opium, taxes, corvée and usury, to mention only some of the worst—were none of them new. Nor were any of them likely to have decreased rather than increased even had the Dutch not intervened. It served in part, at least, to offset these evils that the Dutch introduced clinics and schools, abolished slavery and suttee, built roads, bridges, dams and other important works, and quite definitively imposed law and order. The feuds of the rajas, which had resulted in much turbulence in pre-Dutch times, did not die out, but they no longer climaxed in widespread violence. And the raja's Kerta, the court of final appeal, undoubtedly meted out justice with less regard than ever before for caste, creed or cash.

The Kerta enjoyed, in fact, the reputation of being a reasonably impartial and objective court even before the Dutch Controleur joined or replaced the Raja as the presiding dignitary. The accused, upon being brought into court, had the privilege of calling in spokesmen and witnesses. The jury, which consisted of learned *pedanda*, listened in total silence but checked all proceedings against remembered and recorded precedent and in the end validated or invalidated the judge's verdict. The Controleur made sure that the sentence did not involve cruel punishment, such as blinding and maiming, and that fines were collected and prison terms served. The majesty of the Raja, the prestige of the Controleur, the dignity of the judge and jurors, the sanctity of the oaths to which all witnesses were called upon to subscribe, and the awfulness of the maledictions which were pronounced upon malefactors—all combined to make the Kerta a body in which something close to the truth generally came out and something close to justice would prevail. One especially memorable curse of the Kerta went as follows:

Wherever they may be, let them [the perjurers] be overtaken by all evils. If they go into the forests, let them be entangled by creepers, let them be lost, running hither and yon without finding the way out, let the tigers pursue them and drive them against the rocks where their skulls will be cracked and their brains dashed out. On the roadway between villages, let them fall to the earth or be crushed by a falling tree. In the fields, let the lightning strike them from a clear sky, let them be bitten by venomous serpents, let them be gored on the horns of the water buffalo. Let them fall into the river bed on rough rocks so that their breasts are pierced, their bones are broken, their veins are drained of blood and their corpses are lost in the depths of the water. If they put out from land, let them be attacked by crocodiles, let the sharks and the barracuda attack them, let the venomous lamprey bite them, let the marine monsters devour them. When they are in their homes, let them be afflicted with all maladies, let them die unnatural deaths, let no one attend them. Let it be even so whether they are standing or sitting, eating or drinking. Let not them nor their children nor their grandchildren nor their great-grandchildren be reincarnated as human beings on the face of the earth. Let them be reborn as maggots, snails, worms, serpents. Such is the malediction upon perjurers. Let the great Gods attest it, the Gods of the North, East, South, West and Center, and the Thirteen Divine Revelations. Let them and their children and their grandchildren and their great-grandchildren enjoy no good from this day hence.

NEW TRADITIONS Nyepi, the "Day of Silence", is one of Bali's most important religious celebrations, held each March and bringing the entire island to a complete standstill for 24 hours. On the evening before Nyepi begins, there are dramatic parades of huge papier mâché or Styrofoam monsters known as *ogoh-ogoh*, meant to represent the demons to be cleansed from the island.

Today most visitors assume that the ogoh-ogoh are an ancient Balinese tradition. But in truth they are a very recent innovation, first appearing in Denpasar in the 1980s. There is no better illustration of the vibrant dynamism of Balinese culture on the one hand, and of how quickly new inventions can come to be regarded as fixed "traditions" on the other.

Even during their short existence, the ogoh-ogoh have undergone reinvention. In the 1990s and early 2000s many of the individual monsters were modeled on figures from modern popular culture—from terrorist bombers to Hollywood villains. Today, however, these pop culture ogoh-ogoh have become markedly less common, thanks to calls from conservative religious authorities for people to restrict their monster-making to "traditional" subjects, namely demons from Hindu-Balinese mythology. (Photo © Tim Hannigan)

CLASH OF CIVILIZATIONS This colorful depiction of fighting between Dutch and Balinese soldiers during the decisive Lombok campaign of 1894 by the Dutch painter Jan Hoynck van Papendrecht offers a striking glimpse of late nineteenth-century European images of Bali and its people. The Balinese as they appear in van Papendrecht's painting are not the beautiful, artistic, peace-loving figures popularized in the expat and tourist literature of the 1930s; instead they are violent, terrifying, and perhaps scarcely human (and in obvious contrast, in the artist's eyes, to the heroic Dutchmen).

This hostile European image of the Balinese was very much the norm at the time, thanks in part to the violent clashes that typified Balinese-Dutch encounters in the late nineteenth century. Of course, the view from the other side was often similarly negative, and local architects sometimes saw fit to include gruesomely caricatured Europeans as demonic guardian statues in Balinese temples. (Lombok 1894 © J. Hoynck van Papendrech, Wikimedia Commons)

A RITUAL PASSION One thing which has remained constant in Bali over many centuries has been the significance of cockfighting in local culture. The pitting of haughty roosters against one another in brief but intense battles to the death is not simply a form of entertainment in Bali; it can also serve a ritual purpose. Cockfights are staged as a form of blood sacrifice during many Hindu-Balinese ceremonies. The sport also has a long-established economic significance.

In the precolonial era, when Bali was famous as a source of slaves, debt was often a certain route to slavery. Custom decreed that debtors could legitimately be seized and sold as slaves by local rulers, and the high-stakes betting that accompanied cockfights made personal debt an endemic problem. In fact, Balinese rajas sometimes organized huge cockfighting festivals just to ensure a ready supply of debtors.

The later Dutch colonial authorities—like the modern Indonesian government—looked askance at cockfighting, but stopped short of banning it outright. In fact, they subjected it to taxation, and made plenty of money out of the practice as a result. Today huge sums are still gambled on cockfights. (iStockphoto © Rares Kovesdi)

THE WATER PALACE When the Dutch achieved outright control of Bali, the island's rajas lost their true sovereign power. But as Dutch vassals they retained significant status, and in some cases significant riches with which they were at times able to forge manifestations of a new hybrid Balinese-European culture. One of the most striking examples of this is the "water palace" at Ujung in Karangasem.

Gusti Bagus Djilantik, the last raja of this once powerful kingdom, built three water palaces around his state capital during the early decades of the twentieth century. That at Ujung is the most extensive. Its complex of pools, walkways and pavilions displays a subtle blend of Dutch and Balinese architecture. The buildings were severely damaged during the 1963 eruption of Mount Agung, and were left in ruins until the late 1990s. Today they have been sensitively restored to their former glory. (Shutterstock © dmitry islentev)

THE QUEEN OF THE WITCHES History, religion and folklore can sometimes combine in Bali to create something completely new—and in the case of the legendary Rangda, completely terrifying.

Rangda is the foremost figure in Bali's legion of supernatural horrors, a ghastly demoness with a penchant for eating babies. But she has her origins in a real-life tenth-century queen named Mahendradatta, wife of King Udayana and mother of the mighty Airlangga. The patchy historical records suggest that Mahendradatta may have been a domineering and ambitious woman, and after her husband's death she seems to have become embroiled in some sort of succession dispute with her son. In folk memory this conflict became an epic struggle between good and evil, with Mahendradatta recast as Rangda—which simply means "widow"—and raining pestilence on Bali before finally being defeated by a powerful holy man, a story echoed in the celebrated Calonarang dance.

The figure of Rangda also has links to Indian theology. She bears an obvious physical resemblance to Kali, the fierce aspect of the goddess Durga. During her reign, Mahendradatta is reputed to have promoted the worship of Durga in Bali. (Photo © Tim Hannigan)

THE MOUNTAIN BALINESE In isolated spots beneath the misty ridges of Batur caldera lie a handful of villages apart from the Balinese mainstream. These are the realms of the Bali Aga.

The Bali Aga are often described as the "original Balinese" and presented as some kind of aboriginal race, last survivors of a proto-Balinese people from before the coming of Hindu masses from Java. In fact the word Aga comes from *arga*, or "mountain", and these "Mountain Balinese" are not a distinct ethnicity. Instead they represent the uppermost end of a long cultural cline stretching all the way from modern Hindu orthodoxy to their own earthy traditions. Like the Tenggerese people in neighboring Java, whose rugged upland territory was isolated from Islamic influence, the Bali Aga were subjected to far less Indianization than their lowland counterparts—a difference clearly demonstrated by the fact that they recognize no caste distinctions and do not cremate their dead.

The Bali Aga villages around Lake Batur are difficult to reach, and some have a reputation for being hostile to outsiders. But another Bali Aga community, Tenganan near Candidasa, which has a distinct culture of its own, is accessible and welcoming to visitors. (Dreamstime © nayla14 photography)

WATER OF LIFE The Balinese landscape is itself a masterpiece of human ingenuity. Over hundreds of years the natural flow of water from the island's mountain core has been redirected into a stupendously complex network of canals, ditches, and bamboo aqueducts, maximizing its irrigation potential, and ensuring that lowland fields have as much access to water as those further upstream.

Irrigation is traditionally organized by *subak* associations. There are over a thousand of these across Bali, and everyone who owns rice-growing land within the boundaries of an individual subak is bound by customary law to be a member of the association. Each subak is responsible for the management and maintenance of its own network of channels, and doubles up as a religious fraternity with its own temple dedicated to Dewi Sri, the rice goddess common to both Bali and Java, and thought to predate the coming of Indian religious ideas to Indonesia. Today subak organizations are under increasing pressure from non-agricultural water users in urban areas and the tourist industry. (Pixoto © Gede Suyoga)

THE MOTHER TEMPLE Of all Bali's thousands of temples, the single most important is the mighty Pura Besakih, the so-called "mother temple", 900 feet up on the southern slopes of Mount Agung. The central part of the complex here is the Pura Penataran Agung, with its forest of towering meru pagodas. This was once the state temple of the old Gelgel kingdom, which held sway over all Bali until the eighteenth century; today it is an important place of worship for all Hindu-Balinese people.

But Besakih's origins stretch back far beyond the rise of local rajas. The foundations of the Pura Penataran Agung are megalithic terraces of great antiquity, probably at least 2,000 years old and likely representing an indigenous place of worship long predating the arrival of Indian religious traditions. Elsewhere in Indonesia, particularly in the islands east of Bali, there are similar megalithic shrines, dedicated to the worship of ancestral spirits, on high mountainsides. In Bali such places have simply been absorbed into the complex and syncretic Balinese religion. (Shutterstock © WitthayaP)

CEREMONIES AND CELEBRATIONS Bali is home to a vast array of religious ceremonies and festivals—from island-wide annual celebrations, to events rooted in a single place, such as this *odalan*, or temple anniversary, on the outlying island of Nusa Penida. Every temple has its own odalan, celebrated on the date of the temple's consecration according to the 210-day Pawukon calendar, which runs alongside the 12-month Hindu Saka calendar and the official secular 365-day Gregorian calendar.

Far from fading away under the influence of tourism and modernity, according to many older residents most ceremonies are actually more extensively celebrated today than in decades past. Improved incomes provide cash for more lavish offerings, and a sense of cultural pride—arguably bolstered by decades of cultural tourism—encourages more ostentatious religious displays, while directives from the religious authorities have created new ideas about appropriate dress and practice during ceremonies.
(Photo © Tim Hannigan)

THE ISLAND OF BARE BREASTS The authorities of the Dutch East Indies were quick to identify the key selling points for Bali as an exotic tourist destination, as featured in this 1939 poster: smoking volcanoes; dramatic temples; and, of course, bare-breasted women. The significance of Bali's reputation as "the island of bare breasts" in its early development as a tourist destination can sometimes be exaggerated. But there's no doubt that pictures and descriptions of local women—who often went topless in public in those days—are certainly a regular feature of early tourist literature.

Various factors are "blamed" for the fact that local women covered up in subsequent decades: conservative Dutch colonialists; fear of rapacious Japanese occupiers; disapproving Indonesian officials; and the prurient gaze of camera-toting tourists. In fact there are many other parts of Indonesia where women went about in a similar state of dishabille in decades past, but where they now cover up in public. The change was a gradual and inevitable one, carried out under their own agency as Indonesia modernized, and as isolated communities became better connected with the rest of the country and the rest of the world. (1930s travel poster, copyright holder unknown)

THE HIGH ROCK Perched high above the driving Indian Ocean swells, Pura Luhur Uluwatu is probably the island's most spectacularly located temple. It is also one of the *Sad Kahyangan*, Bali's most important directional temples.

Local tradition dates the origins of the temple to the eleventh century, but like so many of Bali's major places of worship the headland may have already been a sacred place hundreds or even thousands of years before that. The current temple dates mainly from the sixteenth century. Uluwatu—

which means "high rock"—was long under the control of the Rajas of Badung, who jealously guarded access to the temple, which, with its location on the barren Bukit Peninsula, was far from major population centers. Today, however, it is open to all comers, and is one of Bali's most popular tourist attractions—though visitors have to watch out for the resident troupe of kleptomaniac monkeys. (Dreamstime © Aqnus Febriyant)

EXPAT VISIONS Many of the popular international images of Bali as a place of great physical beauty laced with a mysterious spirituality have their origins in the works and words of a small circle of bohemian Western expats in the 1930s. The godfather of this group—which included artists, writers, musicologists, anthropologists and sundry others—was undisputedly the aristocratic German painter Walter Spies.

Today Spies is mainly remembered for his role in developing the vision of Bali as an otherworldly paradise, and for helping to lay the foundations of Ubud as an expat and tourist hotspot. But he was also a seriously talented artist, recording Balinese scenes in a highly distinctive style. Many of his finest works, such as this, 1934's *A View from the Heights*, were inspired by the landscapes around the village of Iseh in the Sideman valley in eastern Bali, to which he retreated when he felt that Ubud was already too crowded with visitors. His work had a significant influence on the generations of local Balinese painters who came after him. (A View from The Heights © Walter Spies, Wikimedia Commons)

THE TALLEST TOWER Towering over the Sanur seafront, the Bali Beach Hotel (now the Inna Grand Bali Beach) is still the island's only true high-rise, well over half a century since President Sukarno launched its construction. Before the place was even properly open for business a bylaw had been decreed demanding that, in the quaint touristic retelling of the tale, no future building in Bali should stand higher than the tallest palm tree.

There's some disagreement over who exactly came up with the regulation. Some claim that it was Sukarno himself, who realized with horror what he had done to the beautiful Bali skyline as the stories of the hotel stacked up; others say that it was the last Sukarno-era governor, Sutedja, who made the call. But whatever the case, Bali's provincial zoning laws still contain a stipulation restricting building heights to a maximum of 15 meters. A challenge calling for the limit to be raised to 33 meters was seen off a few years back. The bylaw certainly helped encourage the "Bali Style" architecture that typifies many of the island's hotels. But in recent years, with low-rise resort areas sprawling far beyond their original limits, some have begun to question its wisdom. (Pixoto © Chomink Schoemi)

THE BOMB MEMORIAL The 2002 terrorist bombings in the heart of Kuta killed 202 people, most of them Australians and Indonesians. They also sent the Balinese tourist industry into a tailspin, and for months afterwards Kuta—usually the island's brashest and busiest resort—was eerily empty of visitors. During this slump there was a considerable amount of introspection about what some regarded as the crass commercialism that had come to typify tourism in southern Bali, but before long visitor numbers were rising once again, and the tourism-related construction boom was back on track.

Today the space where the Sari Club, destroyed in the bombing, once stood is an incongruous gap at the very heart of a Kuta, with plans for a memorial park—or proper commercial redevelopment—stymied by uncertainty over ownership of the plot. Across the street, close to the site of Paddy's Pub, also destroyed in the bombing, is a memorial to those killed in the attacks. (iStockphoto © gionnixxx)

CHAPTER 13

EUPHORIA AND TRAUMA
(1930-1955)

Recurrent Problems of Christian Missions and Converts
The aspect of their Bali policy in which the Dutch take greatest
pride and for which the Balinese give them greatest credit was their
protectionist and conservationist stance with regard to the island's culture. In certain quarters at the time this policy aroused severe criti-
cism, among Dutch Christian missionary bodies, for instance, which
eyed Balinese Hinduism as an especially abandoned brand of hedonistic paganism. Certain Balinese leaders themselves felt at times that
more rather than less Dutch intervention would be desirable, especially in helping to rebuild shrines and temples which earthquakes
and volcanic eruptions, not to mention customary Balinese standards of maintenance, caused to fall into ruins. Certain Chinese and
Western business interests, furthermore, felt that the Resident and
the Controleurs were unduly vigilant in excluding them from potential profits.

The question of Christian missions recurred again and again after
the doleful 1881 incident of the murder of Rev. de Vroom by his disciple Nicodemus. Powerful church groups, both Protestant and Catholic in Java and the Netherlands, put pressure upon the colonial
government to relax its ruling against missionary activities, claiming

at times that it was not the Balinese themselves but the Resident and the Controleurs who were hostile to Christianity. In 1891 the Jesuits received permission to establish a post in Bali, this order being thought to be more sympathetic to Balinese ritualism than other Christian bodies, but the Jesuits lacked the personnel at the time and the permit lapsed. In 1920 the Apostolic Prefect of the Lesser Sundas, who was in charge of a very active program in Flores, negotiated with the Resident to convert one of the two new government secondary schools into a private church school, but again lack of personnel caused the project to be dropped. In 1924 the Apostolic Vicar for Java revived the plan, then modified it to propose the establishment of a new church school in Klungkung, a proposal which caused such grave offence to several of the rajas and other prominent Balinese that it had to be withdrawn. The Balinese decried the possibility that Klungkung, the center of traditional Balinese culture, should become the base of mission penetration and challenged the concept which the church then entertained of building both clinics and schools in various parts of the island. The rajas were stirred, in fact, to raise money for a school of their own in Klungkung and the government made amends for the distress they had suffered by granting the school a subsidy.

Missionary enterprise took a new departure in 1930 with the appearance in Bali of representatives of an American fundamentalist sect, the Christian and Missionary Alliance, which had long been active in Sulawesi and more recently in Lombok. Rev. Jaffray, the head of the mission, visited Bali and assigned one of his catechists, an Indonesian Chinese named Chang, to live there to work with the minute Chinese Christian community. The Resident gave his reluctant approval, and Chang, taking advantage of contacts arranged for him by the Balinese wives of certain of the Chinese, promptly extended his work into certain Balinese villages in Mengwi and Jembrana. In 1932, after less than two years, he reported that he had made some 300 converts. This piece of ecclesiastical and evangelical intelligence electrified the missionary world of Java and the Netherlands. It profoundly shocked the Balinese rajas and the Dutch Controleurs, who immediately began to receive

The Kerta Gosa (Hall of Justice) in Klungkung, the place for the administration of traditional justice in pre-colonial times, as it was ca. 1920.

The original ceiling paintings in the Kerta Gosa, which tell of the punishments awaiting evil-doers in Hell, and of the delights of the gods in Heaven. The paintings were restored and modified in 1960.

or to accumulate complaints from converts and non-converts alike. It was alleged that Chang had promised his prospective converts that Christianity would bring relief from taxes, corvée and all the community obligations to which the Balinese Hindus were subject; also cures for all illnesses and other afflictions. The wages of conversion proved instead to include the branding of all Christian apostates from Hinduism as community outcasts, already dead from the point of view of their villages and disqualified from any traditional village benefits, forbidden even from cremation. It was also said that Chang had inflated his statistics by counting as Christians all members of the household of any individual who could be persuaded to repeat after him the sentence, "I believe in Jesus Christ."

The Resident expelled Chang, whose presence had posed a threat to the "peaceful calm" which all administrators were expected regularly to report. But he still had to deal with the conflicting pressures of other church groups which argued for admission of Dutch missionaries to undo or redouble the work of the Americans, and that of the rajas, who demanded that all missionary activity be banned in perpetuity. He adopted the compromise solution of announcing that one Catholic priest and one Protestant pastor might settle in Bali to minister to the European, the Chinese and now also the minute Balinese Christian communities, on the strict understanding that they were not to evangelize.

The Catholic priest J. Kersten, SVD, was the first to arrive, in September 1935. On Easter Sunday, 1936, he baptized his first two Balinese converts, young men from the town of Tuka, Mengwi, who had sought him out for spiritual guidance. They had already been converted by Rev. Jaffray and Chang. After the expulsion of the Christian and Missionary Alliance, they had declined to affiliate themselves with the East Java Church, which sought to create one new Protestant body in Bali by uniting the Mengwi converts with Javanese Christians living in Buleleng. By 1940 Father Kersten could report 250 converts, made not by himself, for he observed the prohibition upon evangelism, but by his two original disciples and the 20 other ex-followers of Chang whom they soon brought with them. The East Java Church could claim about the same number of Protestants.

Soon the Christian and Missionary Alliance cautiously resumed its work and made a few more converts. The new agent was Rev. Brill, who traveled periodically from Lombok to Bali and became a familiar figure in Denpasar and Mengwi, from the Dutch point of view half sinister, half ludicrous. Rev. Brill trudged about under the hot tropical sun clad always in a heavy black coat, which quite unmistakably distinguished him from the white-jacketed Dutch colonial officials and made it all the easier for them to trace his movements through the reports of the observant Balinese. Rev. Brill's deportment seems to have been discreet, as was that of the very few other foreign mission representatives who appeared in Bali in pre- or post-war days. Deliberate proselytizing had been both officially and privately discouraged, but the Christian population increased nevertheless to a total of about 100,000 people, preponderantly non-Balinese, although allegations are still heard about wooing the poor with promises of rice and jobs.

Cultural Conservationism and Continuity

The Dutch policy of cultural conservationism resulted in large part from the circumstance that in preparing themselves better to fulfill their functions, certain of the Dutch colonial officials became distinguished scholars and appreciative connoisseurs of many aspects of Balinese life. Diligent Dutch research refreshed the Balinese memory with regard to traditions and customs which might otherwise have begun to lapse. Whether Dutch policy and practice did or did not have anything much to do with it, Balinese culture seems to have experienced a quickening influence which made the early part of the twentieth century an era of quite distinguished achievement in art and architecture and in all the ceremonial manifestations of Balinese life, which the greatly increased wealth of the rajas could the more readily finance.

The Balinese culture is a self-contained, self-renewing system which, like the human body, regenerates its own vital tissues, but, unlike the human body, does not—or did not—as a whole perceptibly age. Balinese temples are built in the expectation that they will be rebuilt a generation later. The stone, like the timber, disintegrates in a tropical climate under conditions of very little if any maintenance other than sweeping of the grounds. The extravagantly ornamented tufa, which is worked when freshly cut and easy to carve, hardens into apparently impervious stone upon prolonged exposure to air, but after a decade or two it begins to scale and flake. The wooden superstructures and the thatch roofs are good for half a century to a century at most before they too have to be extensively repaired or replaced. Each new generation of craftsmen and artists, therefore, recreates the masterpieces of its predecessors with variations which may spell either decadence or refinement. The same is true to a lesser degree of the workers in metal and bone and ivory, whose media are more durable but whose traditions are constantly revitalized. It is even more true of the actors, the musicians and the dancers, who take great pride in innovation. No such sweeping generalization can be made about the writers and the thinkers, who were also the priests, but in an era when the temples flourished as never before, so too did the whole religious and intellectual establishment.

Reports began filtering out to Europe and America that Bali, not Fiji or Samoa or Hawaii, was the genuine, unspoiled tropical paradise, known as yet, even by reputation, only by the cognoscenti, a category with which all of the more affluent world travelers sought to identify themselves, as did a certain number of more or less learned scholars. The Dutch colonial establishment in Bali was flattered by the attention which the island was beginning to receive and by the generally favorable notices regarding Dutch altruism, but it entertained grave misgivings about the effect upon Bali and the Balinese.

The Residency had sheltered Bali from missionaries and merchants. It now sought to shelter it from world travelers. It undertook also to shelter the travelers from exposure to what might be the irresistible temptation to settle in and to stay, perhaps to corrupt, or to be corrupted by, the presumably innocent but hedonistic Balinese. It was not President Sukarno, as has frequently been stated, but pre-war Dutch officials who, whether out of consideration for Balinese dignity or Dutch prudery, first required the women of Denpasar to cover their breasts when they ventured out into the streets. In both pre- and post-war days the Dutch administrators several times rounded up and deported a few foreign nationals who were thought to be misleading the island's youth. But foreign anthropologists, archaeologists, ethnologists, artists, musicians, dancers and actors, eventually sociologists, economists and political scientists of more or less reputable professional credentials, not to mention numerous drifters and occasional diplomats, inevitably and eagerly sought out Bali on missions ofttimes indistinguishable from tourism. Pre-war numbers never became genuinely significant, and the Dutch themselves were spared any painful decision on control of tourism by reason of World War II and the Indonesian national revolution.

Tourism and Tourist Agents; Artists, Writers, Expatriates

Tourism came to Bali in the 1920s. By 1930 as many as 100 visitors a month were experiencing the delights of the island. These early pioneers reported so happily to others that by 1940 the total had climbed to about 250 per month. This figure does not include the passengers on the *Stella Polaris*, *Lurline*, *Franconia*, *Empress of Britain*, *Reliance* and a few other cruise ships which advertised and delivered a day or two in Bali as the high point of their winter schedules. Except on days when the cruise ships put in and some one hundred carloads of sightseers careened about the island, tourism never caused much stir. The cars were hired mainly from private Balinese or Chinese owners. The itinerary was virtually the same as it is today, except that it included luncheon—always a 20-course *rijstafel*—at the Bali Hotel in Denpasar, instead of Bali-burgers at the Bali Beach, and the cost per person was only about $3.50. For the other tourists, those who stayed a full two days, or long enough to be counted in the statistics, a visit to Bali meant a much more leisurely round of scenic and cultural attractions. Their travel agents provided motor cars (Essex or Hudson five-

A Balinese girl at a temple gate, photography by Thilly Weissenborn, ca. 1923, a typical image from "the island of bare breasts."

to seven-passenger touring cars or sedans, which rented for $10–15 daily); accommodations (ranging from an austere government rest house at $2.50 to the luxury Bali Hotel at $7.50 double, tout compris); and advice and assistance on all incidental problems (for instance, comfort facilities, then, as now, frequently meant "the rice paddies for the ladies," "the coconut trees for the gentlemen").

Bali tourism began, to be quite precise, when the Koninklijke Paketvaart-Maatschappij (KPM), the Dutch steamship line, decided to attract passengers to fill up the cabins of the ships which it sent to Buleleng to load copra, cattle, coffee and pigs. But KPM was almost scooped by the activities of an enterprising clique of friendly rivals. These included a Balinese "princess," Mah Patimah; a Persian-Armenian entrepreneur, M. J. Minas; an American adventurer, André Roosevelt (son of Cornelius by a French wife); and later an Anglo-American romantic, Miss Manx (eventually to become famous first as Surabaya Sue, a radio propagandist for the Indonesian revolution, and then as K'tut Tantri, author of a highly imaginative autobiography, *Revolt in Paradise*).

Mr Minas was a kinetic cinemast who introduced Western moving pictures to enraptured Balinese villagers by traveling with a portable projector and soon made himself the wealthy theater king of Buleleng (one house). He was also the first really to perceive the tourist potential. In about 1920 he started picking up passengers off the KPM ships who had been put ashore by rowboat at Buleleng with a little advice and repeated admonitions to avoid Mr Minas' attentions. Mr Roosevelt, who arrived in Bali in about 1924 with very little money but very good connections, threw in with Mr Minas and brought American Express and Thos. Cook patronage with him. KPM, in riposte, opened a tourist office of its own in Buleleng (1925), bought the government rest house in Denpasar and rebuilt it as the Bali Hotel (1928), which it soon expanded with deluxe wings and an annex, while also acquiring the Kintamani rest house as a mountain resort adjunct. After Mr Roosevelt's departure in the mid-1930s, KPM wooed and won American Express and Thos. Cook. KPM thereafter dominated the tourist scene, experiencing some discomfiture but no serious damage from the activities of Mah Patimah, Miss Manx and a few later comers.

Mah Patimah was romantically reported to have been a wife of the late Dewa Agung and to have escaped from his funeral pyre just as she was about to be forced to commit suttee, a story which she did not contradict. She was known to be from Karangasem, to be married to a Buleleng Armenian, and to have built up a profitable business in silver and an impressive fleet of taxis. She was given to having herself rowed out to sea to meet all ships, armed with flowers and a bottle. She tended at times to become a bit forgetful about business while dallying with the officers and the crew, so her personal fleet of half a dozen vehicles was generally available to KPM on hire. Miss Manx was somewhat more worrisome. She joined an American named Robert Koke in operating a small beach retreat at Kuta, then built a much more exotic resort of her own on a spot close by and made it her practice to visit the Bali Hotel bar to lure KPM clients with visions of her seaside Eden. But by pre-war standards tourism was booming and there were visitors enough for all. If there was any overflow from the hotels, there was always space in one of the dozen or so little government guest houses which had been built to accommodate traveling or newly assigned officials, of whom there were still only a very few.

Pre-war tourists came to Bali almost always by sea, with KPM ships putting in at Buleleng, or in the event of heavy seas, at more sheltered spots nearby, the cruise ships calling at Padang Bai in the south. Travel by motor car from Java became possible in the mid-1930s when a ferry service was started up between Banyuwangi and Gilimanuk by a pair of energetic German beachcombers, and a road was put through from Gilimanuk to Denpasar by a Controleur who surveyed it by occasional reference to a compass and built it by reliance upon hand labor. But the trip was strictly for the adventurous. The car ferry might take days to arrange and then, if currents, winds or waves proved unfavorable, the one-mile crossing might take not half an hour but half a day, and by night the Gilimanuk road was infested with tigers. Air travel also became possible in the 1930s, but it was never

Legong dancers in Denpasar, ca. 1920. Said to have been created by the King of Sukawati, I Dewa Agung Made Karna (1775–1825), who during meditation saw two celestial angels resplendent in glittering gold costumes, the Legong is an exquisite abstract dance performed by two young girls.

very highly recommended. The first survey flight (August 16, 1932) of the KLM affiliate, the Royal Netherlands Indies Airways (Koninklijke Nederlandsch-Indische Luchtvaart Maatschappij, or KNILM), crashed into Mt Batukaru (without serious casualties), and the first airport, built on the Bukit Peninsula, was much too risky for landing except in the calmest weather. With the completion in 1938 of a new airport at Tuban, the site of the present airport, Bali became an overnight stop on the weekly KNILM flights to Australia and to Makassar. This added only very modestly to the monthly number of visitors.

The tourists came to Bali for a few days of romantic escapism, while an assortment of artists and writers, aesthetes and expatriates came to stay. The most famous and almost the first of them was the German musician and painter Walter Spies, who moved to Bali in 1926 after having already spent a few years as bandmaster in the court of the Sultan of Yogyakarta. Walter Spies, who was interned in 1940 and perished when a Japanese submarine torpedoed the ship on which he was being transferred to Australia, built himself a simple house on the edge of a scenic ravine just outside the town of Ubud, Gianyar. He proceeded to produce two or three paintings a year of such radiant and revealing beauty that he established a new aesthetic which the Balinese have since made their own.

Walter Spies was joined in the early 1930s by the German novelist Vicki Baum, who wrote *Tale of Bali*, a story sufficiently romantic, tragic, exotic and authentic to rate as one of the classics of Balinese studies. The Mexican artist-ethnologist Miguel Covarrubias and his American wife Rose moved in nearby to produce the great study, *The Island of Bali*, which remains unrivaled in English as an exposition of the Balinese culture. There came also Colin McPhee and his wife Jane Belo, who wrote *A House in Bali* and *Trance in Bali*, respectively, and Margaret Mead and her husband Gregory Bateson, who carried out important anthropological inquiries. The painters, however, usually outnumbered the writers. These included the Dutch painter Rudolf Bonnet, who returned on short visits in the 1970s; the Swiss Theo Meier, who moved to Thailand but visited Bali frequently; and the Belgian Le Mayeur de Perpres, who died in 1958, leaving his home with its splendid murals to his Balinese dancer wife Ni Pollok, the property eventually to revert to the state. All of these early European painters and most of their successors accepted Balinese understudies who have created their own schools of painting which now flourish throughout the island. There were also dancers and photographers, among them Jack and Katharane Mershon. Almost all of these early cultural colonists established reputations for insight and empathy which later comers rarely matched.

Life in the 1930s; Japanese Occupation

Life in Bali in the 1930s was agreeable for affluent foreigners, who could and did live very comfortably on an income of about $150 per month, which was the average for the official and the expatriate. It was quite sufficient to allow for a home and a car, a staff of half a dozen household servants and a bountiful table. The large and numerous Balinese royal families were also wealthy and privileged, enjoying every Balinese amenity and imported luxuries as well. Their *puri* were equipped not only with comfortable living quarters but with splendid reception pavilions, and their treasuries were well stocked with gold and jewels. The ordinary people had on the whole plenty of rice and relatively few complaints. Many of their troubles they attributed to the Chinese money-lenders rather than to the Raja or the Dutch, a circumstance which may help to explain why the Chinese were officially tolerated. The rajas themselves, thanks to a much acclaimed and self-acclaimed Dutch administrative reform, the Zelf Bestuurs Regelen of 1938 (Rules of Self-government), recovered what seemed almost like autonomy by reason of separation and division of powers between the central and the regional government and the demotion of the Controleur to status of consultant. The very small element of the population which made up the emerging Balinese middle class—the employees, for instance, of the government offices—might earn no more than about fl. 25–50 per month ($10–20), but they were treated with respect and they could live quite well. They had to pay only a

The official government guest house at Klungkung, ca. 1930, one of a dozen such establishments built to accommodate traveling or newly assigned Dutch officials. They also accommodated the overspill of tourists from Bali's hotels.

Residence of the Dutch Controleur, Gianyar, ca. 1925. The gambrel roof (a hipped roof with gable-like ends), central porch, masonry columns and tiled roof show Dutch influence.

few guilders in rent for a decent house, and 25 guilder cents would easily buy a day's provisions for an entire family.

Among the foreign residents at least, the only really serious cause for concern in Bali of the 1930s was the prospect of war in the Pacific, a threat which suddenly became a reality in December 1941. Japanese troops then began their march down the Malay Peninsula to capture Singapore, the key to the whole of the region, including the danger-ously exposed and weakly defended Indonesian archipelago. When war broke out, most of the European population of Bali sought refuge in Java and onward passage to Australia. As the Japanese moved ever closer, the Dutch officers of the small Balinese-manned military gar-rison joined the civilian exodus, in fact deserting their posts and ex-posing themselves to post-war court martial. A small Japanese expeditionary force appeared off Bali on February 14, 1942, and sol-diers landed at Sanur on February 18. The demoralized garrison sur-rendered without offering any resistance. The Japanese occupation of Bali began several weeks prior to the occupation of Java and ended in 1945 without having caused any great bloodshed or destruction such as occurred elsewhere.

The victorious Japanese administered Bali in accordance with the system already established by the Dutch, reverting, in fact, to the situ-ation prior to the 1938 administrative reform. Japanese military gov-ernment officials occupied the offices vacated by the Dutch, and a Japanese District Officer (*bunken*) was attached to each of the royal courts with powers at least equal to those formerly exercised by the Dutch Controleur. The Raja of Gianyar proved to be intransigent and he was deposed and exiled to Lombok, his elder son replacing him on the throne. None of the other rajas invited the same treatment, and only Gianyar, where the new young Raja was not exactly subservient, suffered much deliberate Japanese retribution. To a very limited extent, not by any means as notably as in Java, the Japanese put the Balinese themselves into relatively responsible positions to replace the Dutch.

For the most part the Japanese did not very actively intervene in Balinese affairs because there was little reason to do so. The small modern segment of the island's society and economy continued to function mainly on momentum, gradually running down, and in the end grinding to a halt when the few public services of the larger towns all but disintegrated. The most serious effect of the occupation resulted from the requisition by the Japanese of rice and other food-stuffs and their failure to supply textiles, pharmaceuticals, manufac-tured goods and replacements or spare parts for such modern machinery as had already been introduced. By the time the war ended the Balinese were experiencing severe privations and were faced with the very immediate prospect of famine and epidemic. It was not until four months after the end of the war that the first representatives of the victorious allies appeared—a small party of British and American officers who arrived, it seems, by submarine in late December and spent only a couple of days on the island. They had come to accept the surrender of the Japanese and to look out for Dutch and other pris-oners of war who might have been interned on the island. But there were no internees and the Japanese had, in effect, already surrendered to the Balinese, willingly or unwillingly, turning over to them most of their weapons.

Return of the Dutch; Nationalist Revolution

The Dutch returned to Bali in early March 1946, first as a small party of civil administrators together with the Gajah Merah (Red Ele-phant) Regiment of ex-KNIL (colonial) soldiers, mainly Ambonese, under Dutch officers recently released from Japanese prison camps in Burma and Siam. In re-establishing their political and military au-thority in Bali the Dutch encountered relatively little resistance. A Bali-nese liberation movement had already started, had aligned itself with the newly proclaimed Indonesian Republic and had established a ru-dimentary administration of its own staffed by former understudies of the Dutch or the Japanese. It was backed by a fledgling army made up of men who had been trained by the Dutch or the Japanese military contingents, plus numerous inexperienced but fiery young volunteers, all of them eager for combat.

The movement dated from the summer of 1945 when the Japanese assembled in Batavia a representative group of Indonesians from all parts of the archipelago in order to prepare for the establishment of an independent state under Japanese sponsorship. Bali sent two representatives, who remained in the capital after the end of the war and the declaration of independence and became members of the national parliament. The new Indonesian government regarded Bali as a province of the Republic and named a prominent Balinese, I Gusti Ketut Pudja, as Governor. It was under his leadership that local self-government began to develop. A Balinese military officer, Colonel Ngurah Rai, meanwhile converted the Prayoda Corps, or island defence force, into the Balinese army, recruiting also various volunteers. When the Dutch returned many of the civilian officials were jailed, together with a small clique of intellectual elite who had joined them. But the Prayoda Corps under Colonel Ngurah Rai withdrew to the hills, from which the members emerged at times to create small incidents and to indoctrinate or intimidate certain influential citizens. Within a very short time, however, still in early March, they encountered a much stronger body of Dutch troops in the neighborhood of Tabanan. In what seemed in certain respects like a modern *puputan*, that is, self-immolation in a battle already clearly lost, the Colonel and most of his followers were killed, to be buried on the spot, which is now a heroes' cemetery marked by a shrine. All organized resistance to the Dutch collapsed with the elimination of the army. Small-scale disorders continued until the end of the year, sometimes directed against the Dutch, more often, however, Balinese fighting Balinese. No few of the islanders seemed willing to seize the opportunity in troubled times when arms were readily available to settle old scores relating more to personal, family and village feuds than to revolutionary politics. But Bali was virtually pacified well before the outbreak of the more serious and sustained fighting in Java.

The return of Dutch colonialism, destined as it was to be of brief duration, resulted in Bali both in restoration of old forms and experimentation with new ones. The island became again a Residency administered by a Dutch official and his staff, with new headquarters not in Buleleng, however, but in Denpasar, close to the airport. The staff was much larger than ever before and it included many professional personnel—doctors and teachers, engineers and agronomists, economists and political scientists and propagandists—all of them backstopped by a regiment of troops. A Dutch District Officer, no longer endowed with the power and prestige of the Controleurs of pre-1938 days, was assigned to each of the eight rajadoms. The rajas themselves ruled their little kingdoms again in their own right in accordance with the colonial reform regulations of 1938, but they cooperated closely and on the whole willingly with the Dutch Residency authorities.

Bali as Member of Federal System and New Republic

In 1946 the Dutch constituted Bali one of the 13 administrative districts of the Republic of East Indonesia (capital: Makassar) which they were sponsoring as a rival state to the revolutionary Republic headed by Sukarno and Hatta. They also created the Dewan Raja-Raja, or Council of Rajas, a consultative and advisory body with which the Dutch Residency officials regularly conferred and to whose judgment they frequently deferred. In 1948 Bali became an autonomous state within the Republic of East Indonesia and the Dewan Raja-Raja succeeded the Dutch Residency as the overall authority. The Dutch administrators, remaining thereafter as advisors to their Balinese successors, set themselves to complete the rehabilitation of the island. They sought to make Bali the showpiece state of the Republic of East Indonesia and thus the conclusive evidence of the possibility and the advantages of genuine Indonesian–Dutch cooperation.

It seems a fair objective judgment in which most Balinese would concur to state that the post-war Dutch administrators, starting in 1946 and redoubling their efforts in 1948, achieved a great deal more success in Bali than anywhere else in Indonesia. They shipped in adequate quantities of food, clothing, pharmaceuticals and other supplies, inclusive both of daily necessities and luxuries—more than enough to put Bali back in good operating order. Roads and irrigation systems were repaired and agricultural services were restored and extended. Particularly urgent attention was given to schools, clinics and hospitals, all of which were soon much more numerous and much larger than ever before. Bali even began again to export rice, a sure sign that conditions had dramatically improved, although the export was dictated more by Dutch propaganda considerations than by any genuine agricultural surplus.

The Dutch succeeded so well in Bali that some Balinese themselves were genuinely disposed to collaborate in the demonstration that fruitful Dutch–Indonesian cooperation was possible and that Dutch-sponsored states could peacefully coexist with the Indonesian Republic. Balinese leaders, and other leaders of the Republic of East Indonesia, proved willing to work with the Dutch up until the point where the Dutch attempted not just to compete with the revolutionary leaders but to wipe out the Republic by resorting to military action. They then helped to tilt the balance against the Dutch in favor of the Republic. Their influence was especially important before and during the Round Table Conference in The Hague (1949), which resulted in Dutch recognition of Indonesian independence. In the newly emerging Republic of the United States of Indonesia (*Republik Indonesia Serikat*, or RUSI), a union under the Dutch Crown of the Republic and the one-time Dutch-sponsored states, Bali was still the leading member of the Republic of East Indonesia. But RUSI was not fated to last, nor was the union with the Dutch. The unitary Republic of Indonesia, inclusive of all the one-time members of RUSI, was created in mid-1950. It renounced the Dutch union in 1956 and soon embarked upon the highly adventurous Sukarno guided course which led to civil war, international disrepute and economic and political catastrophe. In no part of Indonesia was the transition from colonialism to independence an easy one. In Bali it was even more difficult than elsewhere by reason of mutual suspicion on the part of Jakarta and Denpasar.

The reasons for suspicion and lack of cooperation were as numerous as they were dolorous. The Republican leaders in Jakarta resented the fact that the Balinese had not very actively participated in the violent phases of the revolutionary struggle but had collaborated with the Dutch and had greatly benefited thereby. They regarded the rajadoms as fossilized feudal states, artificially resuscitated by the Dutch, which perversely refused to relax their traditional hold upon their people's loyalty even when they were officially dissolved, as happened upon the creation of the unitary state. As the years went by and national troubles multiplied, the Javanese-dominated, Jakarta-centric Republican establishment fell into disrepute throughout the nation for its incompetence and corruption. This was especially true in Bali. President Sukarno, his cabinet ministers, his state guests and his chosen civilian and military cronies paid all too frequent and well-publicized visits, making such unseemly spectacles of themselves as to prove that they were morally and spiritually unfit to rule. The Balinese-Hindu concept of the just and therefore the legitimate ruler is that he is one who conforms to the laws of man, nature and the gods, as, within a decade of his achieving the presidency, Sukarno quite certainly did not.

CHAPTER 14

DECADE OF DISASTER (1955-1965)

Nationalists, Communists and the Later Sukarno Years

During the later Sukarno years (1955–65), Bali underwent profound political, economic, social and cultural change which seriously troubled many of its people. A clique of Sukarnoists, civilian and military, more of them Javanese than Balinese, dominated the island, competing vigorously with one another for power and wealth. They exercised administrative authority mainly to reward themselves and their friends and to punish their enemies, a category of people which came to include many of the island's leading citizens. Their offices were packed with badly trained and badly paid bureaucrats who demanded bribes before performing even the most routine services. After having been one of the best administered regions of the archipelago in the late colonial period, Bali became one of the worst neglected and most exploited provinces of the new Republic.

The one most significant political development of the period was a process of massive and sinister politicization. Prior to the mid-1950s the Balinese were not much interested in national politics and not much attracted to the national parties. Regarding themselves primarily as Balinese and only secondarily as Indonesians, they remained aloof from the great Nationalist Party (*Partai Nasionalis Indonesia*, or PNI), whose ultra-nationalistic leaders, in fact, regarded the Balinese as anachronistically non-revolutionary. As Hindus they were not much disposed to associate themselves with the major Muslim parties, either the traditionalist *Nahdatul Ulama*, or NU, or the modernist *Masyumi*. The Communist Party (*Partai Komunis Indonesia*, or PKI) seemed to them to promise only the desecration of all their cultural institutions. Their leaders tended to affiliate themselves, if at all, with the Socialists (*Partai Sosialis Indonesia*, or PSI), the small clique of intellectual élite headed by Sutan Syahrir. But in the 1950s the Balinese Socialists, like their counterparts in Java and Sumatra, were much too rational for their own comfort or even safety under an irrational regime increasingly dominated by the PNI and the PKI, the chosen instruments of the demagogic Sukarno.

In the 1950s, as economic conditions very seriously deteriorated, the PNI began to win many Balinese converts, and so too, soon afterwards, did the PKI. The PNI was able to offer the quick, easy profits of official appointment or favor, and there proved to be many Balinese who were happy, as new PNI loyalists, to acquire goods and properties at artificially cheap prices, and to exercise influence on behalf of their friends and to the dismay of their enemies. The PKI adopted subtler tactics. It patronized the arts and the artists, employing as its early vehicle of penetration the cultural foundation LEKRA (*Lekra Kebudayaan Rakyat*), upon whose members were bountifully bestowed the paints, canvases, musical instruments, dance costumes and other goods which were otherwise almost unobtainable. Both the PNI and the PKI thus undermined public and private probity, at the same time posing as benefactors of the people and advocating the very reforms which their own activities made the more vitally necessary. In Bali in the early 1960s, virtually no village was without its conspicuously identified PNI office and its PNI-sponsored activist movements of peasants, women and youth, all of which the PKI duplicated and not always by any means in a spirit of fraternal cooperation.

Politics in Culture and Land Reform

Thanks to LEKRA, the PKI succeeded remarkably well in injecting politics into culture and making political capital of cultural change. Balinese actors, renowned for their skill at improvization, began lauding the Sukarnoists and attacking their opponents, frequently doing so with such polished wit that they commanded an amused hearing even from those people who most deplored what was happening. Dancers performed propaganda-packed people's dances which might have been choreographed in Moscow or Beijing. Painters adapted the verbal slogans of the Sukarnoists as visual symbols. To those who knew and loved the genuine traditions of the island, these manifestations were quite frightening. What was most disturbing of all was that Bali, the island of religion and culture, was being drenched with the most poisonous of politics. The mystical Balinese were being converted into political zealots, mouthing the Sukarno slogans about death to all demons and monsters, suddenly no mere mythical creatures but actual living people.

What LEKRA was to the arts, land reform was to agriculture, a fraudulent promise of the fulfilment of the people's wishes. In Bali ever since the turn of the century, the pressure of a rapidly expanding population upon an inelastic supply of land had resulted in a great annual increase in the number of landless people who had to eke out a living by combining tenant farming with day labor. Perhaps as much as 15 percent of Bali's land had come into the possession of landlords, mainly the scions of the high caste families whose own numbers had increased so remarkably that holdings were generally small and income modest. These were precisely the people who were most likely to have acquired education and position in colonial days, to have been associated politically with the Socialists rather than the Sukarnoists, and to have eyed the PNI–PKI rise to power with gravest misgivings. They were easily targeted as feudalists, colonialists and counter-revolutionary conspirators whose properties should be distributed forthwith among the people. The landlords were therefore deprived of their land, sometimes receiving token payment years later in rupiahs which had lost at least 90 percent of their value. The lands were more or less parceled out among the people—the people, that is, who had proven themselves most loyal and active in the PNI–PKI cause. This redistribution of lands, rewarding some and victimizing others and ignoring both the agrarian and the social consequences, lighted delayed-action fuses which ignited demolition charges throughout the island in 1965 and 1966, when the fall of Sukarno and the eclipse of the PNI and the PKI signaled that the time had come for retribution.

Economic Manipulation; Rice Supply

The Balinese economy, meanwhile, suffered setbacks at least as serious as those which occurred in other Indonesian provinces. The central government had rejected the conventional and hence reactionary and non-revolutionary concepts that income should equal outgo, exports should balance imports and expenditures should be contingent upon calculation of resources and returns. Political favorites, civilian and military, plundered the island by taking advantage of ruinous economic controls. They were able to buy up produce or property at a small fraction of its value, sell it at enormous profit and repeat the cycle as frequently as opportunity presented itself. Labyrinthine economic regulations made it possible, as inflation escalated and foreign exchange operations became more and more fanciful, to buy an automobile for Rp. 10,000, sell it for Rp. 10,000,000, then use the rupiah profits to buy up coffee and copra at low official prices for export to foreign countries against payment in good hard currency. Or one could merely pocket official funds and abscond with official equipment for which accounting procedures were rudimentary and easily obscured. While the few became very, very rich, the many suffered hardships which began to remind them of the evil days of the Japanese occupation.

Rice, the one most essential commodity, was in short supply at inflated prices despite—or rather because of—government efforts at control, and the politicians rather than the farmers reaped the rewards of the flourishing black market. Clothes, medicines and all other necessities were so scarce that much of the island reverted to barter. The transportation system deteriorated so desperately and all conditions became so unsettled that even tourism almost came to a stop.

Sukarno's Visitations and Affronts

The frequent visits to Bali by President Sukarno and his entourage did nothing to dispel but served only to intensify the apprehension of many of the Balinese that the island had fallen under a curse. President Sukarno, whose mother was Balinese but whose father was Javanese, made Bali his favorite retreat and built himself a showy palace and guest house. He chose the site of an earlier Dutch official rest house on a superbly beautiful hilltop site above the especially sacred Tampaksiring Temple. It gave special offence to the Balinese that he built his private quarters to overlook the temple springs and baths. Sukarno frequently called upon the priests to stage ceremonies of welcome for himself and his guests when they landed at the airport or arrived at the palace. He called command performances anywhere and everywhere of the actors, musicians and dancers. For his own collections he appropriated the finest works of the painters, the sculptors, the woodcarvers and the other artists and craftsmen. In his palace he allegedly staged night-long parties which deteriorated into orgies.

Sukarno affronted the Balinese by converting their sacred ceremonies into government theatricals and by requiring tens of thousands of common people to line the roadways to wave, smile, sing and shout as he passed. He outraged them even more by allegedly dispatching his aides to collect the prettiest young girls to be delivered to the palace, there to be debauched by himself and his party. The President, his state guests, who included many of the world's notables, his one hundred ministers, his very numerous generals and his male and female camp followers, were not welcome in Bali except among those who profited enormously from their visits. This category did not include many of the common people. The ordinary Balinese can recall all too vividly the occasions on which an advance party of military personnel would shoot the pigs and the dogs which the Hindu Balinese love. They did so in order to avoid any possibility of giving offence to a fastidious Muslim visitor for whom any contact with a pig or a dog was a contamination and even the sight distasteful. Most Balinese preferred pigs and dogs to state visitors.

Premonitions of Evil; Plague of Rats

In Bali, to an ever more marked degree than in the other parts of Indonesia, there was premonition of disaster. Prevailing circumstances were so unusual as to seem ominously unnatural. The supernatural powers, it was feared, were being provoked to some truly dreadful visitation and retribution. Human beings would somehow be compelled by acts of nature or the gods to revert to the standards and the values of the past and to impose order upon the present. The first unmistakable signal that the divine powers were seriously displeased, and that their displeasure would be even more disastrously manifested unless there were indications of human repentance, came in 1962 when a plague of rats infested the fields and the granaries. Rats by the thousands and by the millions, huge, insatiable rats such as had rarely been seen before, feasted upon the ripening grain and then upon such grain as remained to be harvested. The destructive hordes seemed to multiply rather than to diminish as a result of the efforts to destroy them. The government proved totally incapable of rising to the emergency. It promised but could not provide rat poison, which was not a commodity in which the corrupt economic operators chose to deal. Eventually, the farmers and their families engaged in a war of extermination which terminated the affliction. They then piled up token mounds of corpses and gave them symbolical cremations in order to atone for taking even rodent lives, the rat being regarded, in fact, as the familiar of the rice goddess. But the conviction persisted that the gods were displeased. The conclusive and awful evidence came in 1963 with the first eruption in modern times of the sacred Mt Agung.

Eka Dasa Rudra Celebration and Eruption of Mt Agung

In late 1962 and early 1963 the people of Bali began to prepare for the celebration of the Eka Dasa Rudra, the most sacred of all Balinese temple festivals, which occurs only once in a hundred Balinese 210-day years. The Eka Dasa Rudra is held in what is regarded as the most ancient and hallowed of the island's shrines, the magnificent Besakih temple complex on the slope of Mt Agung. It still evokes the prehistoric animistic worship of the spirits of the great volcano which dominates the island and signals the attitude of the gods toward the people by its own serene or violent aspect.

In Bali in 1962 and 1963 there was abundant reason to fear that the original tutelary deities of the island were far from pleased with recent developments. There was great consternation on the part of the priests as they made their calculations to determine on exactly which days the festival should be held—or whether it should be held at all. The learned authorities differed widely in their readings of the omens, and casting and recasting of the horoscope led only to greater confusion in its interpretation. It was a matter of especially grave concern when the high priest, as was required by custom, made his ceremonial ascent to the very brink of the crater to draw lustral water from a sacred spring. He discovered that the spring had gone dry and that the fumes from the crater itself were alarmingly pervasive.

Bali's religious authorities went into prolonged and agitated consultation with each other regarding postponement or even cancellation of the ceremonies and how such an unprecedented decision could be justified on the basis of divine revelation. The signs, they feared, were not auspicious, and to schedule the island's most sacred festival under unpropitious circumstances would constitute a sacrilege. But everyone knew that the time was nearly at hand for the observance of the sacred centennial. The civil if not the religious authorities were determined that the celebration must be firmly scheduled. The prestige of the state was at stake, since even hesitation seemed to be an admission of lack of confidence in Sukarno's much acclaimed new era.

President Sukarno had already publicly announced his intention of attending and of participating. In one of its sporadic attempts to promote tourism the government had also invited travel agents from nearby countries to hold their annual conference in Jakarta and to attend the Eka Dasa Rudra as the climax of their visit. The priests were constrained to defer to official decree. The Eka Dasa Rudra was scheduled to begin on March 8 and to continue for about one month as a sort of command performance for President Sukarno and his state guests.

On February 18, just as the preparations at Besakih were getting well under way with the construction of a special archway honoring President Sukarno and other works of ornamentation at the temple site, Mt Agung suddenly began to emit smoke and ash, and occasional earth tremors could be clearly felt. In the course of the next several weeks volcanic activities continued and intensified. Again the religious authorities argued for reconsideration; again they were overruled. On March 8, therefore, although swirls of smoke and a dusting of volcanic ash were perceptible in the immediate Besakih area, the ceremonies began. But the priests were fearful of profanation of the sanctuary; the crowds were apprehensive rather than festive; Sukarno himself failed to show up. The Eka Dasa Rudra, which started as a disappointment, turned into a disaster.

On March 12, while the ceremonies still continued, Mt Agung began to throw out mud and rock. By March 17 great rivers of molten lava were pouring down the mountainside. Flames leaped higher and higher into the sky and smoke and volcanic ash blotted out the sun and darkened the countryside. The Besakih temple complex, situated on a sharp ridge and bracketed by deep valleys through which the lava flowed, escaped the main line of destruction. But it was covered deep in hot ash. The palm fiber thatch of the shrines was set ablaze, as were some of the wooden superstructures. The main sanctuaries themselves were miraculously spared, but the very first casualty was the ornamental gateway built to honor Sukarno. By then not only Bali but the whole of the nation was aware that Mt Agung had terminated the ceremonies which Sukarno had ordered. Javanese as well as Balinese interpreted this as a divine judgment upon the Sukarno regime. Not only the island of Bali but the eastern end of Java, including the city of Surabaya, was darkened at midday by dense clouds of smoke and ash such as no one could remember ever having experienced before.

The volcanic eruptions of early 1963, which had been preceded by a frightening plague of rats, were accompanied by scenes of horror and terror and followed by widespread famine and disease. The year 1963 is indelibly engraved upon Balinese memory as the worst in historic times—at least, that is, up until the even more dreadful years of 1965 and 1966. Entire villages were wiped out, and thousands of hectares of rich farmlands were covered deep in lava, boulders and ash. Over 100,000 refugees were driven from their homes and farms. Many of them died of asphyxiation when trapped by blocked paths and roadways. Others died later of injuries, exposure or starvation. For many months famine prevailed over wide areas and epidemic was a constant threat. National and international bodies attempted to mount relief operations, but the agencies came into serious conflict. Personnel and supplies sent from abroad were not properly utilized and often did not reach Bali at all, Indonesian agencies of the Sukarno period being both jealous of prerogative and corrupt in handling valuable medicines, foodstuffs and other relief goods. During the worst of the crisis, Jakarta officials authorized planes, which were desperately needed for relief, to fly the visiting tourist agents to view the scenic spectacle by moonlight and firelight.

GESTAPU Coup and 100,000 Killings

The island's disasters of 1962, 1963 and 1964 were still fresh in Balinese memory in late 1965 when disaster very suddenly, but so far as the Balinese were concerned, not unexpectedly, struck the entire nation. The Sukarno regime had obviously long since passed the point of no return on the road to self-destructive folly. During the night of September 30, 1965, a clique of pro-Sukarno conspirators staged an abortive coup d'état. The most gruesome aspects of GESTAPU (*Ger-*

akan September Tiga Puluh, or the 30 September Movement) were the kidnapping and murder of five top army generals and one lieutenant (mistaken for General Nasution, the Commander-in-Chief). It was a tactical blunder which provoked popular revulsion and military vengeance so prolonged and widespread that the conspirators themselves were virtually wiped out and the Sukarno regime collapsed. But it required the better part of a year after GESTAPU for the nation really to begin to steady itself with the clear emergence of Suharto as Sukarno's unchallenged successor. In the meantime there had occurred a nation-wide bloodletting, nowhere more frightful than in frightened little Bali.

At the time of GESTAPU, Bali was under the control of a PKI-sympathizing Governor of the royal family of Negara and a strongly PKI- and PNI-infiltrated and indoctrinated clique of civil and military officials, all of them deeply implicated in the excesses and the extravagances of the Sukarno regime. The Governor himself fled from Bali to Jakarta together with all of his immediate family. In Jakarta President Sukarno provided him with shelter, assigning him a house within the well-guarded Senayan sports complex, then virtually a military cantonment. It was only a few weeks, however, until the Governor vanished—picked up by a party of Balinese activists, according to a well-informed report, and taken off to a nearby rubber plantation to be executed.

The events of late 1965 and early 1966 in Bali have never been fully reported and perhaps need not and should not be. A total of some 100,000 people were killed, thousands of homes were burned and immense damage was done to the island's economy and its morale. One of the special causes of convulsion in Bali was that the PKI and the PNI, the two strong political parties which had maintained an uneasy but mutually profitable alliance during the late Sukarno period, turned upon one another, and everyone who had a grievance to settle settled it then. After years of wretched misrule and exploitation, Balinese grievances were numberless. The military supplied logistic support for vigilante squads which rounded up people accused of being

Sukarnoists, Communists, corrupt or mere sympathizers with the coup. Truckloads of victims were lined up on the river banks to be machine-gunned or beheaded. The bodies were buried in shallow graves or merely rolled into the river. These very numerous Balinese dead, having never been cremated, have no chance of reincarnation in human form. In Bali the thought frequently occurs that the spirits of the guilty and the innocent alike cannot be expected to submit indefinitely to such impious neglect, and that the island may not even yet have atoned sufficiently for its sins, including the 100,000 1965–66 killings. The divinities, who have already visited a series of catastrophes upon the island, may still be unappeased.

After the events of the early and middle 1960s, times in Bali could scarcely have grown worse and they did, in fact, improve. The new government of President Suharto undertook and achieved major reforms of administration and minor miracles of rehabilitation. The government offices were purged of the more incompetent and corrupt of the Sukarnoists, and a new spirit of responsibility was infused into the civil service. The government undertook a program of development which enabled the economy and the society to function at least as well as in the 1950s. This was far from good enough for the 1970s, but it was much better than might have been anticipated in 1965. One of the most significant achievements, the result as much of the people's initiative and energy as of government assistance and encouragement, was the repair of much of the damage wrought by the 1963 eruption of Mt Agung.

In the late 1960s a visit to the state of Karangasem, which Mt Agung dominates, was no longer the dismaying experience of the post-Mt Agung eruption when one traveled over ruined roads across a blighted landscape. The road to Besakih revealed very little evidence of the volcanic action save that a fine new bridge, one of the most important provincial construction projects, crossed a river bed deeply overlaid with lava. The temple complex itself had been largely restored to its earlier state, and the view from the temple terraces was again one of scenic splendor unmarred by evidence of devastated fields. Other areas much more adversely affected by the eruption could not be said to be beautiful, but life was much more than faintly stirring in the ruins. The town of Karangasem was being so rapidly rebuilt that new structures masked old houses and shops which stood several feet below ground level. On the edge of the town it was still possible to see the dramatic contrast between rich rice fields and an adjacent expanse of what seems like pock-marked moonscape. Such contrast was not so sharply apparent in the more distant rural areas where the transitions were much more gradual. With the help of the patient farmers, the eternally verdant life forces of Bali were vigorously reasserting themselves. It is prophetic, one trusts, of triumphs over other and even graver problems that the Balinese were surmounting a natural disaster of major dimensions. In Bali to a much greater degree than anywhere else in Indonesia, recurrent natural convulsions such as volcanic eruptions and earthquakes have conditioned the people to rely for regeneration upon divine favor and their own vigorous efforts. Both will be required to the fullest degree for the island to meet the all too predictable emergencies of the late twentieth and twenty-first centuries, in which, as yet, productivity cannot keep up with population nor achievement with aspiration. The new formula for restoration of Bali's former fortunes is the vigorous promotion of international tourism, a prescription which may adversely affect the rich but ailing culture it is meant to preserve.

IN TRANSIT

T owards the end of his romping narrative of Bali's past, Willard Hanna makes a very strange comment: "The events of late 1965 and early 1966 in Bali have never been fully reported and perhaps need not and should not be."

The idea of any writer with a lively interest in the past suggesting that one of the most significant and traumatic events in the recent history of his chosen subject should not be examined and explained is peculiar, if not a little disturbing. But the reason for Hanna's peculiar attitude to the anti-communist pogrom of the 1965–66 rainy season is not difficult to discern. He was an American from an official background writing at the height of the Cold War; and after bringing clarity, wit and a healthy smattering of cynicism to his view of Bali's more distant past, when it came to the most recent years—those of which he had direct experience—he lapsed into partisanship.

The view that Willard Hanna took of Indonesia's first president, Sukarno, was very much that of American officialdom at the time: that he was a dangerous, communist-sympathizing, West-hating demagogue, who would be best removed from the presidential palace. During the late 1950s, the CIA backed abortive regional rebellions against Sukarno's government and reportedly engaged in all sorts of black propaganda against his person. Hanna's own AUFS reports from the turn of the 1960s sometimes had the character of anti-Sukarno screeds, and when it came to his account of the Sukarno years in Bali he made no effort to hide his bias. He gave the president the character of a monster and made his trips to Bali sound like visitations from the demon-witch Rangda, repeating the most lurid of rumors about his personal conduct without any qualification. However, despite Hanna's suggestions that the waving, smiling Balinese crowds who greeted Sukarno's arrivals were essentially press-ganged, there are plenty of other accounts of the genuine excitement his visits to Bali prompted. Sukarno was a man of almost supernatural charisma, and right to the very end he enjoyed a remarkable degree of personal popularity all over Indonesia, even as the country lurched towards crisis.

In his version of the so-called "30 September Movement" or GE-STAPU, which precipitated the anti-communist pogrom, Hanna's bias also shows through. The real facts behind the 30 September Movement haven't been fully explained, and given the surrounding maelstrom of claim and counterclaim there may never be true clarity. But the bones of the affair are these: during his years of "Guided Democracy," Sukarno, whose own politics had always tended to the left, but who had never been and was never likely to become a communist, attempted to hold the various political forces at work in Indonesia in balance. The idea was that this would allow for calm consensus, but instead it created terrible tensions, particularly between the Indonesian Communist Party or PKI and the nationalist and religious groups, as well as between the PKI and the conservative military elite. The 30 September Movement is often called an "abortive coup," but in fact it was more of an internal military putsch, intended to secure, rather than topple, the ruler of the day. It was organized by a clique of junior, Sukarno-supporting officers who had left-wing tendencies and wished to remove the right-leaning, anti-Sukarno top brass, but who were not themselves members of the PKI. In the event they failed to get control of the army, still less the country. That fell instead to Suharto, the most senior of the surviving rightwing generals, and a powerful narrative, aided by powerful propaganda, emerged, placing the blame for the 30

September Movement squarely at the feet of the PKI. A nationwide massacre of PKI members and supposed supporters ensued, very much orchestrated by the military, for all that it was often civilians who wielded the guns, the knives and the sharpened bamboo staves.

In Bali, the scale of the massacre was particularly appalling. However, oft-told stories of a spontaneous, island-wide rampage are untrue. The military orchestration was as essential in Bali as anywhere else, and mass killing did not begin until December 1965 when troops arrived from Java, where the pogrom had already been underway for weeks. Likewise, distasteful exotic tales in which the massacre in Bali took on the character of a gruesome dance-drama, with the murderers as calm religious functionaries and the victims as repentant sinners, dressed in ceremonial white and offering themselves up as willing sacrifices in the name of "cleansing" the island, need to be taken with a large pinch of salt. Credible reports suggest that victims were indeed sometimes offered the chance to *nyupat*, to repent and thereby save their souls, before death. But this generally came once they were already seized, bound and lined up for execution.

The total death toll will probably never be known. Modern scholars tend to go for a conservative figure of 500,000 for the whole of Indonesia, but other estimates which push the total towards 2 million are by no means beyond the realms of credibility. Willard Hanna's 100,000 estimate for Bali is actually at the upper end of the scale; 80,000 is the most frequently cited Balinese death toll, which still amounts to around 5 percent of the entire population of Bali at the time. Ultimately, all that really matters is that thousands upon thousands of people were killed, many of whom had little to do with communism, and none of whom had anything to do with the 30 September Movement. In the aftermath of the massacres, Suharto and his supporters, with the approval of the USA and other Western powers, carefully maneuvered Sukarno out of the presidency and established the New Order regime which was to rule Indonesia for the next three decades.

As well as being peculiar and discomfiting, Willard Hanna's suggestion that the events of 1965–66 should not be fully reported, and thus not be fully explained, is rather ironic, for he had himself already gone some way towards providing a convincing explanation.

The connecting thread of this book is that of Bali's interactions with the outside world. But its other abiding theme is that of violent conflict. From the disintegration of the Dewa Agung's pan-Bali realm in the mid-eighteenth century until the ultimate Dutch triumph in 1908, Hanna's tale seethes with feuds, double dealings and pitched battles, all of which was eminently political, even if the players were royal *puri* and colonial armies rather than modern political parties. Political conflict kicked off again in the immediate aftermath of the Japanese occupation during World War II, and continued sporadically right up until the awful rainy season of 1965–66.

Given all this, then, the pacific interlude of Dutch rule during the 1920s and 1930s begins to look more like an aberration than a true, tranquil reflection of the "natural" Balinese state of affairs. Indeed, even the calm surface of those Dutch-ruled decades, with Walter Spies and company making hay while the sun shone, belied turbulent tides beneath. While the Ubud set were sipping their cocktails and the early sightseers were seeking out bare-breasted beauties on the beach at Sanur, even Dutch officials were privately admitting that thanks in part to the colonial tax obligations local peasant farmers could "scarcely make ends meet," and counted themselves lucky "if they manage to eat one decent meal a day." The clever Dutch system of administering Bali through the surviving royal courts, however, meant that any bitterness this state of affairs created was likely to be directed at the local aristocracy, rather than at the European "elder brothers." Tensions were being created which would still be rankling in the 1960s.

Even the Dutch desire to formalize Bali's status as a place of peaceful "culture" and "tradition," and in doing so to isolate it from the modern politics of the nascent independence movement in Java, was inadvertently priming future conflict. They sought to rationalize the boundaries of villages and banjar into neat geographical blocks, ignoring subtler communal and agricultural factors; and their effort to gain a legalistic fix on caste, religious practice and even temple architecture was an attempt to stop fluid Balinese culture in its tracks, never an easy thing to do without creating a certain amount of tension.

Despite all this, however, the Dutch years were, for the most part, calm, and one of the most convincing explanations for this state of affairs, and for the turmoil that came before and after, has it that Bali was only ever likely to be free from political violence when there was some sort of strong overarching, or even external, authority. When the old Balinese realm fragmented into separate fiefdoms, and when the Japanese occupation gave way to the fractious divisions of the revolution and the early years of Indonesian independence, there was turmoil. During Dutch rule, however, for all that the daily administration was filtered through the rajas, those paramount "elder brothers" were an unavoidable, island-wide presence. Local leaders could no longer feud openly amongst themselves, and should any peasants decide to resist the burdens of tax or corvée labor, as they occasionally did, the police and army that came to deal with them belonged to the Dutch East Indies.

The name of Suharto's New Order regime was a double entendre. As well as a fresh government, it also presented itself as offering a fresh sense of orderly calm after the chaos of the late Sukarno years. In short, it amounted to precisely the sort of strong, overarching authority which had long been lacking, and which in Bali, arguably, offered the best chance for peace. In the early 1970s, then, it was unsurprising that many, both Balinese and outsiders, were quietly optimistic. What was more, the New Order had already made "development" its watchword and economic progress its theme, and in Bali that meant tourism, which seemed to promise a prosperity unimaginable just a few years earlier.

But as Willard Hanna prepared to leave the scene, heading off for a well-earned retirement in New Hampshire, where he died in 1993 at the age of 82, casting one final disapproving scowl in the direction of the hippies in Kuta, one last baleful backwards glance at the Sukarno legacy and one optimistic departing nod at Suharto, ominous questions remained. If Bali had a chronic tendency to political violence, could anything prevent it from resurfacing in the years to come? And would tourism, ultimately, prove any less dangerous an outside impact than those of the previous decades and centuries?

BALI UNDER THE NEW ORDER (1966-2000)

The Morning of the Earth

They came picking their way through the scrub in the heat of the day: half a dozen long-haired foreigners, a couple of them carrying single-fin surfboards, another lugging a movie camera. They had ridden out from Kuta in a pair of chartered three-wheeled bemo to the end of the bumpy road outside the gates of the Pura Luhur Uluwatu temple, perched on its high promontory. Now they were working their way north along the cliffs, half led, half followed by an excited gaggle of thin-limbed local children. It was June 1971.

This southernmost extremity of Bali, the Bukit Peninsula, was not the postcard world of rice terraces and drooping palms. The limestone soil here was thin, and there were cactuses and thorny bushes crackling in the hot breeze. The children following the foreigners belonged to the poorest of poor communities, scratching a meagre living at Bali's bleakest limit. Eventually, the little cavalcade reached the head of a shallow cleft in the coastline, a dry valley with a short cliff rising to the right. At the seaward end of the cleft, a bamboo ladder made by local fishermen led down into a cave of the kind where the earliest Melanesian hunter-gatherers had once squatted to chip their pebble tools and shell scrapers. Beyond it was the corrugated ocean, with waves unfolding in blinding white lines over the reef. The two surfboard-toting members of the party, a 28-year-old Californian by the name of Rusty Miller and an Australian teen called Steve Cooney, made their way down through the cave and out into the roiling water. The rest of the party gathered on the bluff above, where their leader, Albert Falzon, set up his movie camera. Through the lens he saw Cooney's dark silhouette race left-handed along a glittering silver-green wall of water. It was the first wave ever ridden at a spot which the surfers, ignoring the local name Suluban, would christen for the clifftop temple a mile to the south: Uluwatu.

The language of surf exploration, with its talk of "discovery," its staking of claims and its giving of names, can have uncomfortable imperialist parallels in a post-colonial world. But these pioneering surfers belonged to the fringes of the nascent hippie scene in Kuta, and such thoughts never occurred to them. As far as they were concerned they really had discovered something beautiful in a corner of Bali which was either utterly unspoiled or grindingly impoverished, depending on your point of departure.

Back home in Australia, Falzon cut the scenes he had shot in Bali into his new surf documentary. He called it *Morning of the Earth*, borrowing from Jawaharlal Nehru's misty-eyed comment about Bali. It premiered in Sydney in February 1972, and soon surfers all along the east coast of Australia were trying to find Bali on the map. By the end of the year, the kids from Suluban had taken to hanging around at the roadside just short of the Uluwatu temple, waiting to flag down the bemo that were now coming past several times a day with surfboards protruding at odd angles. For a cannily negotiated fee, they would carry the gear and lead the visitors by a shortcut to the bamboo ladder in the cave. Before long, one of their enterprising elders had built a bamboo-and-thatch shack in the lee of the little cliff in the valley and taken to serving drinks and snacks.

By 1978 there was a billboard advertising cigarettes by the trailhead on the Uluwatu road. At the other end of the path, meanwhile, one disappointed visitor who had arrived primed with the pristine vision of *Morning of the Earth* reported that "On the side of the hill facing the break was a row of concession stands while in the water forty surfers battled to drop in on each other's three foot waves." Two years later they held the first Om Bali Pro Am surf contest at Suluban. The contest had the warm approval of the authorities, and they decided to build a direct road to the surf spot in time for the second Pro Am in 1981. Soon the rough lot at the top of the cliff was packed with minibuses and rented motorbikes. An attendant was on duty to collect a parking fee from the drivers.

Sometime around the turn of the twenty-first century, someone took away the bamboo ladder in the cave and replaced it with a flight of concrete steps. In the countryside between the surf spot and the temple, the bare huts of the local farmers were now solid compounds with red-tiled roofs. There were several dozen cafés tucked under the cliff, many owned by the boys who had once led surfers on foot through the fields, grown men now with children of their own, some keen surfers themselves.

Then surveyors started to pace out plots of land all the way along the clifftop and back into the scrub beyond. And then the bulldozers moved in, and broke the ground beside the parking lot, and by the middle of the first decade of the new century there was a kidney-shaped infinity pool on the very edge of the cliff, its water a cobalt monochrome against the variegated Indian Ocean below. And then, somehow, the pace quickened, and suddenly the cafés had gleaming espresso machines and Wi-Fi instead of old kettles and stacks of dog-eared surf magazines. East and south of the parking lot a small city sprouted, with bone-white masonry and tinted glass and pipe-fed palm trees where no palms had ever grown before, and a hundred frangipani flowers delicately placed on a hundred king-sized beds in a hundred ice-cool guest rooms.

Offshore, the deep ocean groundswells were still unfolding in white lines over the reef.

New Order; New Directions

Suharto has often been described as a "dictator" and, indeed, his New Order regime, which survived until 1998, was profoundly undemocratic in its organization. But he was no cartoon tyrant, and though the New Order was born out of a period of astonishing slaughter, its own public pose was that of quiet paternalism rather than despotic swagger.

The New Order had inherited an economy on the verge of total meltdown, a national infrastructure that was falling apart and an impoverished population. A group of American-educated economists, later to be known as "the Berkeley Mafia," was charged with getting things back on track. But if the economy was to be heated up, then the political scene was to be cooled right down. The Indonesian Communist Party, the PKI, had, of course, been banned and virtually its entire membership and wider constituency annihilated. But that wasn't enough. The surviving parties were ushered into two bland, toothless umbrella groupings: Partai Persatuan Pembangunan, the "United Development Party" or PPP for all those with a politically Islamist approach (of which there were, naturally, very few in Bali), and Partai Demokrasi Indonesia, the "Indonesian Democratic Party" or PDI, for everyone else. Meanwhile, the New Order created its own electoral vehicle in the form of an enormous pseudo-party named Golkar, initially made up of a "joint secretariat" of such "functional groups" as trade unions and farmers' collectives. Indonesia's democratic experiment in the 1950s had proved the country incapable of electing a majority government in a free and fair fight, but now the New Order could hold a general election every five years and be absolutely certain that the essentially apolitical Golkar would win, and that the tame parliament in Jakarta would then return Suharto for another uncontested presidential term. If Willard Hanna had been alarmed by the "process of massive and sinister politicization" in the 1950s, now the opposite was happening: Indonesia was being thoroughly depoliticized, every last drop of meaningful electoral ideology drained out of it, a sinister process in its own right.

An Island Apart?

On November 1, 1967 Suharto appointed a new provincial governor for Bali. He was a bespectacled 42-year-old former military man. His name was Soekarmen and he hailed from the East Java mountain town of Malang.

The idea is sometimes expressed that under both Sukarno and Suharto, and even today, Bali has been dominated by a sort of imperial "Javanese" elite. But, in fact, since it first became a province of the Republic of Indonesia, from the provincial level downwards the island has been overwhelmingly governed by its own. Soekarmen was the only non-Balinese, and the only non-Hindu, ever to occupy the governor's office in the leafy Renon neighborhood of Denpasar, and his appointment prompted little discernable grumbling. This was probably partly down to the sense of numbed shock suffusing the island in the wake of the terrible things done there just two years earlier, and a quietly relieved acceptance of the paternalistic new regime. But it also draws attention to the fact that the idea of Bali as an island apart from the Indonesian mainstream, a last bastion of Hindu tradition holding out in a great green tide of Islam, can sometimes be overdone. The notion of a non-Balinese, non-Hindu governor might be unimaginable today, but it may not always have been considered quite so outrageous.

The idea of Bali as a "living museum of Indonesia's Hindu past," first conceived by nineteenth-century orientalists, ignores the soft edges, the fluidity and the ever-shifting dynamism of local cultures throughout the region. Until very recently, the lifestyles, beliefs and cultural practices of Bali's rural masses were not a million miles removed from those of their brethren across the water in Java, which was no particular stronghold of Islamic orthodoxy in the nineteenth century, or even in the 1960s.

Even the term "Hindu" as a designation for Bali's religious identity, distinguishing it utterly from the "Islam" of the surrounding islands, is by no means straightforward. The concept of "Hinduism" as a religion only really came into being in the eighteenth century when Europeans began using it as a catch-all term for the huge diversity of interconnected traditions in India. Amongst the Balinese people themselves, the term was largely unknown until the Dutch arrived in the early twentieth century. Prior to that, if they needed a name for their faith at all, they sometimes called it Agama Siwa or Agama Buda, "Shiva Religion" or "Buddha Religion," depending on which strain of the priesthood they had in mind. But more often they simply called it Agama Bali, "Balinese Religion," just as many notional Muslims across the water in Java referred to their own syncretic, uniquely local religious practices as Kejawen or Agama Jawa. During the 1920s, as the Dutch sought to define Bali's "traditional culture," there was some disquiet at the phrase "Hindu-Bali" that was now being used by the European authorities; better, some Balinese felt, to call it "Bali-Hindu," thereby placing the stress on the more significant word. As late as 1949, some senior Balinese priests were arguing that Agama Tirtha, "Religion of Holy Water," was actually the most appropriate name for the island's unique creed. It was only in the 1950s, as steps were taken to gain recognition for the Balinese religion as one of Indonesia's five officially sanctioned faiths, all of them "world religions" rather than traditional indigenous belief systems, that the uncontested idea of the Balinese as "Hindus" finally bedded in.

Sukarno had been happy enough to buy into the relatively new notion of "Hindu" Bali as a uniquely artistic representation of Indonesia's classical past. He was every inch the renaissance man and he was always keen to patronize the arts (according to some accounts, the admiring attention that Sukarno gave to Balinese dance performances during his visits helped turn dancing into a respectable profession for adult women; previously professional dancers tended to be girls with decidedly dodgy reputations). But he also made a great effort to place Bali and its traditions at the center of his new nation. It was part of the national core, and Java *and* Bali were the places from which economic transmigrants would be shipped to the furthest-flung reaches of the archipelago, ambassadors of *Indonesian* culture whose new communities in deepest Sulawesi, Sumatra and Kalimantan would help bind the nation together.

The new president, Suharto, was far more conservative than the mercurial man he had ousted, far less interested in art and dancing girls and far more insular in his own deeply traditional Javanese worldview. But he had no inclination to overturn the status that Sukarno had established for Bali in the Indonesian scheme of things.

Economic Progress and the Green Revolution

The Berkeley Mafia turned the Indonesian economy around in double-quick time. By the start of the 1970s inflation was back in single digits, international investors had returned to Indonesia, incomes were rising and gross domestic profit was warming up for a decade of 8 percent annual growth. "Development," particularly of the economic variety, was to become the New Order's abiding theme.

Bali, like Java, had long been an agricultural powerhouse, with formidably fertile soils and a complex irrigation network. It was part of the Indonesian bread basket, and in the early years of the New Order it was subjected to the full force of the so-called "Green Revolution." Egged on by international donors and development agencies, the authorities pressed new high-yield rice varieties, chemical fertilizers and pesticides and mechanized techniques on farmers. Eventually, the abandoning of old crop cycles and the overuse of chemicals would reveal fresh environmental problems, but the initial result was a doubling of rice production. Bali, which had struggled to feed itself for decades, was soon exporting surplus rice to the rest of the country. What was more, the new, more efficient style of farming freed up a good number of workers who had previously spent all their days in the fields. In Java, these liberated agricultural laborers, many of them women, were pointed in the direction of new factories churning out garments for export. Had it not been for a certain legacy of the 1930s, this might have been the fate of the former farm workers in Bali too. Vast steel sheds and smoking chimneys could have risen over the coastal flatlands around Denpasar and Tabanan, and a good number of the world's cheap tee shirts and sports shoes in the 1970s and 1980s might have been stitched in an obscure Indonesian province by the name of Bali. But as it happened there was already another potential source of alternative employment in Bali in a very different sort of industry: tourism.

The Master Plan and the Cultural Tourism Debate

Although World War II and the Indonesian revolution had roundly wrecked the nascent tourist industry of the 1930s, there had already been moves to rebuild. In 1963, using funding from the Japanese government intended to make amends for their wartime excesses, Sukarno had kicked off work on a multistory luxury hotel in the still-sleepy village of Sanur. A hulking slice of whitewashed concrete, it towered over the modest cluster of existing tourist bungalows. Sukarno also oversaw the start of a project to expand the old airfield at Tuban, just south of Kuta on the narrowest point of Bali's southern isthmus. The carnage of 1965–66 obliterated the embryonic industry once again, and annual tourist arrivals had only managed to edge back to a measly 11,000 in 1968. But Sanur's Bali Beach Hotel was now fully operational, and in 1969 the upgraded airport was formally inaugurated as an international gateway. They named it after Colonel Ngurah Rai, the revolutionary leader who had led the fierce but doomed resistance to the returning Dutch in 1946. The New Order was eager to exploit these facilities, and so, in 1971, they called on the expertise of a French consortium, the Société Centrale pour l'Equipement Touristique Outre-Mer or SCETO.

The SCETO consultants' six-volume "Master Plan for the Development of Tourism in Bali" contained all sorts of ideas, but foremost amongst them was the notion that tourism was overwhelmingly a thing involving big spenders on short trips, staying in high-end hotels close to beaches. They recommended that the Indonesian government set about creating 4,800 hotel rooms, some neatly corralled into the two nascent resorts already in existence at Kuta and Sanur, but most in a proposed new 425-hectare complex at Nusa Dua, a barren stretch of coast on the bony eastern knuckle of the Bukit Peninsula, far from any local population centers and occupied only by a few fishermen. Underpinning these plans was the belief that tourism was a potentially destructive force in terms of its impact on local culture, best kept quarantined in a limited area close to the airport. Still, the French experts couldn't deny what they thought was inevitable if serious tourism development was to be pursued: by the mid-1980s, Bali's "cultural manifestations will probably have disappeared." The New Order signed off on the official promulgation of the SCETO report in 1972 and, after a few tweaks from the World Bank, in 1974 they set about executing it.

Meanwhile, the Balinese provincial authorities, dominated by upper-caste locals, shipped-in Javanese governor notwithstanding, were getting a little nervous. Tourism might be a nice little earner, they felt, but wasn't the prospect of the total disappearance of "cultural manifestations" rather alarming? They launched their own series of seminars to consider what they viewed as "the challenge of tourism" and its potential to "pollute" Bali. The solution to all this, they decided, was something called "cultural tourism." Instead of simply touting beaches, cocktails, tropical sunsets and the occasional day trip to a temple, the Balinese tourist industry should make "local culture" its main attraction. This, the reasoning went, would turn culture into a kind of concrete economic capital, like a piece of land or a house, thereby creating a powerful motivation to preserve it. It sounded like a very clever idea. Bali now had both a masterplan and a cultural watchword for tourist development, and there seemed to be no reason why the two couldn't go hand in hand.

Of course, all these airy debates demonstrated a very limited notion of what "culture" actually was. Like the Dutch colonialists of the 1930s, they seemed to view it as restricted to religious ceremonies and other "traditional" things. What was more, both the French experts of SCETO and the culturally concerned local stakeholders had failed to realize that, just like "culture," tourism itself is a dynamic, ever-shifting, many-headed thing which will plot its own multiple courses heedless of all projections and plans. Willard Hanna had dismissed the hippies at Kuta as "drifters rather than drivers," but he couldn't have been more wrong.

Hippies, Guidebooks and the Rise of Travel for the Masses

At the start of the 1970s, Jalan Legian, the main thoroughfare of Kuta, was a long straight lane, flanked on either side by banks of thick foliage. Here and there a sandy footpath angled off to a family compound full of pigs and chickens and children. At its southern end the road split, and just around the corner to the right, on the way to the beach, there was a *warung*, a food stall. It was little more than a shack with a few rickety wooden benches and it served up simple meals of rice, vegetables and roast pork. It was run by a local family and it had no real name. But young Westerner travelers had christened it "Made's Warung" after the forthright teenage girl who usually did the serving. Likewise, they had taken to calling the junction at the bottom of Jalan Legian "Bemo Corner," for this was where you could catch a spluttering three-wheeled public bemo to Denpasar, or charter one for the ride out to Uluwatu if you were serious about surfing.

To begin with, there were only ever a couple of hundred hippies in residence at a time, long-haired, barefooted, wild-eyed and, occasionally, stark naked. But they were part of something bigger. And though to an aging American Universities Field Staffer steeped in American establishment values, this tie-dyed tideline stretching from Kabul to Kathmandu to Kuta might have represented the feckless scum of modern youth culture, there were plenty of creative minds and entrepreneurial spirits amongst their number. In the name of stretching their season in paradise to the maximum length, some of them took to smuggling transshipped Sumatran cannabis in hollowed-out surfboards. But others packed their bags with cheap batik shirts from Java to flog at home in Australia, and thus began what would one day be big-time Bali-based fashion businesses. Others took advantage of lackadaisical notions of land tenure, leased beachside plots and set up juice stalls or bungalows. Some of these businesses would vanish after a couple of months, but others endured and became small empires.

And more important still was what all this meant to people like Made Masih, the teenage serving girl at the *warung* near Bemo Corner. The budget travelers could not afford to stay in the Bali Beach Hotel over in Sanur; instead, they found lodgings with Kuta families. Soon some locals had earned enough cash to throw up a few simple bungalows for rent or to open a roadside food stall serving coffee and warm beer and, for those who asked, omelets laced with the psilocybin-rich magic mushrooms that grew in the cow pastures around Kuta.

Some of the young travelers who stopped by in these homestays and *warung* turned out to have educations and observational skills to match those of Willard Hanna, and smart ideas about how to use their talents. One young British-Australian couple who had passed through in the early 1970s, Maureen and Tony Wheeler, knocked together a booklet giving tips about travel along the "Hippie Trail" called *Across Asia on the Cheap*. Another traveler, an American this time by the name of Bill Dalton, provided a good deal more Bali-specific insight in a similarly homemade pamphlet called *A Traveler's Notes: Indonesia*. Up in Ubud, meanwhile, a young German photographer called Hans Hoefer had put together something rather more detailed, complete with lavish illustrations and detailed essays on culture and history. It was called *Insight Guide: Bali*.

A decade later, in the 1980s, a whole new generation of young independent Western travelers with long schedules and short budgets, termed "backpackers" rather than "hippies" now, would arrive in Bali, clutching vastly expanded editions of these Insight Guides and Moon Handbooks and Lonely Planets. Amongst the listings for Kuta they would find a certain "Made's Warung," still standing a short way towards the beach beyond Bemo Corner and with Made Masih still in charge, though now it was a large, split-level building, stuffed with colonial-era furnishings and surrounded by hundreds of other restaurants, hotels, bars and souvenir stalls. It would still be there a decade later, and a decade after that, when the backpackers had given way to hordes of Australian tourists on cheap two-week beach holidays.

As for cultural tourism, that seemed to have worked out well, too. The island had gone from being a relatively poor part of Indonesia in the late 1960s, with per capita incomes well below the national average, to being a solidly prosperous province by the end of the 1980s, with above average annual earnings. Plenty of the extra cash seemed to be being spent on temples and ceremonies, which, many old timers commented, were now more lavishly and colorfully observed than back in the bad old days. And if Sukarno's patronage had made dancing a respectable career, tourism had made it a lucrative one: up in Ubud there was always work for the local dance troupes at tourist performances.

For the local authorities, this was all very welcome. Governor Soekarmen had gone home to Malang in 1978 and he was replaced by Ida Bagus Mantra, a stately former academic from a prestigious Sanur Brahman family. He had a long-standing scholarly interest in strengthening Bali's Hindu identity, and he made sure that his government was a generous sponsor of serious activity in the arts. He also opened up nine new locations across Bali as designated tourism development areas. Mantra's successor, Ida Bagus Oka, decreed fifteen more as soon as he took office in 1988, and a further six a few years after that. By this stage, a quarter of the entire Balinese landmass had been officially sanctioned for tourism development.

In 1990, in what was either the apogee or the nadir of "cultural tourism," depending on your perspective, Rolling Stone Mick Jagger married supermodel Jerry Hall in a Hindu-Bali wedding in Ubud, complete with a presiding priest and a sacrificial chicken...

Cracks Open in the New Order

The New Order government had brought many real benefits to the people of Indonesia. At the start of the 1960s, few had proper access to healthcare or education, and the overall national infrastructure was in tatters. Under Suharto, however, the network of schools and clinics was hugely expanded, and before long Indonesia had near universal primary school attendance, and literacy levels not far behind those of Europe. A highly successful family planning campaign stressing that *Dua Anak Cukup*, "Two Children is Enough," brought Indonesian population growth under control, and was particularly effective in Bali. Meanwhile, the economy, driven by raw materials from the oil and gas fields of Sumatra and Kalimantan, the vastly expanded manufacturing sector and, to a lesser degree, the booming tourist industry of Bali, grew ever larger. Per capita incomes continued to rise and huge numbers of people around the country found themselves edging into the lower ranks of the middle classes. Some started taking holidays in Bali. But by the start of the 1990s the benefits of New Order rule in terms of improved living standards for the masses seemed to have reached their natural limits. The regime's other traits were beginning to become obvious, not least flagrant cronyism and corruption at the highest levels, and some highly questionable financial practices. In Bali this became apparent in the direction of tourism development.

The opening of the new areas for tourism development had started to spread the tourist dollars to parts of Bali that had previously looked jealously at the booming south: Candidasa in Karangasem, Lovina in Buleleng in the north and a smattering of other embryonic resorts around the island. When it came to the hundreds of small homestays, souvenir shops and modest restaurants, much of the tourist industry was still in local hands. But by now there were fat cats from Jakarta and beyond getting their claws into the trade. Since the deregulation of Indonesia's banking sector in 1987, huge sums of poorly secured cash had been swilling around the private sector, and in Bali much of it went into luxury resort developments. Nusa Dua, a gated vision of the SCETO master planners twenty years earlier, finally came into its own as a burgeoning complex of sanitized luxury. Elsewhere, huge tranches of coastal land were taken over for resort developments, some of them with Suharto cronies, including his own tribe of children who by this stage had enormous business interests of their own, pulling the strings. The Balinese governor Ida Bagus Oka earned himself the pejorative nickname Ida Bagus "OK" for his apparent tendency to sign off on even the most ostentatious resort proposal without batting an eyelid. Earthmovers rumbled in to carve out space for a vast villa complex above the Bukit beach that surfers had christened "Dreamland," and the little islet of Serangan, just south of Sanur, was bulldozed flat and attached to the mainland by a causeway for another planned resort.

None of this looked much like a recipe for successful "cultural tourism," and when plans were revealed in 1991 to build a huge golf resort overlooking the Tanah Lot temple in Tabanan, complete with a spotlight to illuminate the temple for the benefit of guests of an evening, protests erupted from both the farmers who would be forced from their land and from the Hindu priesthood outraged at what some considered an infringement on sacred territory. The development eventually went ahead but only after years of wrangling.

Political Protest and the End of the New Order

On a national level, too, political protest was beginning to emerge for the first time in decades. When the New Order held its scheduled five-yearly general election in 1992, Golkar's share of the vote dropped for the first time ever. Its majority was still unassailable, but it was an alarming signal for the leadership. Still more alarming for Suharto, the PDI, the Indonesian Democratic Party which had sucked up most of the swing away from Gokar, then elected as its leader one Megawati. She was a frumpy, middle-aged housewife and nothing about her suggested a revolutionary leader, but for one fact: she was Sukarno's daughter, and by 1992 a good number of Indonesians were starting to look back on the Sukarno era as a time when politicians had a little more honor and integrity. Megawati proved particularly popular in Bali. She was quarter Balinese on her father's side for a start, and though she was no great orator she was still able to tap into the nostalgic popular affection for her father; and her own mild rhetoric appealed to the farmers and the students. She had obvious potential to become a figurehead of popular political protest, and that was something that the New Order couldn't possibly allow. Swinging from gentle paternalism to heavy-handed bullying, they pressured the PDI to oust her from the leadership in time for the next election in 1997. This crude move had the desired effect at the polls: Golkar regained its lost votes and PDI support collapsed.

Meanwhile, the economy had continued to swell, though it now had unmistakably bubble-shaped proportions. The rampant banking sector was borrowing big in dollars to fund local loans in rupiah; and when, shortly after the 1997 Indonesian election, the economy of Thailand collapsed in an avalanche of bad debts, it precipitated a regional crisis which reached Jakarta within a matter of weeks. The rupiah collapsed like the baht before it; the holes in the Indonesian banking sector were suddenly exposed to daylight; and work on unfinished, crony-controlled resorts in Bali came to a grinding halt. By the start of 1998, with galloping inflation, surging unemployment, spiraling food costs and a currency plunging towards rock bottom, real hardship set in across Indonesia. If Suharto had seemed like a safe pair of hands three decades earlier, he now looked like the worst sort of dissipated, incompetent old raja. Popular protest erupted, first amongst the students in Jakarta and then in cities nationwide. On 23 April, a crowd of demonstrating students some 3,000-strong, calling for Suharto's resignation, gathered at the gates of the Udayana University campus in Denpasar. They hurled rocks as armed police gathered across the street; the police responded with tear gas and baton charges; a dozen people were injured.

Finally, on May 21, 1998, the embattled president announced to the world that he was stepping down. Suharto's deputy, B. J. Habibie, was appointed as interim president. He freed thousands of political prisoners and abandoned almost all restrictions on the press and the formation of political parties. A national election was scheduled for July 1999. Across Indonesia there was jubilation, but also deep unease. The New Order's last weeks in Jakarta had been marked by terrible violence, and in the aftermath of its fall communal conflicts that had been simmering in outlying regions of the country came up to a rolling boil. The tormented province of East Timor, meanwhile, was gearing up to split from Indonesia in the most bloodily traumatic of circumstances, and rumors whispered of dark forces that Suharto had once kept in check, now running amok across the nation.

In Bali there was as much cause for unease as anywhere. Though there had been the noisy student protests at the Udayana campus, and further demos in Denpasar in June 1998, which had prompted the resignation of the New Order-appointed provincial government, the island had avoided serious violence. But what might happen next was anyone's guess.

The 1999 Election and the "Ash Thursday" Riots

The vote of July 7, 1999 was only the second truly democratic election in Indonesian history. The first had been in 1955. After three decades during which ballot papers featured only Golkar, the PDI and the PPP, there were now dozens of competing acronyms and symbols. But in Bali one party, one symbol and one politician dominated. After the New Order had arranged to have her ousted from the PDI leadership, Megawati had not gone away. As soon as Suharto fell, she and her supporters announced the formation of a new party, Partai Demokrasi Indonesia-Perjuangan, "The Indonesian Democratic Party of Struggle" or PDI-P. It claimed the political legacy of the old PNI nationalist party, which had been strong in Bali before 1965, and with Megawati as figurehead it claimed the legacy of Sukarno as well. Bali was awash with PDI-P banners featuring a stern black bull frowning from a blood-red background. When polling day arrived, with spectacularly high turnout, the PDI-P took seven of the nine Balinese seats. Nationwide, too, they took the largest chunk of the vote, and though this only amounted to a 33 percent share of parliamentary seats, most people still assumed that Megawati would end up as president. Politics is a funny old business in Indonesia, however, and once all the backroom coalition-building was over, that's not how things panned out. On Wednesday, October 20, the parliament in Jakarta voted to appoint Gus Dur, head of the Partai Kebangkitan Bangsa, the "National Awakening Party" or PKB, to the top job. Half-blind and with a remarkably informal approach to public performance, Gus Dur was actually a very reasonable choice for president given his formidable track record of progressive tolerance and support for religious pluralism. But as far as Megawati's furious supporters were concerned the whole thing had been a stitch-up. In Bali, the mobs hit the streets.

They called it *Kamis Kelabu*, "Ash Thursday." The day after the presidential vote, large crowds surged onto the roads near the ferry terminal at Gilimanuk at the western tip of Bali, dragging burning tires into the road and cutting off interisland transport from Java. In Denpasar, groups of angry young men in PDI-P tee shirts rampaged through the streets. They set fire to a shopping mall, to the provincial assembly building, to Golkar's Denpasar branch office and to the Badung regency offices, and they overturned and destroyed cars with government plates. Columns of black smoke rose over the city. Away to the north in Singaraja, the old port city on Bali's northern coast, the violence had gone on through the night since first word of Gus Dur's appointment came through. Some 15,000 rioters set the official residence of the Buleleng regent ablaze. They destroyed the bus terminal, attacked banks and smashed down the gates of the local prison; 130 inmates fled onto the streets. It was all over by sunset. In far-off Jakarta, Megawati had been elected to the vice-presidency, taking the heat out of the PDI-P supporters' anger. But by that stage the damage in Bali had been done, an estimated 207 billion rupiahs' worth of it. Newsreel footage of rampaging Balinese mobs had flashed around the world.

In the aftermath of Ash Thursday, an anguished debate unfolded amongst correspondents and public intellectuals in the columns of the *Bali Post*, the island's biggest Indonesian-language newspaper. Some plumped for conspiracy theories and pointed to unseen agents provocateurs; others blamed the riots on the influence of "foreign values" (with the "foreigners" in question being Javanese immigrants rather than Western tourists); still others simply wrung their hands and spoke of collective madness. None, however, seemed to connect this violent outburst in a new age of uncertainty with the political violence that had marked Bali in the similarly uncertain years of the nineteenth and mid-twentieth centuries. All agreed that it was thoroughly inappropriate behavior for this, the island of eternal peace.

The violence was bad for business, too. Tourism had been recovering strongly since the national crisis the previous year. But now, with bad news coming specifically out of Bali for the first time, there was a rush of canceled bookings. It was six months before tourist arrivals got back on track. The Balinese economy was overwhelmingly dependent on tourism; tourism was overwhelmingly dependent on Bali's peaceable image; and when it came to deciding whether or not to run amok over a political grievance, the commentators declared, the power to protect that image was in the hands of Balinese people. Or so it seemed in the wake of Ash Thursday. What no one had considered was what would happen if violence was brought to Bali from beyond the island's shores.

EPILOGUE 3

BALI IN THE TWENTY-FIRST CENTURY

A **Night in October**

If you stand on the northern edge of the Bukit Peninsula, where the high limestone plateau angles down to meet the narrow neck of land connecting it to the rest of the island, the urban heartland of modern Bali fans out at your feet. After dark, in the weeks before the wet season in the third year of a new century, it is a vision of lights.

Directly below, the black crescent of Jimbaran Bay is hemmed with a soft glow where the last diners are picking at their seafood dinners on the beach. At the northern end of the bay, a slow pulse of navigation lights shows where the airport runway is wedged in the neck of Bali like a huge splinter. Beyond that the coast sweeps onwards in an arabesque of dancing lights where Kuta and Legian are in full swing, patched with pure darkness as the rice fields reassert to the north of Seminyak, and then fading to black in the direction of Java. To the right, beyond the eastern end of the airport runway, the muddy blotch of Benoa's natural harbor is speckled with boats, their lights showing doubled up on the glossy surface. To the northeast, the coast bends away towards Sanur's cluster of lights, with the Bali Beach Hotel standing proud amongst them, still the only true high-rise on the island. Between these two swelling shorelines is a great smear of illumination where Denpasar is going about its nocturnal business like any middle-sized Indonesian city. And beyond that again Bali rises into pure darkness where the roads and rivers run like unseen veins, past Tabanan and Mengwi and Ubud and Gianyar, from the high mountain core.

From up here on the slopes of the Bukit, not yet barnacled with white villas, the whole vision gives out a low hum: a composite of a thousand woks rattling over a thousand guttering flames at streetside stalls; a thousand motorbikes puttering through the gloom; and a thousand songs pulsing from a thousand barroom sound systems; all underscored by an occasional hollow base note as a late flight bowls in for landing out of the darkness.

And then, at five minutes after 11:00 p.m. on this, October 12, 2002, a flare of unexpected light shows to the north, a sudden bright blot on the skyline beyond the airport. It blooms and contracts in silence and has already faded to an indistinct amber smudge and a darkening pillar of smoke by the time the sound of the blast has traveled the five miles across the perfumed night from Kuta.

Aftershocks of the Bali Bombings

The Bali bombings of October 2002 killed 202 people, including 38 Indonesians and 88 Australians. There were two separate blasts. First, a suicide bomber detonated his explosive vest inside a raucous bar called Paddy's Pub on the eastern side of Jalan Legian in the heart of Kuta. Twenty seconds later, another bomber flicked the switch on a far, far bigger bomb, packed into the back of a white Suzuki van, pulled up on the other side of the street outside the Sari Club. The two bombers appear to have been a youth from Central Java called Feri and a young man named Arnasan from a poor village in Banten. The men who had actually plotted the attack and built the bombs had already faded away into the night. In the months that followed, however, the investigators, headed by a veteran Balinese police chief named Made Mangku Pastika, tracked them down. They were tried, and on a rainy November night in 2008 three of their number were executed by firing squad on the prison island at Nusa Kembanagan off the southern coast of Java. Others were jailed or killed in shootouts with the security forces. They were connected to the Jemaah Islamiah Islamist network, which was in turn linked to Al Qaeda, and they had planned the bombing as an attack on America and its allies. None of them was from Bali.

Beyond the initial carnage, the bombings did grave damage to the Balinese economy. After the jittery months around the collapse of the New Order, and the dips caused by Ash Thursday at home and the 9/11 terrorist attacks abroad, the tourist industry had been surging forward. Three decades earlier, Willard Hanna had been troubled by projections suggesting that Bali would likely receive 500,000 foreign tourists a year by the end of the century. In fact, a grand total of 1.42 million had flowed through the Ngurah Rai Airport arrivals gates in 2001. Jalan Legian still stretched away northwards through Kuta from Bemo Corner, but it was no longer a sleepy lane; it was a roaring thoroughfare flanked with bars and restaurants, and it ran all the way to Seminyak through three miles of unbroken tourism development. Up in Ubud, meanwhile, though Elizabeth Gilbert had yet to swing by on her *Eat, Pray, Love* odyssey, and though there were still open rice fields around the lower half of Monkey Forest Road, there were already hundreds of guesthouses and spas and galleries and cafés crowding the town.

Perhaps 25 percent of the entire Balinese workforce was directly employed in the tourist sector, but that was only a small part of the picture, for tourism had long since surpassed agriculture as the dominant economic activity on the island. It supported a large manufacturing industry, churning out clothing and souvenirs. It paid the wages of taxi drivers, and its dollars flowed through the pumps of the island's fuel stations. Bali's construction workers were supported by tourism, and out in the poor villages of Buleleng and Karangasem, far from any tourist itinerary, there were medical bills and school fees paid with cash sent back from prodigal sons and daughters serving with a smile in the resorts of the south. Even the migrant food hawkers, offering tepid bowls of meatball soup to off-duty taxi drivers in alleyways on the edge of Denpasar, indirectly owed their living to tourism. It fueled a vast web of transactions large and small, spanning the island from one side of the central volcanoes to the other.

In Bali, just four percent of the population eked out an existence below the poverty line; across the eastern straight in the neighboring province of West Nusa Tenggara, poverty levels were almost five times higher. The difference was largely down to tourism, and now, as tourist numbers collapsed in the wake of the bombing, something suddenly became horribly apparent. For decades, hand-wringing observers had been expressing fears that tourism might "destroy" Bali in the abstract sense of an erosion of "charm." But the bombs showed all too clearly that it was the sudden loss of tourism that now had the immediate capacity to destroy the island as a prosperous society.

There might have been a violent reaction to the bombings, for Indonesia at the start of the twenty-first century was frequently a place of communal conflict. Since the fall of Suharto, small civil wars had unfolded between Christian and Muslim neighbors in Maluku and Sulawesi; local Dayaks in Kalimantan had rampaged against long-established transmigrant communities from Madura; and all over the country Indonesia's much maligned but disproportionately wealthy ethnic Chinese community had had reason to fear the mob. And though the scale had been much smaller, Bali had not been immune to this sort of thing.

The growing tourist economy and general urban development had been attracting economic migrants for decades, most of them from the poorer parts of East Java or West Nusa Tenggara. They worked on building sites and as pavement hawkers, hard-laboring young men sleeping five to a room in the grimmest boarding houses of Denpasar, enduring all the immigrant's eternal opprobrium from the settled locals, and inevitably blamed for every criminal act. Back on April 29, 1999, during the heated run-up to the first post-New Order election, a mob of men in traditional Balinese costume had come out onto the streets of Kuta in the early hours of the morning. While the night's stragglers were eking out the tail end of the party in Paddy's Pub and the Sari Club, three-quarters of a mile to the north on Jalan Melasti, the *sarong-* and *udeng-*wearing vigilantes were overturning the food carts and kiosks of Muslim vendors from Java and dragging the smashed pieces to the beach to be burnt. Who exactly had organized the mob was never clear. Kuta community leaders claimed that the migrants had annoyed local residents with their late night trading; but the episode was clearly symptomatic of wider hostility towards "incomers," heightened by the uncertainty of those early months of post-New Order *reformasi*. There had been further violence in early 2002, this time up in Kintamani where locals destroyed the homes of seven Balinese Christian families, always a favorite target for persecution.

After this, after the Ash Thursday riots, and after Bali's older history of violence, some terrible revenge action against the island's Muslim minority, both recent migrants from Java and centuries-old communities of Bugis and Sasak origin, in the wake of the 2002 bombings might have been easy to imagine. But that's not what happened. The anguished response from international media commentators, tourists and expats was predictable: the violence of Islamist terrorism was surely at complete odds with "peaceful Hindu Bali." But local people, too, reeling from the reality of economic hardship, wounded pride and shared trauma, felt exactly the same, and felt it with absolute sincerity. There could be no violent retribution for the Bali bombings because, as the tee shirts hastily printed up in the weeks that followed would have it, "Bali Loves Peace"....

"Strengthening Bali," Identity Politics and Invented Traditions

Though there were no revenge attacks, in the aftermath of the bombings a powerful and potentially belligerent local discourse did emerge in response. Its name was *Ajeg Bali*. The phrase is usually translated from the Balinese as "Strengthening Bali," and it had actually been around for a while by the time the bombs exploded in Kuta in October 2002. Satria Naradha, the head of the Bali Post Media Group, owner of the *Bali Post* newspaper, claimed to have invented the entire concept of Ajeg Bali in a moment of divine inspiration as a meditating schoolboy back in the 1980s. But other senior civil and religious figures from Denpasar clearly played a part in developing the concept. It was first properly unveiled to mark the launch of Naradha's new regional broadcaster, *Bali TV*, in May 2002, but it wasn't until after the bombing, as a particularly intense wet season unleashed its downpours over the ranks of empty restaurants and untenanted guesthouses in Kuta, Seminyak and Sanur, that it gained real popular currency.

Ajeg Bali was as vague as such philosophical concepts in Indonesia tend to be, but at heart it rested on the notion that a return to imagined old-fashioned values and a strengthening of Balinese identity and pride was required. Threaded through this was a disquiet at the encroachment of "outsiders," once again economic migrants from other parts of Indonesia rather than foreign tourists or expats. The extravagantly bearded Hindu-Bali televangelist Ida Pedanda Gede Made Gunung, a *Bali TV* favorite during the station's early years and a firm proponent of Ajeg Bali, reminded his viewers that "Many Balinese sell their land to buy a lot of *sate*, but don't forget that many immigrants sell *sate* in order to buy a lot of land." The movement also played into the rise of the *pecalangan*. Today, these volunteer village "security teams" are found in virtually every *banjar*, the smallest of traditional community structures, in Bali. They are sometimes presented as a timeless aspect of "traditional" village life, but before the fall of the New Order they were virtually unknown, and though they could at times slide into petty thuggery and vigilante violence, they now had a gloss of Ajeg Bali legitimacy.

There was also an explicitly religious component to the discourse, with talk of "strengthening" and "purifying" the Hinduism of Bali, a "Hinduism" which had only really been properly acknowledged as such by its participants half a century earlier. Newsreaders on *Bali TV* took to pressing their palms at the start of their broadcasts and saying *Om Swasti Astu*, an invented "Hindu" version of the Muslim salutation *As-salaam alaikum*. The Parisada Hindu Dharma Indonesia, the national Hindu council, meanwhile, had taken to issuing edicts tell-ing people how to pray "correctly," what color to wear for ceremonies, and what was, in fact, "proper" Hindu practice.

In short, Ajeg Bali, with its call for a return to traditional values, its religious conservatism, its undercurrent of hostility to immigrants and its association with sinister volunteer security teams, had unsettling parallels with aggressive populist right-wing movements the world over. But it also had woven into it that idea first properly voiced during the public soul-searching after the Ash Thursday riots and then emblazoned across tee shirts and bumper stickers as the smoke from the 2002 bombings cleared: "Bali Loves Peace."

Ajeg Bali, as both an organized movement and a popular catch-phrase, faded away somewhat in subsequent years. But its core concept remained: of a faintly belligerent chauvinism tempered by a sincere and absolute commitment to the image of Bali as a peaceful place. When, on a still evening in 2005, eleven days short of the third anniversary of the Kuta attacks, two new suicide bombers walked out amongst the dining tables on the beach at Jimbaran and detonated the explosives in their backpacks and a third bomber followed suit further north in a restaurant in an upscale shopping precinct in Kuta, killing 20 people and sending a barely recovered tourist industry reeling back into crisis, no one was surprised when no revenge attacks on Muslim migrants ensued.

The Man of the People and the Regencies' Resurgence

In 2008, the people of Bali went to the polls to elect their own governor for the very first time. All the previous provincial heads, including the most recent, Dewa Made Beratha, had been appointees, but now, in the ongoing era of post-New Order reform, Indonesia had gone democratic with a vengeance.

The Balinese popular choice for the ultimate top job, Megawati, had actually ended up as president in 2001 after Gus Dur was impeached. But she served a lackluster half-term, and lost out during the first directly democratic presidential election in 2004 to a retired military officer with significant reformist credentials, Susilo Bambang Yudhoyono, better known in the interests of brevity as "SBY." This time there was no popular backlash in Bali after Megawati's national defeat. As for the 2008 gubernatorial elections, here the popular vote did go to the candidate with PDI-P backing, none other than the police officer who had gained international plaudits for his investigation of the 2002 bombing, Made Mangku Pastika.

Pastika was the son of a village schoolteacher from Sanggalangit in Buleleng in northern Bali. He came from a poor background and he had to work selling flowers and cutting grass from a young age. When the 1963 eruption of Mount Agung destroyed local rice fields, his father signed the family up for a government transmigration program, and they shipped out to Sumatra. It was there that the young Pastika, having already worked as a houseboy for an ethnic Chinese family and learnt to speak Chinese as a consequence, and having also done time as a street vendor in Palembang, joined the Indonesian police force. A stellar career followed, and his role in bomb investigation gave him a high, and highly positive, public profile in Bali. The shift into politics was a natural one, and he was a genuinely popular choice. What's more, during his first five-year term, his promise as a man of the people seemed to come good. He initiated an ongoing "home improvement" program to bring gimcrack dwellings in isolated communities far removed from the tourist hotspots up to minimum standards; he made Bali the first Indonesian province to deliver free healthcare to the poorest members of society; and he even took steps to initiate a modern public transport system though this element of his governance occasionally lapsed into fancifulness, not least in an abortive plan to build a round-island railway line. But perhaps Pastika's greatest credential when it came to man of the people status was his background: he was the first Sudra governor of Bali, the first to come from the majority "commoner" caste. Of the eight provincial heads who had gone before him, all bar the single Javanese transplant had been members of the Triwangsa, the trio of topmost caste designations from which came the priests and the kings.

After Indonesia became an independent republic, the old Balinese aristocracy had not gone away. The outlines of the rajadoms as they had existed under colonial rule—Badung, Bangli, Buleleng, Gianyar, Jembrana, Karangasem, Klungkung and Tabanan—remained as the borders of the *kabupaten*, the regencies, the level of local governance beneath that of the province. Under both Sukarno and Suharto, and indeed under the new democratic system, members of the old princely families and the priestly elite often headed up the regency administrations as well as being prominent in business and civil society in general. And by the time Made Mangku Pastika was elected governor, the regencies had more power than they had enjoyed since the days of the rajadoms.

B. J. Habibie, the stop-gap Indonesian president who took over when Suharto resigned, had rushed through a great raft of political reforms. Amongst these were new laws devolving extra power and funding to the regency level of government, a move prompted by long-running complaints about Jakarta's centrist arrogance and nervousness about secessionism after East Timor embarked on its bloody separation from Indonesia. The laws were enacted by Habibie's successor Gus Dur in 2001, and the regency governments across the country got their hands on such matters as transport infrastructure and planning, not to mention much, much bigger budgets. Decentralization did assuage some of the grumbling about Jakarta's high-handedness, but it also quickly created new problems of its own. Critics pointed out that it had simply provided fresh opportunities for corruption and cronyism at a local level. And even without the problems of graft, effective, province-level planning could now be hampered by intransigence or ineptitude in the regencies, an issue that Pastika sometimes ran up against during his time as Bali's governor. Decentralization, then, represented a sort of political fragmentation, an erosion of strong, central governance, and in Bali that had ominous historical connotations.

New Tourism Directions

On January 5, 2011 Governor Pastika announced a moratorium on the building of new tourist resorts in southern Bali.

In the wake of the 2002 bombings, with tourism development temporarily stalled by a rush of canceled bookings, there had been a brief pause for reflection. Some, both foreigners and locals, had wondered aloud whether Bali really had gone too far, pushing beyond the sensible limits of cultural tourism into crass commercialism, and whether the island ultimately bore some kind of responsibility for the terrorist outrage visited upon it. It was an idea that had queasy parallels with the terrorists' own notions about Kuta as a den of Westernized debauchery. But such worries were quickly forgotten and the serious wobble caused by the second bombings in 2005 notwithstanding, tourist development was soon surging forward afresh. The year before Pastika announced the resort moratorium, foreign tourist arrivals had topped two million for the first time, and everyone expected the numbers to keep rising. But at the same time, average hotel occupancy rates had actually started to fall. The simple fact was that there was too much tourist accommodation in Bali.

The vast majority of the development was still concentrated in the south, in the regencies of Badung and Gianyar, and in the municipality of Denpasar which includes the resort at Sanur. The southern infrastructure was groaning under the strain. Much of the Kuta-Legian-Seminyak strip, which had grown up organically over the previous four decades with little proper planning, was in a state of near permanent gridlock. Water, electricity and sewerage systems were also struggling to cope. Meanwhile, some other Balinese regencies, in particular Karangasem, Jembrana and Buleleng, still suffered high unemployment rates and a serious paucity of development. Pastika's idea was that a ban on new resorts in Badung, Denpasar and Gianyar would not only relieve the pressure there, it would also help push tourism development into these neglected outlands. But he was fighting a lost cause, not least because he didn't have the empowered regencies on his side. The regents of Badung and Gianyar and the mayor of Denpasar had no desire to see investment for construction, and rates from established tourism business, go elsewhere. They kept signing permits for new resorts regardless of any paper moratorium issued at the provincial level. From the other direction, meanwhile, the provincial administration was faced with a national tourism ministry determined to see overall tourist arrivals continuing to rise, with optimistic projections heading into the tens of millions by the early 2020s.

What was more, by the start of the second decade of the twenty-first century, tourist development in Bali had developed new characteristics. For a start, there were now dozens upon dozens of modern "city hotels," typically two- or three-story blocks without the slightest hint of "Bali Style" in their architecture, crowded into Tuban, Kuta and Legian. These were a step well above the old homestays that had served generations of backpackers and surfers, and many of their guests were Indonesian. When the planners and predictors of the 1970s had laid out their schemes, they had largely ignored the potential of the domestic tourism sector. Indonesia, they presumed, was a Third World country and the inhabitants of Third World countries didn't go on holiday. But under the developmental auspices of the New Order, and then during a fresh surge under SBY's democratic government, the Indonesian national economy had grown dramatically. Some excitable commentators were now proclaiming the country a new economic superpower, a superpower which happened to have the fourth largest national population on the planet and where many people now had significant disposable incomes and an inclination to travel for leisure. Domestic tourist numbers are always far harder to track than those for foreign visitors, but most observers estimated that by 2010 Bali was receiving around twice as many Indonesian tourists as foreign visitors.

Then there were the villas, which were now thickly scattered across the vanishing rice fields north of Seminyak, throughout the palm groves around Ubud, and all over the stony heights of the Bukit Peninsula. At first, in the wake of the terrorist attacks, many officials were inclined to look on this particular type of development favorably.

Luxury villas seemed to represent that elusive "high quality" tourism that had long been regarded as a holy grail, with proportionally lower numbers and higher spends. What was more, many of the villas were being directly built by or leased on long terms to foreigners, or to wealthy Indonesians from the big cities of Java. Unlike travelers on cheap two-week packages, those with long-term investments would be far less likely to abandon Bali in the wake of a new terrorist atrocity or some other disaster, or so the reasoning went. Many locals, too, were delighted to get big lump sums by selling off for villa projects plots that had only ever returned a few hundred dollars a year as rice fields. But it soon became apparent that compared to traditional hotels, villas swallowed up a huge amount of land and sucked up vast quantities of water while providing accommodation for a relatively small number of visitors, and by now everyone could see that Bali's environment was struggling to cope with the pressures of the modern world.

Drying Out: Environmental Impacts

Environmental pressures are nothing new in Bali. Writing of the 1930s, before anyone had built a resort infinity pool on a Bukit clifftop or sunk a borehole to supply a hotel hot tub, Willard Hanna noted that the island was a place with "too many people, too little land, and too few job opportunities." Population pressure had already had some very obvious impacts: the swathes of true wilderness that once covered the interior had contracted to the highest uplands and westernmost hills by the start of the twentieth century, and the last recorded Balinese tiger, sole survivor of Asia's easternmost population of these big cats, marooned in Bali when the rising sea levels isolated the island from Java at the end of the last Ice Age, was killed in 1937. By the twenty-first century, it was not just apex predators but the entire Balinese ecosystem and the entire traditional agricultural system which ran alongside it that was facing an uncertain future. This seemingly waterlogged land, drenched with torrential downpours and buried under thunderheads for several months each year, irrigated by a

1,000-year-old network of channels and ditches, and liberally sprinkled with holy water, was in very serious danger of drying out.

According to some estimates, around 65 percent of Bali's entire water supply goes straight into tourism-related properties, chlorinated for huge swimming pools, blasted from showerheads in some 90,000 hotel rooms, sprayed over lawns and flowerbeds and golf courses and piped out to villas and exclusive resorts in the essentially waterless heights of the Bukit Peninsula. To meet these extravagant needs, water has long been diverted from the delicately balanced *subak*, the traditional irrigation networks that feed the rice fields of the interior, and also sucked straight up from the ground via boreholes. As a consequence, the mountain lakes that have always acted as the ultimate reservoirs for the whole of Bali have begun to dry out; more than half of the island's watercourses now stop flowing altogether during the dry season, and in the low-lying areas where there is much ground-water extraction, particularly in the coastal resort areas, seawater has begun leaching into the water table at an alarming rate.

Elsewhere, the rice fields, which once made more restrained use of the natural water supply, have started to vanish. By some counts, around a thousand hectares of agricultural land each year is converted to other uses, much, though by no means all, of it directly related to tourism. Air pollution on the congested roads, vast volumes of trash and dirty seas are other features of the heavily developed southern regions.

By the time that tourism had fully recovered from the aftereffects of the 2002 and 2005 bombings, there was a definite public awareness of the environmental problems and a sense that, just like a terrorist bomb or a politically motivated riot, pollution and environmental degradation could damage Bali's image. When *Time* magazine ran an only slightly hyperbolic article in 2011, describing "dunes of surf-tossed garbage" on Kuta Beach and a plethora of other environmental horrors, some local politicians and tourist industry chiefs responded in time-honored fashion, claiming that that the article was a conspiratorial plot to discredit Bali. But Governor Pastika reacted more sensibly, pointing out that "If we want Bali to be known as a paradise island, it needs to be like paradise. That's a goal we all need to work on together." By that stage there were already a good number of people working towards that goal: NGOs doing their best to run educational programs and campaigners pressing for more sensible environmental approaches from both government and civil society. But though they could often achieve small triumphs—recycling at village level, the apparent resurrection of the critically endangered Bali starling, and so on—when it came to the ceaseless forward march of big-money tourism development and general urbanization they looked like they were fighting a losing battle.

The wider environmentalist movement seemed to have its unifying moment in the organized opposition to an extravagant plan to fill the natural harbor at Benoa with artificial islands inspired by the similar developments in Dubai. The island complex, first mooted in 2011 and funded by a Jakarta-based developer, was expected to feature luxury hotels, a Disney-style theme park and possibly even a Formula One race track, none of which seemed to have much to do with "cultural tourism." It was also expected to have a seriously detrimental impact on the already battered mangroves around the fringes of the bay, the last surviving strip of truly natural habit in the area. A *Tolak Reklamasi*, "Refuse the Reclamation", movement soon emerged. It had many of the features of the earlier campaign against the Nirwana development at Tanah Lot, with the addition of the more uncomplicatedly admirable elements of Ajeg Bali, plus a dash of 1998-style street cred thanks to the heavy involvement of students, artists and musicians. The sit-ins and marches that the movement organized, with Made Mangku Pastika now cast in the villain's role as far as the campaigners were concerned, thanks to his signing of an initial 2013 permit for the project, were widely supported, but, of course, peaceful.

The Benoa reclamation project itself became bogged down in the muddy challenges, its future uncertain. But it is clear that wider environmental issues constitute one of the biggest challenges for Bali's future, as they do for many other heavily populated, economically boisterous parts of Indonesia.

Paradise Lost and Found

In the twenty-first century, the southern heartland of Bali has become a single conurbation, centered on Denpasar and edged by the main coastal resorts. The once separate communities still have their distinctive characters, from Kuta's hugger-mugger mayhem to Renon's dignified air of Indonesian suburbia. But the spaces in between have filled with homes and businesses, and the urban sprawl has long since begun to leach outwards from the core, the Bukit and Canggu transforming into villa-speckled suburbs and ribbons of concrete and commerce creeping uphill towards Ubud and Gianyar. The population of this region is probably about 1.5 million out of a total Balinese population of approximately 4.2 million, bolstered by tens of thousands of temporarily resident tourists at any one time. It is a city and it has many of the problems you would expect to encounter in any city in any developing post-colonial state. There is poverty and inequality, pollution and buckling urban infrastructure despite some impressive recent improvements, not least a toll road, built on stilts above Benoa Bay. There is also a good deal of crime, from house-breaking to convenience store hold-ups, rising rates of HIV infection and a significant problem with drug use.

Some excitable tabloid journalists from overseas, and some similarly excitable netizens with their own interests in Bali, like to declare that all this is evidence of the island's ultimate corruption. It is a paradise lost, they say, given over entirely to the worship of Mammon. Tourism, as so many predicted for so long, has finally destroyed Bali. But the problems they point to are often exaggerated and are in no way unique to places with a tourist economy. Surabaya, Makassar, Banjarmasin and any number of other urban centers in modern Indonesia also have bag-snatchers, pickpockets, drug addicts, gangsters, bent traffic police and corrupt local politicians, and yet none of these places has an economy founded on tourism. Most of them also have worse levels of urban poverty than the Denpasar conurbation. What's more, there are dozens of other Indonesian cities similar in size to Denpasar—Malang, say, or Padang—which four decades ago still had quiet streets, a certain sleepy charm, a dash of faded colonial elegance and rice fields in easy walking distance of the center, but which are now also gridlocked concrete metropolises, and without international tourism having played any significant part in the transformation. Bali is a part of Indonesia, and a fairly central and prosperous part at that, and Indonesia is a part of the modern world. Had no tourists ever arrived in decades past, Bali would still today look nothing like it did forty years ago. Indeed, an urban periphery of villas and beachfront restaurants is perhaps a pleasanter prospect than one made up of factories, housing complexes and slums.

Those who declare that Bali, or at least the southern part of it, has been spoilt by mass tourism tend not to see beyond their own subjective criteria for an appealing holiday destination, and fail to acknowledge that tourism itself is one of Bali's biggest draws. The characteristics usually cited to explain Bali's unique appeal, from the mountain and rice field vistas to the colorful cultural traditions, and from the beaches to the vibrant arts scene, are often equaled or bettered in other parts of Indonesia. But the island's ultimate trump card is its highly developed tourist industry, and in that it certainly surpasses every other destination in the country. A key attraction for many of the domestic tourists who make up the vast majority of Bali's visitors today is the island's "liveliness" as a bustling resort, as it is for many of those from the emerging markets of Russia and China, and as it always has been for the hordes of Australian package tourists and partying teens. Even those who would look down on the specific areas and specific activities that attract those dominant demographics tend not to stray too far from sophisticated accommodation, service and dining, even if they do seek out more tranquil settings up in the hills. Very few travelers truly want to eschew the beaten track.

In any case, it only takes a brief glance at the map to realize that tourist development is actually still concentrated in a remarkably limited area. Beyond the urbanized south, there are only scattered pockets of significant tourist activity. New hotspots are always emerging, of course, mountain villages like Munduk or Sideman, transformed over a few short seasons so that starry-eyed visitors who find a personal paradise one year might discover disappointment the next. But you only need to cross a single ridge to the east or west of the latest emerging destination to enter a valley as yet untrammeled by outsiders, and in Bali there are still a lot of ridges and a lot of valleys.

When it comes to "culture," meanwhile, no one could convincingly argue that that has been destroyed by tourism. From the most exclusive beach resorts to the humblest mountain hamlets, offerings are still laid out each day, and most temple festivals are actually more lavishly celebrated than in the past. None of this is a tawdry charade, meaninglessly performed for camera-carrying sightseers. It is real.

Back in the early 1990s, as the SCETO master planners' prediction of the end of "cultural manifestations" began to look distinctly silly and as "cultural tourism" started to seem like a notable triumph, some observing academics made admiring noises about a supposed Balinese capacity for what they called "boundary maintenance." The people of Bali, they argued, had proved remarkably adept at recognizing which parts of their lives and lifestyles really mattered and which bits belonged to the throwaway field of tourist service, and at maintaining the "boundary" between these supposedly discrete realms. But this interpretation still rests on that restrictive view of what "culture" is, making it exclusively a thing of religious worship and traditional practices rather than allowing it to encompass the full gamut of life, fluid, unbounded, acquisitive and ever shifting. If you accept this broader, more dynamic understanding of "culture," then it stands to reason that tourism itself is as much an authentic part of Bali today as rice farming. And perhaps tourism as an authentic part of modern Balinese culture has had a more profound impact than simply raising living standards and reinforcing traditions by giving them value as touristic "capital."

The nineteenth-century history of Bali which Willard Hanna so vividly described was one of endless turmoil and frequent bloodshed, not to mention piracy, slavery, opium and guns. No one at that time, Balinese or outsider, would have for a moment suggested that the island was a place of peace and harmony. That idea was a product of the 1920s colonial domination of Bali, its 1930s "discovery" as an expat paradise, and its later promotion as a cultural tourist destination. The episodes and events described in this book strongly suggest that, historically, whenever Bali has been without stable, overarching governance it has had a tendency to lapse into political violence. In today's post-New Order era, Bali is freer and more democratic, but it also has less sense of certainty and security, even without the myriad pressures of chaotic urbanization, immigration and environmental degradation. Thanks to decentralization, it is also far more politically fragmented than it was during Suharto's thirty-year centrist reign. Judging by past precedent, this seems like a recipe for disaster, and yet, beyond the brief flare-up of Ash Thursday, there has been no widespread rioting, no pogroms, no serious attacks on minorities. Violence does still occur, of course. Conflicts between villages over "customary issues" such as access to a disputed temple or burial ground sometimes degenerate into street fighting, and village *pecalangan* can turn from security team to lynch mob if they get their hands on an "outsider" suspected of a crime. But there's a sense that such things cannot be allowed to get out of hand, because a wider conflagration would not only be bad for tourism, it would also be somehow "un-Balinese." The idea that this is an island of peace, once little more than a colonial and touristic cliché belied by the hard facts of history, has become a reality, a part of Bali's very identity.

Bali has been constantly changing since the moment the seawater first flooded across the shallow valley west of Gilimanuk and made it an island. Traders, immigrants and itinerants have changed the place. Javanese overlords and Indian ideas have changed it. Dutch colonialists, Japanese imperialists and Indonesian ideologues have changed it. The Balinese people themselves have changed it, over and over. And tourism, most certainly, has changed it too, though not always for the worse.

FURTHER READING

B ali comes with a vast literature attached, from entertaining expat memoirs to heavyweight anthropological treatises, and from sensationalist tabloid journalism to revisionist academic history. The following recommendations, a mix of scholarly and popular books, are good places to start if you wish to learn more about the island's history.

Island of Bali, Miguel Covarrubias. Eight decades after it was first published, this is still *the* book about Bali in more ways than one. Covarrubius, a portly Mexican cartoonist married to an impossibly glamorous and much older American woman, was a sometime member of the 1930s expat scene. The book he penned about Bali was beautifully written and delicately illustrated, and it packed in history, ethnography, travel writing and more. It probably did more than any other publication to introduce Bali to the Western world and also to introduce popular ideas about the island's character and culture that still endure today. Walter Spies, who had provided Covarrubius with much of the information for the book, later quipped that "to everyone who asks me something, I say: look in Covarrubius...."

The Spell of Power: A History of Balinese Politics, 1650–1940, Henk Schulte Nordholt. For a heavyweight history of Bali to the end of the colonial period, you can do no better than this book, which manages to corral all those feuding rajas into a comprehensive yet comprehensible scholarly narrative. Schulte Nordholt is also the author of *Bali: An Open Fortress, 1995–2005*, one of the few histories specifically covering the end of the New Order and the process of democratic reform in Bali and the associated social changes.

Bali: A Paradise Created, Adrian Vickers. If Covarrubius wrote the book to establish the popular legend of Bali, Vickers, half a century later, wrote *the* book to scrutinize that legend. It's a scholarly work, but thanks to the author's sharp prose it is thoroughly readable, and it convincingly shows how enduring, though not always accurate, ideas about Bali came into being. Its greatest strength is in highlighting the gap between foreign ideas about Bali and local experiences over the centuries.

The Dark Side of Paradise: Political Violence in Bali, Geoffrey Robinson. Fiercely argued, formidably researched, immaculately referenced and suffused with a certain iconoclastic energy, this is the very best sort of academic writing. The book examines the troubled history of Bali from dawn of Dutch rule to the massacres of 1965–66, and in doing so roundly overturns many of the perennial myths, not least the idea that the island was a paradise in the 1930s.

Bali: Sekala & Niskala, Fred B. Eiseman, Jr. There are countless books purporting to explain Balinese religion and culture, but this one makes a particularly good starting point. Authoritative without being overly scholarly, and displaying an obvious personal affection for the island, it's a little dated, well over a quarter of a century after its original publication, but it is still packed with meaningful insight.

Bali Heaven and Hell, Phil Jarratt. The cover and title might suggest yet another lurid exposé of terrorism and drug smuggling, but this is actually a highly readable and very well researched narrative history, combined with engaging personal memoir and insightful modern reportage. It's particularly good on the birth of the budget travel and surf scenes in the 1970s, scenes of which the author had first-hand experience.

A House in Bali, Colin McPhee. The expat memoir has very long form in Bali; there are whole shelves full of books about creating a new life amongst the palm trees. This one, from the early days, stands head and shoulders above most of the more recent offerings in the genre. McPhee was an American musicologist, a fully paid-up member of the louche 1930s expat scene, but also a serious and scholarly connoisseur of Balinese music, which he more or less single-handedly introduced to the wider world. His book, penned during World War II when Bali was under Japanese occupation, is both a rich introduction to that subject and a passionate personal testament to what seemed like a lost paradise at the time of writing.

BIBLIOGRAPHY

Arntzenius, J. O. H., *De Derde Balische Expeditie in Herinnering Gebracht*, The Hague, 1874.

Bawono, Rochtri Agung et al, "Mesolithic and Neolithic Cultures of the Karst Landscapes at Jimbaran," *IPPA Bulletin 28*, Canberra, 2008.

Begin ende Voortgangh van de Vereenigde Neederlantsche Geoctroyeerde Oost-Indische Compagnie, Amsterdam, 1646.

Bloemen Waanders, F. L. van, "Aanteekeningen omtrent Bali," *Tijdschrift van het Bataviaasch Genootschap V & VII'*, Batavia, 1855 & 1857.

_____, "Aanteckeningen omtrent de Zeden en Gebruiken der Balinezen, inzonder-heit die van Boeleleng," *Tijdschrift van het Bataviaasch Genootschap*, Batavia, 1859.

_____, "Bijdragen tot de Kennis van het Eiland Bali," *Tijdschrift voor Nederlandsch Indie*, Batavia, 1859.

_____, "Dagverhaal eener Reis over Bali in Juni en July, 1868," *Tijdschrift voor Nederlandsch Indie*, Batavia, 1870.

Blom, Govert, *Lotgevallen op mijne Reis naar Java*, 1841.

Boogaard, F. H., *L'Expédition de Lombok*, Paris, 1896.

Booms, P. C., *Précis des Expéditions de l'Armée Néerlandaise des Indes Orientales contre les Princes de Bali de 1846–1849*, Breda, 1850.

Booth, Anne, "Splitting, splitting and splitting again," *Bijdragen tot de Taal- Land- en Volkenkunde 167*, Leiden, 2011.

Carnbee, P. Melvill de, "Essai d'une Description de Bali et de Lombok," *Le Moniteur des Indes Orientales*, Batavia, 1846–47.

Connor, Linda and Adrian Vickers, "Crisis, Citizenship, and Cosmopolitanism: Living in a Local and Global Risk Society in Bali," *Indonesia 75*, Ithaca, 2003.

Cool, W., *De Lombok Expeditie*, The Hague, 1896.

Covarrubias, Miguel, *Island of Bali*, New York, 1936.

Eck, R. van, "Een en ander over Bali," *De Indische Gids'*, Amsterdam, 1880.

Friederich, R. H. Th., "An Account of the Island of Bali," *Journal of the Royal Asiatic Society VIII*, London, 1876.

Gelman Taylor, Jean, *Indonesia: Peoples and Histories*, New Haven, 2003.

Gerlach, A. J. A., *Fastes Militaires des Indes Orientales Neerlandaises*, Paris, 1859.

Helms, Ludvig Verner, *Pioneering in the Far East*, London, 1882.

Hoëvell, W. C., van, *Reis over Java, Madura, en Bali in het Midden van 1847 Vols I-III*, Amsterdam, 1849–54.

Jacobs, Julius, *Eenigen Tijd onder de Baliers*, Batavia, 1883.

Jarratt, Phil, *Bali Heaven and Hell*, Melbourne, 2014.

Kammen, Douglas and Katherine McGregor (eds), *The Contours of Mass Violence in Indonesia, 1965–68*, Singapore, 2012.

Kemp, P. H. van der, "Verslag nopens het Eiland Bali," *De Oosterling Tijdschrift van Oost-Indie I*, 1835.

Kielstra, E. B., "Het Eiland Bali," *De Indische Gids IV*, Amsterdam, 1893.

Kol, H. H. van, *Dreimaal Dwars door Sumatra en Zwerftochten door Bali*, Rotterdam, 1914.

_____, *Uit Onze Kolonien*, Leiden, 1903.

_____, *Weg met het Opium*, Rotterdam, 1913.

Lauts, G., *Het Eiland Bali en de Balienezen*, Amsterdam, 1848.

Lekkerkerker, C., *Bali en Lombok: Overzicht der Litteratuur omtrent deze Eilanden tot Einde 1919*, Rijswijk, 1920.

_____, "Het Voorspel der Vestiging van de Nederlandsche Macht op Bali en Lombok," *Bijdragen tot de Taal-, Land- en Volkenkunde 79*, Leiden, 1923.

Leupe, P. A., "Het Gezantschap naar Bali onder den Gouverneur-Generaal Hendrik Brouwer in 1633," *Bijdragen tot de Taal-, Land- en Volkenkunde 5*, Leiden, 1856.

Lewis, Jeff, and Belinda Lewis, *Bali's Silent Crisis: Desire, Tragedy, and Transition*, Plymouth, 2009.

Liefrinck, F. A., *Bali en Lombok: Geschriften*, Amsterdam, 1927.

_____, "De Residentie Bali en Lombok na het Jaar 1894," in *Verslag der Algemeene Verhandelingen van het Indische*, 1902.

Lingensz, Hernout, "Bali 1597," *Bijdragen tot de Taal-, Land- en Volkenkunde 5*, Leiden, 1856.

Medhurst, W. H., "Short Account of the Island of Bali, Particularly of Bali Bailing," in J. H. Moor, *Notices of the Indian Archipelago and Adjacent Countries*, Singapore, 1837.

Miksic, John (ed), *Indonesian Heritage Series Volume I: Ancient History*, Singapore, 2003.

Nielson, Aage Krarup, *Leven en Aventuren van een Oostinjevaarder op Bali*, Amsterdam, 1928.

Nieuwenkamp, W. O. J., *Bali en Lombok*, Edam, 1906–10.

Nijpels, G., *De Expeditiën naar Bali in 1846, 1848, 1849, en 1868*, Haarlem, 1897.

Picard, Michel, *Bali: Cultural Tourism and Touristic Culture*, Singapore, 1996.

———, "Balinese religion in search of recognition," *Bijdragen tot de Taal-, Land- en Volkenkunde 167*, Leiden, 2011.

Pringle, Robert, *A Short History of Bali*, Crows Nest, 2004.

Raka, I Gusti Gde, *Monografi Pulau Bali*, Jakarta, 1955.

Reuter, Thomas (ed), *Inequality, Crisis and Social Change in Indonesia: The Muted Worlds of Bali*, New York, 2003.

Rietschoten, C. H. van, *Algemeen Verslag van den Chef van den Staf der Expeditie naar Bali, 10 September–30 October, 1906*, 1910.

Robinson, Geoffrey, *The Dark Side of Paradise*, Ithaca, 1995.

Schulte Nordholt, Henk, *The Spell of Power: A History of Balinese Politics, 1650–1940*, Leiden, 1996.

———, *Bali: An Open Fortress, 1995–2005*, Singapore, 2007.

Schwartz, H. J. E. F., "Aanteekening omtrent het Landschap Gianyar," *Tijdschrift van het Bataviaasch Genootschap XIX*, 1900.

Swellengrebel, J. L. (ed), *Bali: Studies in Life, Thought, and Ritual*, The Hague, 1960.

Swieten, J. van, *Krijsverrigtingen tegen het Eiland Bali en 1848*, The Hague, 1849.

Utrecht, E., *Sedjarah Hukum Internasional di Bali dan Lombok*, Bandung, 1962.

Verster, J. F. de Balbian, *Een Amsterdammer als Pionier op Bali*, Amsterdam, 1911.

Vickers, Adrian, *Bali: A Paradise Created*, Singapore, 1990.

———, "Bali rebuilds its tourist industry," *Bijdragen tot de Taal-, Land- en Volkenkunde 167*, Leiden, 2011.

Vickers, Adrian (ed), *To Change Bali: Essays in Honour of Gusti Ngurah Bagus*, Denpasar, 2000.

Vlijmen, B. R. F. van, *Bali in 1868*, Amsterdam, 1875.

Weitzel, A. W. P., *De Derde Militaire Expeditie naar het Eiland Bali in 1849*, Gorinchem, 1859.

Zollinger, Z. H., "Verhal eener Reis over de Eilanden Bali en Lombok Gedurende de Maanden Mei tot September, 1846," *Verhandelingen van het Bataviaasch Genootschap XXII*, Batavia, 1849.

"Books to Span the East and West"

Tuttle Publishing was founded in 1832 in the small New England town of Rutland, Vermont [USA]. Our core values remain as strong today as they were then—to publish best-in-class books which bring people together one page at a time. In 1948, we established a publishing outpost in Japan—and Tuttle is now a leader in publishing English-language books about the arts, languages and cultures of Asia. The world has become a much smaller place today and Asia's economic and cultural influence has grown. Yet the need for meaningful dialogue and information about this diverse region has never been greater. Over the past seven decades, Tuttle has published thousands of books on subjects ranging from martial arts and paper crafts to language learning and literature—and our talented authors, illustrators, designers and photographers have won many prestigious awards. We welcome you to explore the wealth of information available on Asia at **www.tuttlepublishing.com**.

Published by Periplus Editions (HK) Ltd.

www.tuttlepublishing.com

Copyright © 2004 Institute of Current World Affairs

First published as *Bali Profile: People, Events, Circumstances (1001–1976)* by American Universities Field Staff, New York, 1976 First Periplus edition as *Bali Chronicles*, 2004 Second Periplus edition 2016

Library of Congress Control Number: 2016943603

ISBN 978-0-8048-4731-5

Distributors

North America, Latin America & Europe
Tuttle Publishing
364 Innovation Drive
North Clarendon, VT 05759-9436 U.S.A
Tel: 1 (802) 773-8930
Fax: 1 (802) 773-6993
info@tuttlepublishing.com
www.tuttlepublishing.com

Indonesia
PT Java Books Indonesia
Jl. Rawa Gelam IV No. 9
Kawasan Industri Pulogadung
Jakarta 13930, Indonesia
Tel: 62 (21) 4682 1088
Fax: 62 (21) 461 0207
crm@periplus.co.id
www.periplus.com

Asia Pacific
Berkeley Books Pte. Ltd.
3 Kallang Sector #04-01
Singapore 349278
Tel: (65) 6741-2178; Fax: (65) 6741-2179
inquiries@periplus.com.sg
www.tuttlepublishing.com

Japan
Tuttle Publishing
Yaekari Building 3rd Fl 5-4-12 Osaki
Shinagawa-ku Tokyo 141 0032, Japan
Tel: 81 (3) 5437-0171
Fax: 81 (3) 5437-0755
sales@tuttle.co.jp
www.tuttle.co.jp

26 25 24 23   8 7 6 5   2311CM
Printed in China

TUTTLE PUBLISHING® is a registered trademark of Tuttle Publishing, a division of Periplus Editions (HK) Ltd.